D1274400

# ON MIRACLE GROUND

# ON MIRACLE GROUND
## Essays on the Fiction
## of Lawrence Durrell

Edited by

## Michael H. Begnal

Lewisburg
Bucknell University Press
London and Toronto: Associated University Presses

Associated University Presses
440 Forsgate Drive
Cranbury, NJ 08512

Associated University Presses
25 Sicilian Avenue
London WC1A 2QH, England

Associated University Presses
P.O. Box 488, Port Credit
Mississauga, Ontario
Canada L5G 4M2

The paper used in this publication meets the requirements of the American National Standard for Permanence of Paper for Printed Library Materials Z39.48-1984.

**Library of Congress Cataloging-in-Publication Data**

On miracle ground : essays on the fiction of Lawrence Durrell / edited by Michael H. Begnal.
    p.  cm.
    Includes bibliographical references.
    ISBN 0-8387-5158-X (alk. paper)
    1. Durrell, Lawrence—Criticism and interpretation.  I. Begnal, Michael H., 1939–  .
PR6007.U76Z78   1990                                    84-3051
828′.91209—dc20                                         CIP

PRINTED IN THE UNITED STATES OF AMERICA

# Contents

6 Contents

# Introduction

MICHAEL H. BEGNAL

These essays represent a collaborative attempt to assess the major fiction of Lawrence Durrell. With the completion of *The Avignon Quintet* in 1985, Durrell has capped an artistic career that spans almost fifty years, a career that continues to unfold in its explorations of space, time, consciousness, identity, and modern love. As accomplished a poet, a critic, and a traveloguist, Durrell in his novels can rightly claim the status of one of the most distinguished and significant practitioners of the discipline of fiction. Almost always at odds with the literary establishment, as a supporter of Henry Miller and Anais Nin and almost anyone else who writhed within the confines of conventional morals and mores, Durrell has sought a way out of the constrictions of the labyrinth. His novels continue to dazzle his readers with the sensuosity of their language and the daring of their insights.

Though Durrell had been recognized for many years by writers the likes of T. S. Eliot and Dylan Thomas, the publication of *The Alexandria Quartet* (1957–60) vaulted him into the public eye. Thousands upon thousands of readers came under the spell of Durrell's four-novel Egyptian adventure, his "investigation of modern love," and his reputation was assured. Yet, strangely enough, his subsequent fictions have received nowhere near the same kind of attention and respect in the English-speaking world (though Durrell continues to be revered in France). Reed Way Dasenbrock has recently suggested that the waning of Lawrence Durrell's literary reputation is not the fault of the later works themselves, but instead the reading public has not kept pace with the new direction of Durrell's narratives.[1] In the essays that follow, several of the writers continue the ongoing exploration of *The Alexandria Quartet*, but many are also concerned with *The Revolt of Aphrodite* and *The Avignon Quintet*. These last two groupings have certainly not received the critical attention that their structural and thematic complexities deserve. It is beginning to be clear that in these three major fictional sequences Durrell has made his major contribution to the development of the novel.

7

The commentators here strive to examine Durrell from as many diverse contemporary perspectives as possible, from metafiction to close textual analysis to deconstruction to reader-response theory. The wide and eclectic nature of Durrell's own reading makes each of his novels a mine of underlying reference, whether scientific or esoteric. A quick glance at this volume's bibliography reveals sources that range from Egyptian mythology to the history of the Templars to the philosophy of Buddhism. The more one delves into Durrell's fictions, the more one realizes there is to know. Though none of the essayists claims to have the final word, this collection seeks to mark out some of the boundaries that encompass Durrell's art, to provide avenues of insight into just how the work coalesces into a coherent statement on the condition of culture.

The "Overture" is an edited transcript of remarks Durrell made when he was enticed to leave his home near Avignon for a conference held in his honor at the Pennsylvania State University. Back in the United States for the first time in more than ten years, he offered these initial comments on his literary career, and he charmed everyone involved with his patience and his kindness. These supposed off-the-cuff remarks provide a view of the man and his work that may help to illuminate the mind behind the very considerable array of work. With a characteristic wit and grace, Lawrence Durrell ranges back over his beginnings and illustrates some of the basic concepts that inform his idea of the value and the role of literature in the modern world.

In the opening section of essays entitled "Metaphysics and Metafiction," Ian S. MacNiven provides an overview of Durrell's early fiction, as a starting point or a transition from which to gauge the experimentation that was to follow. Chiara Briganti traces Durrell's links with the so-called metafictional novelists and contemporary thinkers, such as Foucault, Barthes, and Lacan, while Candace Fertile explores the relationship of the act of writing to love and social responsibility. Corinne Alexandre-Garner confronts the controversial role of incest in Durrell's writings, seeking to relate the taboo to artistic insight with the help of structural anthropology.

Carol Peirce's essay, the first in "Portraits of the Artist in Fiction," unearths the archetypes of Isis and Osiris in *The Alexandria Quartet*, and David M. Woods pursues the implications of the Buddhistic background of the *Quartet*, arguing that the hostile response of some of the early criticism is the result of a misunderstanding of Durrell's motives. Proust is cited as a model for the narrative stance in *Mountolive* by Eugene Hollahan, thus tying Durrell more directly to the tradition of European fiction. Moving on to *The Revolt of Aphrodite*, Frank Kersnowski discusses the interaction between Felix Charlock as the narrator of the two volumes and Lawrence Durrell as the author of the books. Donald P. Kaczvinsky, as well, concentrates on *Tunc* and *Nunquam,* underlining the influence of D. H. Lawrence's theories of culture and civilization on Durrell, who has acknowledged Lawrence as a literary mentor.

The final group of essays, "Myth, Mystery, and Dirty Tricks," confronts *The Avignon Quintet* head on. In an investigation of the murky history of the Knights Templar, Michael H. Begnal seeks to clarify their role in Durrell's contemporary version of a search for spiritual knowledge. This is initial spadework, and much is left to be done on the historical and symbolic backgrounds of the *Quintet.* Susan Vander Closter looks to Durrell's alter-ego, the painter Oscar Epfs, and to art history to illuminate the many tableaux that are studded throughout these five novels, and James R. Nichols turns the concept of the Fortunate Fall upside down to show how Durrell's supposedly fallen women lead the way to virtue and to love. Finally, in an attempt to arrive at a rationale for Durrell's narrational technique in the *Quintet,* William L. Godshalk demonstrates Durrell's constant and effective violation of the conventions of storytelling, providing the reader with some initial footholds with which to begin the ascent of *The Avignon Quintet.*

Throughout his career, Lawrence Durrell has always been an experimental writer, blending the theories of Freud with those of Einstein, manipulating the intricacies of form and narrational point of view, yet he always remains intent upon the relevance of the here and now. Tantric Buddhism is just as central to his work as is field theory, the spiritual intertwines easily with the physical, and the central goal is the resolution of opposites. Paradox is implicit in his writings—the romantic impulse is incorporated into the formal classicism of James Joyce. It is our hope that these essays may help to rekindle a reader's appreciation for a writer who is certainly a major practitioner of twentieth-century fiction. Throughout it all, Lawrence Durrell remains simply what he began as: a consummate artist.

## NOTE

1. Reed Way Dasenbrock, "Lawrence Durrell and the Modes of Modernism," *Twentieth Century Literature* 33 (Winter 1987): 515–27. Alan W. Friedman makes much the same point in his introduction to the essay collection *Critical Essays on Lawrence Durrell* (Boston: G. K. Hall, 1987).

# Overture

## Lawrence Durrell

Ladies and gentlemen, I feel a terrible fraud. I've prepared absolutely nothing because I've never been in this position before in my life, and I wanted to test the novelty of it and the singularity of it. The thought that my characters, my projections, the people I fabricated out of my own isolation as a writer, have penetrated the known world and are making babies everywhere, so to speak, is something so intoxicating that it's very bad for my narcissism. And it's with trepidation that I came today, but I've been much reassured by the eloquence and the incisiveness and the cleverness of the insights, and I really feel that perhaps I've been doing quite a good job.

But this said, it led me to go back in my mind and over my own life, and to try to evaluate how it all came about. And I was wondering if perhaps the simplest thing, as a commentary, would be to describe my biography very simply to you, and to explain that it really isn't as difficult as all that. There are no original ideas in what I've done. What I wanted to do was to end my life as a poet by leaving behind a travelogue of my experiences, my psychological and practical experiences in the world, and this couldn't be done unless I chose a medium. As I was not good enough to be a painter, I had to content myself with words.

I was born, as you know, in India, and I lived there until I was eleven. Somebody has remarked that the terrible thing about life is that we have to live it forwards, but it can only be evaluated backwards. In other words, while I was in India I was not conscious of what India was doing for me or to me. I lived the life of a colonial, a typical *pied noir*, an English *pied noir*. My father was a civil engineer, and we were not very rich, but he traveled all over the place and we went with him. The result is that I've lived in tents and in jungles, and I lived a pretty wild life in India. I had not been at all conscious, being so British, that India had rubbed off on me at all, until I became about fifty years old, and I reevaluated the Buddhism in which and with which we had largely lived without being conscious of the fact.

A series of curious Buddhist events have taken place in my life. For

11

example, with my first wife—at the age of three—a man came to have dinner with her father, and, when he left, he left her his entire estate. When she was twenty-one, she inherited a book called *Burma: The Soul of a People* by E. Fielding-Hall. This book, which continues to sell, and which brings in a little bit of money, enabled me to borrow some money from her in Paris in 1940 and become the publisher of Henry Miller and Anaïs Nin. It was this money of the Fielding-Hall estate with which I published *Max and the White Phagocytes, The Black Book,* and *The Winter of Artifice* of Anaïs Nin. This was what the French would call an *enchaînement* of some kind. And then the war broke out, and we were all catapulted into different domains to live through this distressing but unbelievably rich period with which I attempted to do something.

But all through this period I had been unconsciously doing yoga, having watched my father do it. At that epoch, the colonials didn't believe in anything mystical, and they were perfectly determinist in their attitude, you see, and yoga was regarded as one would regard aspirin. In other words, when you were ill you asked the local carpenter to come up and give you a few lessons, and you learned half a dozen asanas. You did it therapeutically, but not religiously, not in any profound sense. But I imitated the asanas, and I discovered how to heat myself, which, later when I went to Darjeeling, I found extremely useful in the cold. Even more when I went to England, because there they specialized. They knew nothing about lamas, but they went one better. The English cold really went to the bone, and in St. Edmund's, which was a normal and a rather happy school really, the cold was so intense that the snow used to blow in on the foot of my bed. I was very grateful to have learned how to draw my knees up to my chin, and breathe on them, and warm myself up by in-breathing, by redistribution of oxygen.

But there was another factor, and this is perhaps the more cogent part of such a biography, I had decided early on to become a poet. I don't quite know what I meant by that, but I realized that it was a role that had a function which was quite different from the business function of my parents, my family, and so on, and our rather materialist and determinist attitude to the world. The idea was applauded because it was regarded as not dangerous, not obnoxious, and so I was encouraged to continue to believe that it was OK as an ideal. In some curious way, I made the conjunction in my mind between what was taking place in the yoga world and what was taking place in myself as somebody evolving towards a nature of poetry. I hadn't learned to write then. I started writing poetry at the age of eight, doggerel really, but I was grateful for Kipling as somebody in the same subcontinent who was exercising the function of a poet, and I offered myself as a sort of student to him. But the Buddhic and yogic function seemed to me to tie in somehow with this poetic function, and I suddenly realized—I hadn't conceptualized the whole matter—it seemed to me that the whole poetic function, the poetic equation, was what, in fact, my yoga teacher was trying to sell.

Life being so short, it was clear that we really had to hurry up and try to achieve a kind of realization, to hook in with reality, and to start using it, instead of moving along parallel tracks. The yogic asanas seemed to me to relate absolutely directly to that, and, if Buddhism was more satisfying than the Protestantism of my parents, it was because you could check it on your physique. You used your body like a piano, and, with the help of your yoga teacher, you could check out the states of mind described by these people. I saw in all this a relevant field of action, a field of development, which kept me nourished during a period when the whole of life seemed to me to be entirely deterministic, materialistic. People paid a rather perfunctory attention to religious observance, in terms of going to church for five minutes on Sunday but then forgetting about the whole matter. Where exactly this came from I didn't realize for many years, but one of the assignments that my father had was to build a railway in Burma, and we lived there while he did it. We lived for nearly a year there in tents and in forests. It was called the Himalayan railway, and the Burmese were ardent Buddhists at that time.

It is something that is so extraordinary when the national ethos of a country is devoted to seeking out states of calm and states of harmlessness and states of good nature, because after all if you want those sorts of results you must really work for them. Goodness can't just be inherited; it's got to be earned, in a way. If you live in a Buddhist country, it is so extraordinary. You wake up without being afraid of your neighbor, as you do in the countries we inhabit. The whole of nature seems permeated by a sense of harmless good will, and it opens a field for self-development which is not accessible in a country where you have very rigid, theologically oriented people with a national ethos that's repressive or restrictive in any way.

In fact, Christian theology is such; it's poisoning in the restrictive sense. Well, my father built this railway, and he had for the children a nurse called Miss O'Farrell, who was a lugubrious Irishwoman who took us for walks. One day we strayed into a Parsee graveyard, which was simply a little forest with a whole lot of corpses lying all over the place. I suddenly realized how much the corpses represented something of which we were afraid and which we had repressed, because Miss O'Farrell reacted immediately. Meanwhile, in the graveyard itself, there were a couple of men who were cutting up the corpses in the most genial way, perfectly charming, and they were distributing them in the trees to attract the birds. They were making signs to the birds to come and get their lunch, so to speak. Also, on the ground there were fires. Some people were burning their relatives, a little bit, and there were vultures lying about, like literary critics, making that sort of curdling noise that one makes after a heavy lunch. I didn't exchange a word, but I felt that my nurse was absolutely paralyzed with fright. She snatched at me, and raced back home to the camp with me, and then she confessed to my mother that she had strayed into this little reserve which was a graveyard.

I suddenly realized without formulating the fact that the basic factor, the basic neurosis, the heart of distress, was this repression about the nature of death. When I came on to Buddhist practice, I realized that that's their point of departure. They realized that, unless you get on top of the distress caused by the fear of death, you cannot advance creatively in your business of self-realization. You start with the notion of impermanence, and the necessity of impermanence, and you turn it into something positive. And this clears the way for every kind of positive emotion, for love, for abstract thought, and for everything. I hadn't realized the force of death.

It's come back to me so frequently since I became a lecturer, because when one's talking about poetry one's talking about a privileged experience, and the unhappy thing is that it's an experience which really cannot be compassed in words. You can only exclaim and point, and keep on pointing until they get it. But you can't confer it. And however logically brilliant you are, all your formulations, poetic or otherwise, are only indications—they're the outer skin of something. You can't actually confer it—it can only be self-conferred. And it can only take place with a real effort, real work on yourself in that tantric sense. It's a problem that we're facing, both as a national ethos, as an ethos of the West, and as individuals here, because Christianity has failed, which might have had a possibility of evolving in this sense. Owing to lack of method, I think it's failed us. If the Buddhistic element seemed to me richer, it is because, as I say, you can test it. You don't have to take anything for granted. When you think of the Christian rigamarole, all that you have to believe and subscribe to without any proof, it's naturally a cause of great distress. Whereas in the Buddhist thing, you test it on yourself, the states of mind, you can achieve them by breathing, by redistribution of your oxygen. In a matter of a month, no matter how preposterous the propositions of your yoga teacher, you can verify them for yourself. So it's a great consolation to be responsible for your own feelings, for your own theater of operations, in the world, especially if you're a creative artist, and you want to confer—what? You don't want to confer theology. It's perfectly terrifying. At the same time, language is totally inadequate to deal with this particular thing, this particular notion, this inspired view which transcends the given logic of the day, and which infuses oxygen into you, and which, as they say, changed my whole life in a matter of a breath.

This has happened to everyone, and will continue to happen to everyone, and we are hunting through various forms to provoke this, so that writing, and poetry particularly, is a sort of challenge. I've noticed this recently because sometimes, depressed by an audience when one is lecturing, and one brings up this matter, one sees from the faces that there are people who have been programmed out of this type of sensibility, which makes this experience particularly viable, so that you're wasting your breath and your time. If you are lecturing on this sort of matter and trying to propound the poetic view, the poetic equation in relation to life and to living, you'll have to try to find a way that's therapeutic to do it. I suddenly asked at one lecture in Geneva, how many people have seen somebody dead. Four people put up their hands. Then recently I had a small seminar of people, and I had the same problem of understanding, and they had never assisted anybody to die, and, so to speak, helped them away. I suggested to them that they get in touch with a doctor friend or a hospital, and therapeutically try that out. It completely changed their sensibilities. Two promising neurotics have become almost normalized by the simple experience of being forced to accept death as a reality. They'd been funking it, unconsciously, and something like this same process is, I think, necessary when one talks about poetry.

Fundamentally, our education, the whole business of our ethos, our culture, should begin with death and with birth. To the same people, I suggested that they assist at the delivery of some children. They did that too, a group of four ladies, and completely changed their whole conspectus of things. Now they suddenly find what they'd considered mysterious, and perhaps not very alluring, in the *Quartet* accessible to them. In other words, they began to follow the argument, from their own experience, not from anything I had to tell them, because it had been there all the time. The fact of helping to deliver a few babies and helping shut the eyes and lay out a couple of people deepened their feeling of reality, which engaged them immediately on the poetic path, which, with yoga, starts from there. All education should really start with death, and the proof of our enormous repression about this matter is that we put screens around the dying. I don't know anybody who's helped deliver children except me. I think we all should have had that. Navigating through these general ideas, and with the notion that everybody was a poet—in fact, my yoga teacher, in trying to describe what he regards as Taoism, said everybody has it, but it's so amusing because it's like somebody walking around the house looking for his spectacles, when they're on his head. Because everybody's got it, but it's a question of how to mobilize a way of getting in touch with it. Well, this I think is the function of art.

When I turned out my playbox at the age of eighteen, when I wanted to start practicing as a writer, I took this matter tremendously seriously. We were brought up as pre-Raphaelites, in a sense, our sensibility was a pre-Raphaelite sensibility. We were brought up rather strictly, not really oppressively. We were taught to revere girls, which is right, a bit too much perhaps, and, at the same time, to work. Nowadays, I'm afraid, nobody seems to be interested anymore. With this raw material, my parents always believed that I ought to become celebrated and rather rich, but they sort of saw a Trollope in me. When you're born in a Philistine family, it's very difficult. You can't stake your claim to be an artist, but they were extremely genteel. My father, who didn't believe at all that I should be a writer, bought me a complete Dickens and sent it up on a mule, which was very handsome of him, because he would nominally figure as an honest Philistine. My mother believed in it, but I could see from the way she said, "Yes, dear. Yes, dear. Yes, dear," and passed on to some other subject matter, that they were humoring me. And so I went through the routine of going to school, and going to public school, and going to army crammers, and pretending I was going up to university, when I didn't want to.

At the same time I started writing, and they really didn't believe in me, but I did finish a novel, a very bad novel. I actually took it to London, and I went to see Spencer Curtis Browne who said he would sell it for me, and he did. I told them I had sold a novel, but they didn't quite understand at all, and then one day there was a ring on the doorbell. The postman came with a big packet in brown paper. It was six complementary copies of this novel. I undid the packet at the breakfast table, and they said, "What's that?" I said, "It's my novel." It was just like Hiroshima—I had dropped a bomb. From then on, they looked at me in the strangest way, but they realized there was something serious in all this nonsense. They kept picking this novel up and turning it over, looking at it as an object, a sacred object, a tantric object. I had proved my case, and I received every support from them.

I then discovered that I was unhappy in England, because of the cold feet and because of the general ethos. English life is really like an autopsy. It's so, so dreary. Then I set off, and I discovered first Paris and then France. I'd always been keen on the French, and I'd done more work in French, practically, than in English. In fact, I still think that in a real way I think in French and write in English. It gives a sort of grain to English, which tends to be a bit lush. The lucidity of French and the anarchy of its psychological and syntactical motions are a great help to a poet, I find. Then I went to Greece, where I discovered another strange thing. In Greece I had done a lot of work on the ancient Greek philosophers, but not *very* much. There I made a sudden discovery that, really, what was ailing me, why I was neurotic, why I was unfulfilled, and why I was interested in using these various gambits to try to realize myself, was really the enormous trauma of being shut out of India at eight, and found out. It was a great shock. Of course, one learns to pity one's self retrospectively. I hadn't read Freud then, so I really wasn't self-pitying enough.

Anyway, in Greece what was so intriguing was that I discovered that the continuity with ancient Greece was practically perfect. The language had aged so little that Socrates would have been able to read the street signs if he had returned, the signs of the bread shops and the domestic shops, so little has the basic language changed. The only two languages which don't seem to have worn at all are Chinese and Greek, whereas now, even for Shakespeare, we need a dictionary after three hundred years. That was a great astonishment to me, and daily life in Greece was a great treasure, a great pleasure. But then I discovered that the Greek philosophers had all taken their degrees in India, that there had been a continuous message coming through on some sort of wavelength. India had been informing Europe, and this transmission had been broken, like you break an electric current. I suppose historians will be able to explain it to us. I suspect one of the big earthquakes that destroyed Santorini and destroyed the entire Cretan culture might possibly have broken the continuity. Perhaps we could read some of the symbols into the Roman remains of Provence today. For me it was a personal discovery, and I realized with it that what I was trying to do was to find my way back to India, in my personal life to restore the broken context. One couldn't do this because the war was coming, and it was not possible. I took refuge in yoga, and I suddenly realized that India had never left me, and I had never left India.

I was using yoga the wrong way, not sufficiently richly. So I began to take it more seriously, and to try to elaborate a creed of poetry, if you like, which would justify a sort of interior life which seemed to me was necessarily more rich than most people permitted themselves to live. In a sense, they blinkered themselves and kept themselves aloof from the deeper part of their own natures. Of course, it's also the most perilous part of your own nature, because it's where you keep your choice neuroses. One has to go through that. In fact, the yoga teacher will tell you instantly that you must take risks, and that in order to refine and provoke the spark, the poetic spark, the bliss, you risk also a nice schizophrenia if you don't do it carefully. Yoga does need thought and needs extremely concise tuition. It needs some self-dedication; you can't, for example, be a drunkard like me and be a very good yoga man. You run a risk there. If you take your yoga seriously, and your poetry seriously, you have to be a bit of an ascetic which, thank God, I'm not.

What I had vaguely in mind was not only that the work, the oeuvre in the general sense, if it stood up at all, if it was still alive ten years after my death, say, would represent a kind of travelogue of my life, with all its various influences, but that I might by luck manage to refurbish a little bit the English novel, which it seemed to me was showing signs of terrible wear and tear because of its epistemological backwardness. Just as Proust used Bergson and the ideas of Bergson to refurbish his notions of time and continuity, I wanted to see what our contemporary ethos, our culture, was, and see whether I couldn't use it as a kind of symbolic basis for a poem of some sort. In the *Quartet* I chose the relativity proposition because it seemed to me that the ideas that were most interesting and most enriching, and which were leading us, in a way, back to India, were coming precisely out of the heavily deterministic mathematics of these old boys, Freud and Einstein.

To oversimplify horribly, you couldn't regard a field without modifying it. The identity of opposites was a proposition which you came across in Chinese Taoism. It seemed to me that the world was becoming one world, that the transmission was repairing itself, and that if I could do that it might be quite a fruitful way of treating the modern novel. I hoped that it would perhaps be original, but I hadn't any actually schematic notion about it because I felt it might go dead. In fact, one of the basic problems is to keep the transmission going, and not let the thing become dead because it was too theoretical. In a sense, I strayed into this novel with trepidation, holding in mind these philosophic equations and seeing whether they would work out, whether I could get a multidimensional personality which would correspond roughly to the quest that was going forward in the unified field theory.

That, and of course Freud, who had presented us with a new unconscious, which is completely pristine. My grandfather would not have understood *The Interpretation of Dreams*. He would have regarded it as the most excruciating folklore, and yet it seemed to me an absolute reality. I even managed to check it a little bit by analyzing myself. I wrote a series of confessional letters to friends of mine. I monitored some of my dreams, and I was surprised to find that I was cured, simply by the fact of having written to two or three friends of mine, letters accusing myself of things I'd been dreaming, which obviously I wanted to do and hadn't the courage to. I found that the therapy proposed by Freud was really an active working principle. It was a little too simple—the psyche as an impulse inhibition machine was a little too deterministic—but it was such a marvelous breakthrough, breathtaking in its novelty and so useful because one has used it all one's life.

Nowadays, it has sunk into our bloodstreams, into our consciousnesses. We're using it in all kinds of ways, in group therapy, and as far as I can see the original proposition hasn't been at all dented. That, and the propositions of Einstein, seemed to me to constitute our total ethos. There I saw the world coming together, the Tibetans coming to meet the Christians, and the whole thing becoming one world. This is happening so rapidly thanks to the television that by the time I get back to my village it will be entirely populated by Chinese. Now, travel tours pass through my village, with Chinese housewives looking into the windows of the French housewives, and discovering that they have common values in their attitudes towards vegetables and fish and so on. The great danger is that we will find such uniformity coming about in the next ten years that we'll be excruciated. Anyway, that's not my fault.

If I can have done one Tibetan-type novel, and one European-type novel, and left them to marry each other, and made a poetic equation which is a challenge which might offer a toehold to young poets and young thinkers, and a provocation to people who are not growing fast enough, my job will have been done. It's in that sense, really, that I was so thrilled to hear these evaluations and to see how correctly I had laid the trail, because these sparks were in the genuine context. This is really what I meant. The other day, before I came here, I went to see my brother in Jersey, and he said, "Oh, it's terribly bad for narcissism. You know what you'll do, you'll just die of flattery. It's too horrible." I said, "No, I won't. I'll write *My Brother and Other Animals* when I come back."

He said, "Well, listen, old boy, you're going to croak one of these days, so I hope you're satisfied with all this rubbish you've been writing. You'd better think now of what you'd like written on your plaque in the Poet's Corner of Westminster." And that really gave me thought, so I had an enormous think about this, and I was walking in Shepherd's Bush Market the other day, which is a wonderful shanty town, African and Indian and Sikh, and everything. They're selling all sorts of things, and there are some very grave, reverential-looking Indians and Parsees with a huge store full of toys. Among the toys were some beautifully articulated snakes for sale, children's toys, and they were labeled "Oriental Serpent—Authentic Wiggle." I thought, if I had anything in Westminster Abbey, I would like to have "Authentic Wiggle"!

—Transcribed and silently edited by Michael H. Begnal

# ON MIRACLE GROUND

# Part 1
# Metaphysics and Metafiction

# Pied Piper of Death:
## Method and Theme in the Early Novels

### IAN S. MACNIVEN

If ever a first novel was given by its author an unfitting title it is Law-rence Durrell's *Pied Piper of Lovers* (1935). A boy-child survives a diffi-cult birth that results in the death of his mother. The boy is rather a changeling who doesn't fit his father's pukka conception: he is ex-pected to be "English," despite the "native" mother who has given him the "dark eyes" that mark his half-caste blood. Never mind. Dur-rell ignores throughout the novel what in the race-conscious worlds of Anglo-India and *"Belitee"*—England—must have been the indelible marks of "colour." What Durrell shows us instead is a person haunted by death, from his early explorations of Indian burial grounds to the loss of his father. The protagonist's single love affair comes near the end of the novel, and his lover is doomed by an impaired heart. No train of lovers follows him. Death is the leitmotiv of this novel and of Durrell's next two novels as well, *Panic Spring* (1937) and *The Black Book* (1938). Indeed, death is a presence in most of Durrell's writing, from such early poems as "The Death of General Uncebunke" (1938) to the late "A Patch of Dust" (1974); in his verse tragedies, especially *Sappho* (1950) and *Acte* (1964); in the "foreign residence books" (each is given a tragic focus by one or more deaths); and in the major novel groups, *The Alexandria Quartet* (1957–60), *The Revolt of Aph-rodite* (1968), and *The Avignon Quintet* (1974–85).

This brief outline of Durrell's use of death as a dominant theme from his first novel on suggests that *Pied Piper of Lovers* should be looked at as a prefiguring of what was to come, and indeed this novel shares with *Panic Spring* the first indications of many of Durrell's artis-tic methods and themes, developed even before *The Black Book,* the novel in which Durrell himself has claimed he "first heard the sound of my own voice."[1] Durrell's first two novels have never been reprinted due to his specific prohibition. They are available in a very few library special collections or only occasionally and at high prices from dealers. Partly for these reasons they are virtually unknown to the reading

public and have seldom been considered by scholars.[2] It is clear to all
who have looked at Durrell's early novels that they, like the novels that
followed them, are interrelated. Some characters and situations are
carried over from *Pied Piper* into *Panic Spring,* from *Panic Spring* into
*The Black Book.* The journal in which characters in *Pied Piper* carry on
their intellectual dialogues is called "the black book," looking forward
to the title of Durrell's third novel.

As one would expect, in the early novels Durrell is learning to control his material and his talent. His narrative method moves from
third-person limited omniscience with a few editorial asides in *Pied
Piper of Lovers* to the melange of "I" narration, diaries, letters, and omniscient voices found in *The Black Book* and thereafter. He also learns
to place narrative distance between his own experiences and his inventions, while at the same time increasingly denying the difference between fact and fictions. Durrell's characteristic diction appears but
rarely in *Pied Piper,* yet in *Panic Spring* his distinctive voice is common,
especially in his descriptions of place and in his evocations of the horrific. His readings of the English classics have left the pug marks of
allusion everywhere, but such tracking is beyond the scope of this
study, as is Durrell's development of his theory of "heraldry," the establishment by the creative artist of his own world of symbol and
meaning, a topic that has been handled with some thoroughness by
others.[3] After treating the development of Durrell's narrative method,
I shall consider principally such items of thematic importance as the
evidence of Durrell shying away from Christianity; developing the
paired motifs of estrangement and exile; turning loneliness into a personal ethic; evolving his concept of the breakdown of the discrete ego;
becoming, although himself among the healthiest of mortals, almost
pathologically fascinated by disease; taking up death as a powerful
ally and ultimately recognizing it as his greatest theme. All these aspects of Durrell's art appeared by the time he was twenty-five, showing his rapid determination of his artistic direction.

Durrell's first three novels are loosely connected in plot and charac-
ters. *Pied Piper of Lovers* describes the birth and exotic childhood of
Walsh Clifton in India, his public-school education in an abhorred
England, and his love affair in bohemian Bloomsbury with Ruth, like
Walsh a precocious orphan. *Panic Spring* shows a group of castaways
from northern and eastern Europe trying to reconstitute their lives
on a Greek island where Pan rather than Jehovah is the tutelary god.
Walsh is there, recovering from the death of Ruth, with her brother,
Gordon, as a protective presence. The other characters are new to
*Panic Spring. The Black Book* brings a bit-player from *Panic Spring,* the
schoolmaster Tarquin, into major focus, but the continuity here is

more evident in theme than in cast. England and the "English death," a limbolike passive state, are summarily rejected, and Lawrence Lucifer, the principal narrator and thinly disguised spokesman for the author, discovers himself, as a man and an artist, on Corfu.

*Pied Piper of Lovers* is an unabashed *Erziehungsroman,* the tale of the growing up of Burma-born Walsh Clifton in the hill country of northern India (like India-born Durrell, who "saw the Himalayas like lambs there"[4]) through his abrupt translation to the fogs and humours of "Pudding Island." Durrell himself likes to tell interviewers that the true guide to his childhood is Kipling's *Kim,* and in his autobiographical essay "From the Elephant's Back" Durrell describes a childhood paradise.[5] Durrell has made some attempt to open the action of *Pied Piper* with the point of view and language of a six-year-old, Walsh's age when his story proper begins, but Durrell employs an ironic tone that threatens to become quaint: "When he was six, and old enough (sweet privilege!) to be allowed to watch his father shave every morning, he began to consider himself a person of great importance."[6] The same ironic tone is applied to a lazy carpenter, an incompetent doctor, and a tyrannical headmaster. By *Panic Spring* Durrell has abandoned such mannered irony for a carefully balanced ambiguity, as in the presentation of Christian Marlowe, a timid apostle of "Quietism" who has fled from English public school teaching to find excitement. Stranded in Brindisi by Greek civil strife, he observes a plump and wealthy fellow traveler: "Watching her as she wound damp spools of spaghetti upon a fork, Marlowe found himself wishing she would hang herself in the stuff. He watched the disappearance of each writhing forkful with a vague excitement."[7] Is this to be the limit of Marlowe's discovery of excitement? Soon the reader gains confidence in Marlowe and comes to view the Greek world through the glass of his quirky nature.

Durrell's infrequent editorial comments in *Pied Piper of Lovers* seem as mannered as the irony he employs in this first novel, especially where the narrator discourses upon his own words: "Yet, perhaps I wrong him," comments the editorial voice, after a lengthy passage on the imbecility of a Hindu carpenter.[8] Occasionally the editorial comment is phrased as a direct address to the reader, instructing him: "You will find the town on the map (if you care to look)," he is told.[9] The editorial "I" appears about the same half-dozen times in *Panic Spring,* but Durrell abandons the device in *The Black Book* in favor of the commentary of internal narrators and diarists, the method he favors in *The Alexandria Quartet* and thereafter.

*Pied Piper of Lovers* is the most overtly autobiographical of Durrell's novels, yet even here he departs freely from the facts of his life. Walsh

Clifton is an only child who becomes an orphan while in his teens. Durrell grew up with three siblings, and, although his father like Walsh's did die while he was at school in England, his mother lived to an advanced age. The more significant parallels with fact are apparently inward: like Durrell, Walsh disliked England, fiercely resented the brutal school discipline, despised the bohemia of literary London. In his later novels Durrell soon learned to distance himself, to disguise his tracks. In *Panic Spring* only the situation—foreigners together on a Greek Island—and some of the characters are in general outlines traceable to Durrell's life at the time of composition. Benevolent and rich old Kostas Rumanades playing host to a number of casual visitors could have been suggested by several of Durrell's Corfu friends, local patricians with country estates: Count John Theotocki, Dr. Palatiano, the Abrami family, the Soufi family. *The Black Book* shows Durrell up to a sleight-of-hand identity trick: the reader is practically ordered to consider the author's namesake, Lawrence Lucifer, his point-of-view character and spokesman, and then toward the end of the book "Durrell" is referred to by name as separate from Lawrence Lucifer when Tarquin confesses: "Listen, we borrowed Durrell's car and went out of London. Imagine us locked in the back seat, O Christ, buggering each other like a couple of billy goats."[10] Similarly, Durrell later places himself by initial in *Monsieur,* the first novel of *The Avignon Quintet,* as the "begetter" of the sometime narrator Blanford.

Few changes are more startling in the course of Durrell's first three novels than the emergence of his characteristic diction, his phrasing. His fondness for the homely adjectives "slow" and "great" (as in "slow chords" and "great flashing tears"[11]) is evident in *Pied Piper of Lovers,* but only very occasionally in this novel does one come across anything even approaching the surprising word combinations recognized as Durrellian: of the carpenter, Durrell says that "long parings of wood lolled up from his plane, squirming over and about his strong hands."[12] Not too bad, perhaps, but a bit labored. And there are many clichés, as in the description of Walsh's first meeting with Ruth: "He turned and smiled confusedly down at her, feeling at a disadvantage. . . . it cost him an effort to look at her so frankly, so deep into her eyes. . . . His forearm pressed back upon her firm round breasts. . . . He said breathlessly. . . ."[13] However, the language of *Pied Piper* is not usually impoverished so much as stilted: the language of a dictionary addict, of a writer seeking out unusual words yet lacking the artistry to make their appearance credible. Durrell writes of Walsh's father, "The implacable forces could be placated, not by himself, nor by the abruption of conscious action, but by that unflinching acquiescence in himself, which would make room for change."[14] Ouf!

*Panic Spring* is quite another matter. My reading notes list several dozen pages with one or more passages of characteristic Durrellian diction, lines that beg for the typographic distinction of verse, as I have rendered the sample here:

> Wheat like gold foam;
> the ashy rectangles of oats,
> the mustard crop, spittle-bright:
> these were tantalising images of coolness
> and ease focused against the blue water
> and the distance that hid Epirus.[15]

Durrell wrote *Panic Spring* on Corfu, probably while he was staying in the "White House" on idyllic Kalami Bay, and it is tempting to conclude that his skill in presenting a locale was awakened by the Greek world. *Panic Spring* is filled with descriptive similes, sometimes startling, sometimes outrageous, yet invariably apt: St. Benedetto hanging "like a folded bat, in swathes of tranquil blackness";[16] a large Italian lady, "emphatic as a motorbike." Durrell described his conscious use of the formula of pairing a "hot noun" to a "cold adjective" in a 1958 letter to Henry Miller:

> When a Jap writes "cherry" "moon" "grass" the ideogram has a mystical-metaphysical ring quite different from the set of associations we stir by using them; hence the image making that we have to put into it; I work hot to cold like a painter. Hot noun, cold adjective ("mathematical cherry" rather than "sweet cherry"). Or on a sour abstract word like "armature" a warm sweetish one like "melodious."[18]

We find him playing precisely this noun/adjective game in *Panic Spring*: "anonymous lover," "economic winter," "mechanical brain."[19] The "ashy rectangles" quoted earlier pits a "sour" geometric word against the portentous "ashy."

Durrell once wrote to T. S. Eliot, "My job is to throw myself over precipices,"[20] and in *Panic Spring* we see him taking greater and greater chances to gain conciseness and impact. Durrell also pushes at the limits of decorum, juxtaposing the horrific to the mundane and doing it in language that preserves ironic detachment. The last of many parties in the novel concludes with yet another of the sinister Russian Fonvisin's macabre stories. The incredible tale—that Dr. Fonvisin had put his brother into a comatose sleep that is still continuing after twenty years—combined with the storm outside and the copious swigs of alcohol each guest has swallowed, drives all to frenzy:

This state of affairs might have lasted all night, had not Fonvisin been reminded that his flesh, too, was heir to a thousand natural shocks. Crop-sick of a sudden, he reeled to his feet, staggered, rotated, drove the thumb of his right hand into his eye, and began horribly to cat in the fender.

It was a consummation devoutly to be wished.[21]

Recalling Fonvisin's discomfiture provides a suitable transition from language to theme, since it shows Durrell combining in brief compass the natural, the grotesque, and the humorous. The themes that stand out fit together with an inherent logic: Durrell's rejection of Christianity was perhaps the first step in his evolving sense of estrangement and exile, and these factors increased his loneliness. His feeling that he stood alone personally while he was developing multiple personalities in his writing may have suggested to him the breakdown of the discrete ego—who *is* Lawrence Durrell, indeed?—and it is the *discrete* ego that is threatened by disease and death. These themes were apparent in his writing by the time he had completed *Panic Spring*.

In *Pied Piper of Lovers* the secular triumphs over the Christian religious impulse: Walsh first loses faith in the efficacy of prayer, discovering that whining to his father will procure him toys whereas praying to God will not. Whatever doubts he may have harbored about Christianity are resolved by the arrival of his father's mother:

> With the summer came Grandmamma, and with Grandmamma came the plague; both calamities, coming as they did, at exactly the same time, became indissolubly linked in the boy's mind as a double-headed evil. . . . Grandmamma was . . . securely entrenched behind the illusory fiction of her God. . . . She was squat, immense, and obese. . . . She walked, like a spirit of parasitic evil, about the house, murmuring texts and maxims.[22]

According to Durrell, this is a portrait of "Big Granny," as his paternal grandmother was called.[23] When Walsh is sent to public school in England the twice-daily chapel services became dreaded ordeals: "And the organ groaning loudly above the uproar in lachrymose anguish . . . groaning and invoking *Granny's God*. . . . Meantime he must try not to listen: *he must not listen*."[24] While some individual clerics come off fairly well in Durrell's writing—a few Jesuit and Greek Orthodox priests—Christianity was never to be presented as a viable option for faith in his novels. Rather, when a formal religion is described at all sympathetically, it is either an Eastern religion or Gnosticism, the obverse of Christianity.

Thus, in his first novel Durrell proclaims his lasting rejection of Christianity, and he also shows a marked preference for the religions that he now favors, the Taoism of *A Smile in the Mind's Eye* (1980), the Tibetan Buddhism practiced at the temple Durrell now actively supports in Plaige, France. In *Panic Spring* the restoration of a small Orthodox church becomes an element in the plot, but far from having any religious significance in the context of the story, the proposed work is merely a scheme on the part of Rumanades, owner of the island, to keep Francis, a young and beautiful English artist, around with the promise of a mural to be painted. The name of the sympathetically rendered protagonist of *The Black Book,* Lucifer, suggests Durrell's anti-Christian stance.

When Durrell rejected Christianity he took an important step toward his estrangement from both Anglo-India, with its strong missionary bias and its sense of obligation to "carry the White Man's Burden," and the mother country that fostered the convenient colonial rationale of Christian paternalism. Durrell's irony in describing the making of the coffin for Walsh's Oriental mother shows his estrangement from the empire builders: Krisnati, the mistreated carpenter, builds the coffin out of discarded packing crates, and, although he planes most of the surfaces smooth, he leaves "for all to see" the "red, stamped capital letters that herded unsteadily together":

'WITH GREAT CARE'
'THE KULU APPLE'
(The white man's delight.)[25]

The native woman who had been John Clifton's delight is given this "parting tribute" by another native who just might, Durrell informs us, be aware of the irony as well: "Perhaps he had divined the need for an epitaph . . . perhaps, in his fuddled old mind, he remembered the inscribed tombstones of the oppressors of his race. . . . Who can say?" Durrell, loving India and the "hill folk" among whom he lived until age twelve, rejected colonialism in India as he would later in Cyprus.

Although Durrell was then or would soon become estranged from the colonial function, he felt when a youth that his departure from India was in the nature of an exile (young Lawrence did not want to go to England, but his father insisted on sending him "home," against his mother's wishes as well).[26] Durrell gives to Walsh his own sentiments: "He knew, of course, that England was where everyone should go," but the boy admits to his interlocutor, "'It doesn't sound so frightfully nice.'"[27] Walsh feels that he is being exiled when he is finally sent, and he views the cliffs above Dover with no enthusiasm. *Panic Spring* is a novel about exiles, and to an extent so are all Durrell's novels: about the English on Corfu, about Europeans exiled to Egypt, about deracinated wanderers in wartime Europe, and so on. Durrell credits his Indian origin with making him an exile: "I am, and I remain, an expatriate. That vague sense of exile has never quite left me. . . . The expatriate carries his country with him, inside him: everywhere belongs to him, because he belongs nowhere."[28] Lacking the strong national and community roots of a James Joyce or a D. H. Lawrence, to mention two other prominent self-exiles, Durrell has become a cosmopolitan writer in a way they have not. Joyce and Lawrence were to carry Dublin and Eastwood respectively with them wherever they went, but Durrell has no such single locus of reference, and this is already evident in *Pied Piper of Lovers*.

One does not have to be an estranged exile to be lonely, but it helps. Walsh's beloved Aunt Brenda calls him a "solitary little devil,"[29] but all of Durrell's characters in *Pied Piper of Lovers* seem to be solitaries: Walsh's father, John, who cannot talk to his sister; Aunt Brenda, who cannot confide in Walsh. From a speeding train taking him to London Walsh waves to an old man with a scythe: "Walsh, seeing him, was suddenly trapped by an impulse of loneliness and yearning; the doom, the hot agony of the earth filled him with a sudden passion of loneliness."[30] Toward the end of the book we learn that Walsh can be open with one school friend and with Ruth and her brother, Gordon—not such an insignificant tally of intimates after all—but in *Panic Spring* Walsh is again in the main cut off. Writing to Henry Miller, Durrell tied his own loneliness to his condition of self-exile: "I'm one of the world's expatriates anyhow. It's lonely being cut off from one's race. So much of England I loved—and hated so much—I try and wipe it off my tongue but it clings."[31] A few months later Miller commented on "the remarkable obsessive use of the word 'loneliness'" in the then-unpublished *Black Book*. He thought that Durrell derived "from icy clear loneliness a fear of madness—but not truly, not real, only a pose unconsciously assumed in order to re-provoke the marvellous feeling of sheer loneliness, of your rightness."[32] Still later Miller scolded Durrell for complaining of his loneliness: to be an artist is to be lonely. With equal truth we could maintain that the loss of a sense of community is a condition of nineteenth- and twentieth-century man, going back at least to Melville's Ishmael.

A constant theme in Durrell's novels from the very first is the struggle to connect, but he is ambivalent about the value of connection, at least for the artist. The failures to connect are emphasized in *Panic Spring* by the fact that nearly every main character, even the fabulously wealthy host, Rumanades, is living alone in a villa quite some distance from all the others (the only exceptions are Walsh and Gordon, who share a bungalow). Rumanades, Francis, Fonvisin, and Walsh have

each suffered the flight or death of a mate. A survey of the principals
in *The Alexandria Quartet, The Revolt of Aphrodite,* and *The Avignon
Quintet* reveals comparable assortments of solitaries, alone for the
same reasons. The one person to have achieved "happiness" in *Cefalû*
(1947; first published as *The Dark Labyrinth* in 1958) lives as a hermit
on "the Roof of the World," an inaccessible valley in the mountains.
Walsh the bereaved composer of popular tunes seems a prototype for
such later solitary artists as Darley in the *Quartet,* seeing Alexandria
in retrospect from his lonely Greek island, and Blanford in the *Quintet,* "talking in whispers to an empty alcove,"[33] re-creating in his imagination his dead friend Constance. This strikes an eerie personal note:
*Nunquam,* the second title in *The Revolt of Aphrodite,* closes with a
"Postface" in the form of a personal letter to "Dear C.-M.V.," Claude-
Marie Vincendon, Durrell's third wife, who had died over two years
before the publication of the book. Durrell addresses her as if she were
alive: "Well, here it is, the second volume I promised you."[34]

The ability of a lonely artist, an internal narrator, to bring to life
another character suggests that the ego may be multiple and enduring:
is the Constance re-created by Durrell/Blanford any less (or more) real
than the original created by Durrell? Durrell blurs the distinction between "reality" and "fiction," between uniqueness and multiplicity,
still further in *The Avignon Quintet* by having Blanford create an
"alter-ego," Sutcliffe, who retaliates by creating Bloshford as a parody
of Blanford. Sutcliffe in *Constance,* the third volume of the *Quintet,*
thinks:

> We are all fragments of one another; everyone has a little bit of everything
> in his make-up. . . . Yet obstinately I dream of such a book, full of not com-
> pletely discrete characters, of ancestors and descendants all mixed up—
> could such people walk in and out of each other's lives without damaging
> the quiddity of each other?[35]

To view the ego as an assemblage, not a unity, is a concept of Tibetan
Buddhism, which Durrell was studying in 1937; witness the Tibetan
epigraph to *The Black Book.* In *Panic Spring* Durrell may have been
moving toward the creation of nondiscrete egos: just after telling a
story of a rich Pole who had mummified his wife in an attempt to
ensure the survival of her identity after death, Fonvisin sneers, "Personal identity!"[36] Asked to name the woman much later, the drunken
Fonvisin shouts "MANUELA," suggesting an overlapping relationship between the characters in Fonvisin's story and the situation of
Rumanades, whose wife Manuela has recently fled. Did Fonvisin create alternative egos for Rumanades and Manuela, or was he telling

the truth about the Polish couple? The issue is never clarified, and Durrell seems to be implying that *it does not matter* whether or not there was a single, discrete Manuela who died and was embalmed, or one who fled and still lives, or both. Fonvisin himself goes through a startling change immediately following the death of Rumanades, going in moments from being weary, dirty, and hung over into an absolutely blooming sensuality, "ripe as a nut for life."[37]

Shifting egos are more clearly delineated in *The Black Book*. The prostitute Gracie turns respectable, "talking with the hygienic purity of an Anerly matron"[38] under the influence of her lover Horace Gregory's status and the task of presiding over a tea service. The hypochondriac aesthete Tarquin emerges as an open homosexual, "Sexually mature, my dear, and fulfilled."[39] Chamberlain sheds his D. H. Lawrence–imitation ego ("more bowels of compassion!"[40]) in favor of bourgeois tranquillity as a *pater familias*. A quick glance at *The Alexandria Quartet* will reveal many nondiscrete egos in it as well: Balthazar goes from aesthetic adept of the cabala to love-sick fool to would-be suicide to fragile patient; Capodistria goes from libertine to corpse to political intriguer; Justine goes from mistress of Alexandria to droop-eyed failure to controller of the powerful Memlik; and so on. Iolanthe in *The Revolt of Aphrodite* is first a naïve, childlike prostitute, then a film idol; she escapes through death from the possessive mania of the business mogul Julian Pehlevi, is forced back into a simulacrum of life as a robot, and escapes a second time through the destruction of her robot-self. (I should add that her final escape occurs in a fall from the whispering gallery of St. Paul's Cathedral, further evidence of the Durrell's conviction of the destructive nature of Christianity.) The examples already given from *The Avignon Quintet* show that for Durrell the concept of the nondiscrete ego has remained an important theme in his novels.

Linked with the concept of the nondiscrete ego in Buddhism is the belief in reincarnation. In fact, both the nondiscrete ego and reincarnation are methods for defeating death. If the ego is not single and unique, and is shared across time as well, the death of the individual assumes less importance. Witness Scobie, the aged homosexual in *The Alexandria Quartet*. While alive, he leads a life at least tripartite as friend to Clea, Bimbashi in the police force, and transvestite. Dead, he is revered as a Moslem saint and is resurrected through mimicry by Clea and others.

Disease exists in Durrell's work as a state intermediate between life and death. From his earliest writing Durrell has been fascinated by disease, so much so that during his twenties he considered becoming a doctor. His concern with disease amounts to an obsession that goes back to his childhood in India and his subsequent realization of the effort it cost his parents to keep him and his three siblings alive. This consciousness of disease is amply illustrated in his early novels and remains a major theme through *The Avignon Quintet*. The overworked woman doctor in *Pied Piper of Lovers*, Maclean, names the killer diseases of India like a catechism: "Her mind repeated the names as a child repeats verses, without meaning, even without interest: cholera, dysentery, malaria, typhoid, smallpox, bubonic plague . . . was there no end to the catalogue?"[41] India is a deadly land, according to Durrell, with snakes threatening where disease leaves off. A cobra menaces Walsh on his way to his Jesuit school: he kills it—thanks to luck, since he had struck with his eyes closed.

The leitmotiv of *Pied Piper of Lovers*, as I said at the outset, is death: the novel begins with the childbirth death of Walsh's mother, then picks out as Walsh's strongest memories of India the native funerals led by conch-blowing "giant Bhutias," the corpses carried slung in coffins that left the heads exposed; the native burial ground where the boy had seen a "polished" anklebone gleaming among the ashes; the death of a young school friend ("It takes ten years for the worms to eat through the coffin,"[42] his ghoulish grandmother tells him). Walsh is haunted by his fantasy that "he saw with the dead man's eyes the deepest parts of the earth: the labyrinth of ants: the crannies of the lizards."[43] Sudden death threatens the living. It is no surprise when Walsh in England dreams the prophetic nightmare of his father's death at the fangs of a "hamadryad" or king cobra. When Walsh falls in love it is with Ruth, a frank sensualist doomed by a faulty heart. Death is not viewed only as the final affliction of human beings. Walsh when very young pursues a butterfly he covets for his collection into the garden of a neighbor named Sowerby, who shows the boy a room filled with carefully gutted and exquisitely mounted insect specimens, not only butterflies but every variety of entomological species. Sowerby tells Walsh of his idea that the mounted insects may some day be "galvanized" by lightning back into life.

In *Panic Spring* Sowerby's vision is paralleled by Fonvisin's tale of the resurrection during a winter storm of the mummified Spanish wife of the unnamed rich Pole. Durrell introduces the story in the comic/ grotesque mode that he has come to employ in dealing with the morbid. Walsh, Marlowe, and Fonvisin are described night-fishing in the silent moonless sea, a marvelous set-piece worthy of Durrell at the peak of his powers. The trio sits eating in the boat, motionless in a dead calm:

> Fonvisin had broken a large fig in two between his fingers, and was examining the halves, holding them away from his face, minutely pressing the green walls this way and that, cocking his head first on one side, then

on the other. Quite seriously, cocking a mournful eye at his companions who watched him he said:

"Look! Here is an exact resemblance to the anus of an embalmed mummy. See when I move it. Look!" He began to laugh quietly, moulding the suggestive fig between his fingers.[44]

Fonvisin describes the embalming process in horrible detail, including the extracting of the Spanish lady's insides through the anus, reminding the reader of Sowerby's meticulous removal with a needle of the entrails of his insects. Finally the mummy is placed in an open bath of spiced oils, like the "tide of spices" suspending "Cicero's daughter" in Durrell's very early poem "Tulliola" (1934).[45] The mummified woman in Fonvisin's story walks out into a blizzard and is shot in error by her husband who has been firing at wolves. Or so he tells Fonvisin. Durrell presents another "resurrection" in *Nunquam* where Iolanthe is brought to "life" as a robot. The details, including a full description of embalming and the suspension of the robot-under-construction in a liquid bath, recall *Panic Spring*. At one point Felix Charlock, eminent scientist and past lover of Iolanthe, is invited to touch the genitalia of the robot: "Poor Iolanthe, lying there asleep and in pieces, to be fingered over by mousemen! I felt as if I had insulted her dignity."[46]

Death is treated with respect by Durrell, with almost a loving delight, from the boy Walsh Clifton's pleasure in watching Hindu funerals in *Pied Piper of Lovers* to the death-by-mistaken-identity of Affad in *Sebastian*. In 1960 Durrell called for the establishment of a "Science of Death."[47] This appreciation of death is clear too in *Panic Spring*, where the sense of impending death sets into relief the golden indolence of the castaways. The novel is framed by deaths: Ruth's death has cut Walsh adrift to vegetate on a remote Greek island owned by the millionaire Rumanades; and at the end of the novel the death of Rumanades sends his little collection of Utopia-seekers into the outer world anew. Durrell deliberately blurs the distinction between life and death, and this has remained an important theme. The actual death of Rumanades does not bring panic so much as relief: each of his guests is cast back into life. Walsh and Francis make love, Marlowe becomes creative and resumes work on his monograph about "Quietism." Rumanades' death is death in the old ritual, mythic sense: the Priest of Nemi dies so that the new Priest of Nemi may live, Christ's death brings eternal life. After a sleepless night of watching over Rumanades, Fonvisin calls out the news of the old man's death from a window, "gulping in the icy air, purging his weary and dirty body." His mood immediately changes to joy: "Fonvisin turned back into the room, laughing with tenderness at the morning, and patted the dead cheeks of the old man, saying: 'Now if you don't mind, I'll have a bath.'"[48] This bath baptizes Fonvisin for renewed life. As though to emphasize the revivifying nature of Rumanades' death, his body is carried off by a boatman named Christ.

Fonvisin is the forerunner in Durrell's fiction of another character who is resurrected: Caradoc in *The Revolt of Aphrodite*. Caradoc fakes his death in order to escape the clutches of the firm, Merlin. He flees to a Pacific island where he is eventually discovered, living anointed with coconut oil and rejuvenated. It is worth noting that Fonvisin in his roguish humor is close to Caradoc, the man who cannot resist placing suggestive personal advertisements in the *London Times:* "Small pegamoid man, fond of soft clinics, seeks tangible rubber acme. Own plug."[49] Many other characters in *Pied Piper of Lovers* and *Panic Spring* are reincarnated as later Durrell figures: Walsh into Darley, Marlowe into Horace Gregory, Rumanades into Lord Galen, Francis into Clea, and so on.

*The Black Book* continues the death theme, but with an increased complexity. The shadow of death still looms—Gracie the casual prostitute dies of tuberculosis—but Durrell has learned to maintain greater objective distance and detachment. Although doomed by her "wonky lung," Gracie remains more alive after death than the respectable English who once patronized her. Her true epitaph is *"And the same to you with knobs on,"*[50] the phrase, beyond any endearments, that her husband Gregory believes shows she understood his love. The excoriation of the "English death" is a major theme of the book, and Durrell is surely saying that the *real* death of a person who has genuinely lived has meaning and value, while the nebulous condition of the "English death" does not.

Durrell writes in the "Postface," signed with his initials, to *Nunquam*, "As always I have tried to move from the preposterous to the sublime!"[51] The grotesque and death are invariably close in Durrell: death is a ridiculous accident that happens, inexplicably, to human beings. But then, he sees human life as inherently ridiculous, from the humiliating births parodied in his resurrection scenes through the equally humiliating love-making (the woman who "catches hold of you and sort of corks herself up with it,"[52] the man "squeaking in copulation like a frog"[53]) to the final arbitrary snuffing out.

We have considered in some detail the primacy of death in Durrell's first three novels. So too in the others. In *The Dark Labyrinth* each character either escapes from the labyrinth or meets the death that corresponds to his needs and weaknesses. *The Alexandria Quartet* is as filled with death as a Jacobean tragedy, but there are also many resurrections: Scobie is brought back to life in voice through the renditions from memory of his words and in spirit through his bathtub gin; Capodistria is presumed shot and then is shown to have escaped to Palestine; even Narouz strikes from the grave to pin Clea's hand to a submerged wreck. *The Revolt of Aphrodite* revolves around the death of Iolanthe, and of her patron/worshipper Julian's attempt to defeat death by re-creating her as a robot. The death theme reaches its culmination in *The Avignon Quintet,* in which the death cult of an Egyptian gnostic sect attempts to defeat the entropic viciousness of the cosmos, the gnawing predatory unfairness of death, with an elaborate mechanism for cheating irrational death with planned murder/suicides, of which the death of Piers in *Monsieur* is an example. In Durrell man achieves—or attempts to achieve—dignity either by dying well, or by encountering death on his own terms, as in the gnostic death cults. Like Rumanades in *Panic Spring,* Piers in *Monsieur* dies with a smile on his lips. In Piers's case we do not know whether his smile is one of welcome for a friend or for death—or perhaps for both in one.

Durrell as the celebrator of death has covered his tracks well. He has cast himself as a guru of love, not death, as a superficial glance at some of his titles suggests: *Pied Piper of Lovers, Reflections on a Marine Venus, The Revolt of Aphrodite.* And Durrell claims in the preface to *Balthazar* that the "central topic" of *The Alexandria Quartet* is "an investigation of modern love." Death is, however, the third party in many of Durrell's love matches. Ruth in *Pied Piper* is doomed by her faulty heart. The Polish gentleman described in *Panic Spring* embalms his beloved. Gracie in *The Black Book* dies of tuberculosis. Iolanthe in *Revolt* dies once in her human form and a second time as a robot. In the *Quartet* the love-driven who die include Melissa, Cohen, Narouz, and Pursewarden, and Clea is only brought back from her near-death by drowning through the "pitiful simulacrum of the sexual act,"[54] Darley's artificial respiration. Durrell's characters repeatedly attempt to defeat death with love, and they fail, with the qualified exception of Blanford in *The Avignon Quintet,* who can recall and hold conversations with Constance, "Duchess of Tu," although she is long dead. In *Sebastian* the eponymous hero is murdered by a madman who apparently mistakes his fever-wracked sleeping form for Constance's. (Ironically, this death re-creates the most successful love-making of Constance and Sebastian: she is passively laid out on a clinically white table, smeared with menstrual blood, a symbolic *Liebestod.*)

My point is that Durrell has from the very first led his readers to death, but to inform and acclimatize, not terrorize. The boy Walsh, fascinated by the polished anklebone amid the ashes of an Indian cemetery, is father to the mature author constructing his fables about

Monsieur, the Prince of Darkness. It is an adage with Durrell that "A poet's death is never wholly sad, in the sense of a life unlived. . . . Every good death should incite us,"[55] as he wrote of the death in 1961 of H. D. Death is a part of "this munching world,"[56] he has the mystic Akkad proclaim in *Monsieur,* and for the individual to defeat death he must relinquish that very individuality so dear to the western world. This is in part why Durrell rejects Christianity, rejects the primacy of the discrete ego, turns to the multiplicity of Taoism and Buddhism. Durrell's gnostics strive to defeat the external arbitrariness of death by electing to have the decision of death made by members of their own human circle. This is but one of the solutions proposed by the older Durrell to questions posed by the twenty-three-year-old author of *Pied Piper of Lovers.*

## NOTES

1. Lawrence Durrell, "Preface," *The Black Book* (New York: Dutton, 1960), 13.

2. Among those who have written about Durrell's early novels are John A. Weigel, "Lawrence Durrell's First Novel," *Twentieth Century Literature* 14, no. 2 (July 1968): 75–83; Dion Whitney Nittis, "The Heraldic Universe of Lawrence Durrell" (Ph.D. diss., University of California, Los Angeles, 1971); and James A. Brigham, "An Unacknowledged Trilogy," *The Lawrence Durrell Newsletter* 2, no. 3 (March 1979): 3–12.

3. Many have treated Durrell's concept of heraldry in detail, including Derek Stanford, "Lawrence Durrell," *The Freedom of Poetry: Studies in Contemporary Verse* (London: Falcon Press, 1947), 123–35; Eleanor N. Hutchens, "The Heraldic Universe in *The Alexandria Quartet,*" *College English* 24 (1962): 56–61; John Unterecker, *Lawrence Durrell,* Columbia Essays on Modern Writers, no. 6 (New York: Columbia University, 1964); John A. Weigel, *Lawrence Durrell* (New York: Twayne, 1965); Dion Whitney Nittis in the dissertation cited in the preceding note.

4. Lawrence Durrell, "Cities, Plains and People," *Collected Poems, 1931–1974,* ed. James A. Brigham (New York: Viking, 1980), 158.

5. Lawrence Durrell, "From the Elephant's Back," *Poetry London/Apple Magazine* 2 (1982): 1–9.

6. Lawrence Durrell, *Pied Piper of Lovers* (London: Cassell, 1935), 39.

7. Lawrence Durrell [Charles Norden, pseud.], *Panic Spring* (New York: Covici-Friede, 1937), 25.

8. Durrell, *Pied Piper,* 34.

9. Ibid., 46.

10. Durrell, *Black Book,* 204.

11. Durrell, *Pied Piper,* 295, 298.

12. Ibid., 32.

13. Ibid., 198–99.

14. Ibid., 73.

15. Durrell, *Panic Spring,* 99.

16. Ibid., 29.

17. Ibid., 13.

18. Lawrence Durrell to Henry Miller, ca. 27 February 1958, *The Durrell–Miller Letters, 1935–80,* ed. Ian S. MacNiven (London: Faber and Faber, 1988), 308.

19. Durrell, *Panic Spring,* 131, 134, 138.

20. Lawrence Durrell to T. S. Eliot, November 1938, "Letters to T. S. Eliot," *Twentieth Century Literature* 33, no. 3 (Fall 1987): 351.

21. Durrell, *Panic Spring,* 341.

22. Durrell, *Pied Piper,* 133.

23. Lawrence Durrell, interview with author, Sommières, France, 26 May 1988.

24. Durrell, *Pied Piper,* 183.

25. Ibid., 34–35.

26. Lawrence Durrell, *The Big Supposer: A Dialogue with Marc Alyn,* ed. Marc Alyn, trans. Francine Barker (New York: Grove Press, 1974), 25–26.

27. Durrell, *Pied Piper,* 82.

28. Durrell, *Big Supposer,* 24–25.

29. Durrell, *Pied Piper,* 129.

30. Ibid., 248.

31. Lawrence Durrell to Henry Miller, ca. 27 January 1937, *Durrell-Miller Letters,* 50.

32. Henry Miller to Lawrence Durrell, 15 March 1937, *Durrell-Miller Letters,* 60.

33. Lawrence Durrell, *Monsieur* (London: Faber and Faber, 1974), 305.

34. Lawrence Durrell, *Nunquam* (New York: Viking, 1970), 319.

35. Lawrence Durrell, *Constance* (New York: Viking, 1982), 123.

36. Durrell, *Panic Spring,* 167.

37. Ibid., 353.

38. Durrell, *Black Book,* 50.

39. Ibid., 174.

40. Ibid., 38.

41. Durrell, *Pied Piper,* 24.

42. Ibid., 147.

43. Ibid., 145–46.

44. Durrell, *Panic Spring,* 153.

45. Durrell, *Collected Poems,* 33.

46. Durrell, *Nunquam,* 148.

47. Lawrence Durrell, "I wish one could be more like the birds: to sing unfaltering, at piece," in "Three Famous Writers Comment of the Anxieties of our Time: François Mauriac, Jean Giono, and Lawrence Durrell," *Realities,* no. 120 (1960): 56, 58–59, 78.

48. Durrell, *Panic Spring,* 353.

49. Lawrence Durrell, *Tunc* (New York: Viking, 1968), 192.

50. Durrell, *Black Book,* 80.

51. Durrell, *Nunquam,* 319.

52. Durrell, *Black Book,* 132–33.

53. Lawrence Durrell, *The Alexandria Quartet* (London: Faber and Faber, 1962), 654.

54. Ibid., 851.

55. Lawrence Durrell to Richard Aldington, 4 October 1961, *Literary Lifelines: The Richard Aldington–Lawrence Durrell Correspondence,* ed. Ian S. MacNiven (New York: Viking, 1981), 190.

56. Durrell, *Monsieur,* 138.

# Lawrence Durrell and the Vanishing Author

## Chiara Briganti

George Steiner has termed *The Alexandria Quartet* a "Baroque Novel," and has called attention to Durrell's display of an "array of sensuous, rare expressions into patterns of imagery and ideas so subtle and convoluted that the experienced reading becomes one of total apprehension."[1] Steiner, however, has omitted to mention that feature of the baroque that is most crucial to the *Quartet*—the tendency to defy closure. While the Renaissance classic form is static and closed, the baroque form is dynamic and suggests a progressive dilation of space. Its attempt to re-create movement through optic effects never allows a unique, privileged vision; instead it compels the viewer to adjust continuously his or her angle of vision, as if the work were undergoing constant change. If the baroque is seen as the first clear manifestation of modern sensibility and culture, it is because in the baroque form for the first time the individual confronts a world in movement that demands an imaginative response. The work of art is presented not solely to be enjoyed, but it is offered as an object for investigation, a stimulus to the imagination.[2]

That the *Quartet,* this "four-decker novel," a "word-continuum," must be read as an open novel cannot be doubted. As we learn from the prefatory note to *Balthazar,* the four volumes "are not linked in a serial form"; as the "consequential data" at the end of this same volume inform us, the events "collect here and there like quanta, like real life."[3] Indeed the four volumes appear as discrete unities only during the actual process of reading. When the reading is over, the whole combines into a palimpsest in which the lower strata show through and affect the design of the surface without actually changing it. Thus, for instance, Balthazar's interlinear "changes" Darley's narrative and is in turn changed by Mountolive's story and Clea's letters, which, by offering alternative points of view, ripple the surface of the text. Thus, the first three volumes are "open," but since the work is intended to be read as a whole, this kind of openness would hardly surprise anyone. The "workpoints" at the end of the fourth volume indicate that the whole *Quartet* rejects closure and could in fact continue with

41

"Hamid's story of Darley and Melissa," the story of "Mountolive's child by the dancer Griskin," and so on in an endless proliferation of characters and storytellers.

If it is true, as it has been often observed, that a work of art describes the world not only by its choice of subject matter, but especially by reflecting it in its own structure, the openness of the *Quartet* aptly reflects Durrell's epistemology—his conviction that no order can guarantee a definitive solution and that the artist can only offer provisional ones, thereby constantly denying closure. In his search for an adequate form that has led him to conceive a story to be told, "so to speak, in layers," "a series of novels with 'sliding panels,'" or perhaps a novel that would resemble "some medieval palimpsest where different sorts of truth are thrown down one upon the other, the one obliterating or perhaps supplementing another" (*Balthazar,* 177), Durrell has also destroyed the partitions between the several forms of art. Thus the *Quartet* on the one hand reminds us of baroque paintings, but, on the other, each volume reminds us of the performance of a musical piece, where each execution approximates the essence of the work but does not exhaust it. "Each performance realizes the work, but all performances are complementary; each performance, finally, renders the work in a complete and satisfactory manner, but at the same time makes it incomplete for it cannot give us simultaneously all the other possible solutions."[4]

However, the *Quartet* is "open" also in another, and more interesting if less obvious, sense. Along with the declared explosion of the closed form of the novel, we find the related disruption of the unity of self, of the notion of unified personality, which, in turn, affects the very notion of character and author. Durrell introduces a vast array of characters, all endowed with unique traits, yet almost all displaying a curious tendency to merge into each other, as if the very boundaries between the various personae had collapsed. As soon as one stops looking at them as cardboard figures, as playing cards ("She is like the playing cards?" asks Melissa's child about Justine), their very complexity undermines their individuality. As in a cubist painting, the reduction of all forms to a combination of cubes, cylinders, and planes with sharply defined edges, the abandonment of the closed form and the focus on planar structure, allow one to construct the most complex view of reality ever attempted in the visual arts. From another perspective:

> while Cézanne destroyed in art the possibility of a static view of nature, the Cubists went further and found the means of making the forms of all objects similar. . . . If everything was rendered in the same terms (whether

a hand, a violin, a window) it became possible to paint the interactions between them; their elements became interchangeable. . . . The Cubists created a system by which they could reveal visually the interlocking of phenomena. And thus they created the possibility in art of revealing *processes* instead of static states of being.[5]

In a way, each character in the *Quartet* is a cubist painting. Each one is revealed as a process, with a number of constant traits and a few changing and interchangeable ones, exactly as, for instance, in Picasso, all the formal qualities of an object are synthetized into a single characteristic. Justine's unambiguous signs are a hoarse voice and a ring with a yellow stone (but even the ring passes into another character's hands). But then she, like Clea, is shown standing over a sink and peering at a fetus; like Leila, whom, as she admits, she hates for being so much like herself, Justine dreads her husband's jealousy and spends a period of enforced residence at Karm Abu Girg. During this time she too, like Leila, has "fits." Narouz and Nessim are both vision-makers and are different to the very extent that they are complementary: though divided "like twigs of olive. . . . They were of the same branch and felt it" (*Mountolive*, 23). When Mountolive for the first time embraces Leila, we are told that he is like a man stumbling forward into a mirror: "Their muttering images met now like reflections on a surface of lake water" (*Mountolive*, 28). But Leila is also a mirror image of Nessim, whose world of intelligence and sensibility she shares, so much so that, in scrutinizing Nessim's Byzantine features, Mountolive feels that he is looking into Leila's face.

Nessim, we are told, goes through a period of horrible dreams, which "are strangely like echoes of Leila's dreams of fifteen years ago" (*Balthazar*, 139). Consequently, it is not surprising to discover that Mountolive's relationship with his mother is very similar to Nessim's relationship with Leila, which, in turn, is not without sexual overtones. When Leila glimpses Nessim's naked "slender white back," she wonders whether her attachment for Mountolive "wasn't lodged here somehow among the feeble incestuous desires of the inner heart" (*Mountolive*, 52). Balthazar writes in his interlinear that Pursewarden's face in death reminds him very much of Melissa's. Pombal, dressed for the carnival, reminds Darley of Scobie in his absurd Dolly Varden. Melissa's and Justine's daughters are, quite simply, *the* child, the child Justine lost and the child Darley has found, and to a certain extent they do appear as actually interchangeable. The examples are innumerable, and they all point to a merging of characters at some point in space and in time: in space, as if Durrell's cubist multiplication of perspectives was bound to produce planes where one character's concave surface becomes another character's convex surface; and in time, for, while each one is seen in flux, a subject in process, his or her boundaries cease to exist.

Remembering a couple of Pombal's astringent comments on Justine and Melissa, Darley reflects, "He was right, perhaps, yet the true meaning of them resides elsewhere" (*Balthazar,* 18). Darley seems to echo Lacan's notion that the true meaning of an utterance always remains elsewhere, for the subject is a divided entity dominated by an unknowable unconscious. Although, as Pursewarden puts it, to "seek to supplement the emptiness of our individuality through love" is mere illusion, it is true that the "unconscious is the discourse of the Other"—it belongs to the Other and is addressed to the Other, be it reader, analyst, lover, double. The self can be experienced and investigated only in relation to the Other. Thus Durrell's "investigation of modern love" reflects both the Lacanian notion of the conative character of language and of the divided nature of the subject, and his own cubist approach to fiction. Cubism is, in fact, as Berger has said, "an art entirely concerned with interaction: the interaction between structure and movement; the interaction between solids and the space around them; the interaction between the unambiguous signs made on the surface of the picture and the changing reality which they stand for. It is an art of dynamic liberation from all static categories."[6]

One should not be surprised if one of the planes where most of the characters of the *Quartet* meet has to do with writing and storytelling. Most of the major characters share an amazing eloquence. Moreover, most of them are professional writers or aspiring writers who threaten to take over Darley's role as the "reworker" of reality, so that at times he feels that he has become "a sort of postscript to a letter which was never ended, never posted." Arnauti is writing a book on Justine, and Pursewarden, the writer, is trapped in his own aphorisms. Darley is experimenting with different modes of narration in an attempt to encapsulate "the truth." Keats considers himself a writer, although he has never written. Cavafy serves as the quasi-oracular voice offstage, while Carlo Negroponte, the Venetian poet invented by Pursewarden, as mysterious as a character in a Gothic novel, serves to join Venice and Alexandria and to add depth and significance to the Egyptian, vampire-populated carnival. Clea composes wonderful letters, and Leila and Mountolive live almost exclusively by letters through a good portion of the *Quartet* (Leila's features are melted down by smallpox, and all that is left of her is her epistolary ability). Justine does not write, but nevertheless she proves to be a spell-binding storyteller whose theory of fiction echoes Sartre's theory that a being cannot be reduced to a limited series of manifestations, because each of these manifestations depends upon a perceiving subject who undergoes constant change. Therefore, not only does an object present several profiles at once, but the same profile can be observed from several points of view: "Now if I wrote I would try for a multi-dimensional effect in character, a sort of prism-sightedness. Why should not people show more than one profile at a time?" (*Justine*, 16). Even Scobie, between love-trips to the harbor, recites to himself for hours the literature he carries, "like an ancient tribe," in his head. And Balthazar manages to traverse freely the several planes of the text and expands until, from a character, he becomes a coauthor, rectifying, making room for his own perspective, and forcing Darley into accepting his own angle of vision.

"Strings of language extend in every direction to bind the world into a rushing ribald whole," says Donald Barthelme's Snow White. So many voices try to assert themselves, to insinuate themselves into the texture of Darley's narrative, disguised as memoirs, letters, notebooks, notes for an interlinear. Yet, of course, try as these voices may, the world will resist such a compression. Disenchantment with the humanist conception of the subject, which makes us suspicious of any philosophical approach that assumes human capacity for wholeness, condemns language to defeat. While modernists, like the structuralists, see interpretation as a quest for order among the manifold possible meanings which the text discloses to the competent reader, deconstructionists and postmodernist writers like Durrell have shown how any discourse is not a closed system of meaning, but an active production of it. Just as, after Lacan, it has become increasingly difficult to accept the equation between self and the notion of identity, wholeness, unity, continuity, anything more ambitious than the subject in process (and of this Clea seems to be well aware), so it has become more and more difficult to believe that language can offer meaning to reality. This is perhaps why at the end of *Balthazar* Clea will adopt the "we" pronoun, which becomes symptomatic of the lack of unity of the self and of the merging of author, character, and reader. In *Balthazar,* Clea inhabits at once the position of reader, both of Pursewarden's letter and of Darley's narrative, and that of character while also becoming the producer of a text that adds to the manifold perspectives of the *Quartet*:

"We, for our part, very much need to see you again and refresh the friendship which we hope exists the other side of the writing—if indeed an author can ever be just a friend to his 'characters.' I say 'we,' writing in the Imperial Style as if I were a Queen, but you will guess that I mean, simply, both the old Clea and the new—for both have need of you in a future which . . ." There are a few more lines and then the affectionate superscription. (*Balthazar*, 240)

As an author, Clea is not allowed to pronounce the last words. Darley leaves them out to destroy any illusion of completeness, thus enacting the role of the author as repressive figure and also explaining by implication why his own quest cannot end. The notion of a finished product is no longer viable. All that can be accepted as finished is Scobie's mock shrine, from which he manages to escape by continuing to speak through the other personae.

D'ou l'auteur est a releguer a se faire moyen pour un desir qui le depasse. (Jacques Lacan, Radio Interview)

The sense of fragmentation of reality and of the self exposes the tremendous presumption of knowledge implicit in the figure of the author, a figure whose status has been increasingly questioned in the last few decades, especially by French antihumanists such as Pierre Macherey, Roland Barthes, and Michel Foucault. Macherey has spoken of the illusory character of the author's freedom, concluding that "it is the narrative as such which is determining."[7] Barthes has called attention to narrative's historical roots and has described the author as a modern figure, the result of "English empiricism, French rationalism and the personal faith of the Reformation."[8] Michel Foucault has distanced himself from the position of structuralists and poststructuralists, who would grant complete autonomy to the text, and has been mainly concerned with the question of discourse as power. However, he too has contributed to dissolving the notion of the subject as the originator of discourse and, like Barthes, has done so by pointing to its historical as opposed to ontological status. He has argued that "the coming into being of the notion of 'author' constitutes the privileged moment of *individualization* in the history of ideas, knowledge, literature, philosophy, and the sciences."[9] While Foucault denounces the author as a figure of power, for Barthes the author is but a shaman, who does not father the text but is born simultaneously with it. The writer can at best aspire to imitate and combine other writings, for, as Macherey would say, "his narrative is discovered rather than invented."[10]

This argument is corroborated by the preoccupation of so much experimental literature with what have been until recently the unquestionably separate categories of text, author, and reader. The proliferation of writers in the *Quartet* is not the only instance. The same

uneasiness with a monotheistic notion of the "author" runs throughout Joyce's *Finnegans Wake* and Beckett's *Trilogy* and is felt by such
diverse writers as Mario Vargas Llosa, Calvino, Nabokov, and Barth.
Joyce declared himself "quite content to go down to posterity as a
scissors & paste man for that seems to me a harsh but not unjust description."[11] And *Finnegans Wake* explicitly comments on the multiplicity of "identities in the writer complexus (for if the hand was one,
the minds of active and agitated were more than so)."[12] In Mario Vargas Llosa's *La tía Julia y el escribidor,* a writer of radio soap operas finds
himself unable to control his characters and ultimately becomes the
unwilling instrument of their desire to break the fetters of the text
in which he has tried to enclose them. In Nabokov's *Pale Fire,* the obvious irrelevance of the commentary to the poem results in a multiplication, and therefore in a fragmentation as in a kaleidoscope, of the
author-figure. Lost as we are in the room of mirrors that is the book,
we are unable to discern which one of the several reflections is the
original object. Barth's solution in *Sabbatical* is the adoption of the
"we" pronoun, which allows the author to shed his uncomfortable
singleness and become plural, while the text culminates in a vision of
continual storytelling by virtue of the abortion of individuality. What
the novel questions is the univocal relationship of author and text. If
our children are not the ones we have conceived, but rather the sperm
and the eggs that have failed to couple, then the father/mother figure
becomes an ideological figure by which we mark our fear of indiscriminate proliferation. It becomes, that is, the means by which we channel
indiscriminate production. The writer, in short, must assume the role
of the dead man in the game of writing, which is what Barth attempts
in *Sabbatical,* where the pronoun "we" may be said to refer to the players, one of whom, the dead man, is there only to enable the others
to play within the limits of a structured game.

> the books I am using for the present fragment which include Marie
> Corelli, Swendenborg, St Thomas, the Sudanese War, Indian outcasts,
> Women under English Law, a description of St Helena, Flammarion's The
> End of the World, scores of children's singing games from Germany,
> France, England and Italy and so on. . . . (James Joyce, letter to Harriet
> Shaw Weaver, 4 March 1931)

If, as Calvino maintains, the writer succeeds in canceling out the
individual subject to identify with the collective "I" of the great artists
of the past and of the future, the very potential of literature will show
the text's irreducible plurality, by virtue of which the text "answers
not to an interpretation . . . but to an explosion, a dissemination."[13]

In the *Quartet,* Cavafy is certainly part of the artist's collective past, and so in Blake, with whom Pursewarden identifies in the beautiful scene of the dance in Trafalgar Square. As for the great artists of the future, perhaps Darley's aspiration to become one is after all legitimate, since he is the one who "can hear the echoes of words uttered long since in the past by other voices" (*Clea,* 16). And if, as Foucault argues, the author is only a figure of history, the explosion of the author-figure on the part of postmodernist writers is the first important step toward the production of a discourse that will "develop in the anonymity of a murmur." The author-function must not necessarily remain constant in form. The new artist may very well be Clea's new hand, which "has proved itself almost more competent even than an ordinary flesh-and-blood member," and which by its very impersonality "has contrived to slip [Clea] through the barriers into the company of the Real Ones" (*Clea,* 271–72).

It would probably be pure romanticism "to imagine a culture in which the fictive would operate in an absolutely free state, in which fiction would be put at the disposal of everyone and would develop without passing through something like a necessary or constraining figure."[14] However, multiplying narrators, disrupting the linearity of the text, enhancing the reader's role, are all ways of indicating how the author is only one of the dimensions of discourse, the function that introduces principles of causality and order.

It is no wonder that such a figure, once the very notion of the unity of self has been questioned, should be subject to fragmentation. That is why, in the *Quartet* and in all the other novels I have cited, we have a number of would-be writers—Cavafy and Arnauti do not operate on the stage but somehow behind the curtains, and Pursewarden relinquishes his role and becomes ironically effective only through his own death.

More important, all these voices somehow merge into each other; we are not really allowed to single out which voice is Durrell's, Darley's, Pursewarden's, Cavafy's. The intended artistic blurring in Arnauti's *Moeurs* between Claude and Justine is meant to suggest that, in spite of their singularity, all characters are one essential character and all voices one essential voice. They are all compressed into the voice of the aspiring author, and they are all busy putting pieces together, while Alexandria, "the mythical city" from which they are to draw their nourishment, resists encapsulation and appropriation and offers them only fragments, a bit of silver cutlery and white cloth, earrings and flashing jewelry, sleek oiled heads and smiles. Clea, who attempts to recompose the city for Darley, to enable him to "walk back into the painting from another angle and feel quite at home" (*Clea,*

80), must content herself with a series of tableaux that only temporarily freeze the flux, while Alexandria refuses to become "home" and makes them all exiles. Reality appears as a continuum manifold, and Durrell's attitude is the attitude of the musician, for whom the essence of the musical piece can only be suggested during each performance but can never be reached. And it is also the attitude of the scientist, for whom our apprehension of physical reality can never be final, and the "evidence obtained under different experimental conditions cannot be comprehended within a single picture, but must be regarded as *complementary* in the sense that only the totality of the phenomena exhausts the possible information about the objects."[15]

> And yet there is no more commonplace statement than that the world in which we live is a four-dimensional space-time continuum. (Albert Einstein, *Relativity*)

As Darley admits, "these fictions all live as a projection of the white city itself" (*Balthazar*, 96). As the categories of reader, text, and author cannot be separated, and the artist is also "the statue which must disengage itself from the dull block of mable which houses it and start to live" (*Clea*, 110), so Darley must finally conclude that the same freedom to traverse the several planes of fiction that most of the characters have enjoyed can be also rightfully claimed by Alexandria. Durrell's cubist approach merges with his own declared intention of writing a novel based on the relativity proposition.

It has often been argued that cubism is best understood by reading it through the lens of a space-time continuum.[16] It is not mere coincidence that the introduction of non-Euclidean geometry into physics and the breaking away from an occidental perspective occurred almost simultaneously. Or that Einstein published *The Special Theory of Relativity* in 1905 and Picasso painted his first cubist picture, *Les Demoiselles d'Avignon,* in 1906–7. Although exact correspondences between painting and physics can hardly be proved, the new synthesis propounded by the cubists, even if not directly influenced by the theory of relativity, was a result of the same mental climate, and in terms of painting it can certainly be considered "the philosophical equivalent of the revolution that was taking place in scientific thinking."[17] Durrell shares the concerns of both cubists and modern physicists. He too denies the fixed state, and he places instead emphasis on the process, on the infinite referral from signifier to signified, from text to text. It is through the realization that "truth is double-bladed," and that there is no way to express it in terms of that "strange bifurcated medium" that is language, that Keats grows into a writer. As Pursewarden puts it in his letter to Clea, "truth itself is always halved in utterance [and it] disappears with the telling of it" (*Clea*, 135). Yet as Darley suggests, "perhaps buried in all this there lies the germ and substance of a truth—time's usufruct—which, if I can accommodate it, will carry me a little further in what is really a search for my proper self" (*Balthazar*, 222).

With Einstein and with the cubists Durrell shares also the emphasis on the primordial importance of the problem of observation. John Dewey has noticed how the change in science occurred "when it was found that the process of conceptual abstraction could not be carried to the point of excluding the act of observation without the possibility of verification."[18] The same preoccupation with the integration of the kinesthetic experience is found in cubism, where it results in the abandonment of the spatial illusionism of one-point perspective and in the combination of multiple viewpoints into a single form. For both the scientist and the novelist, truth is not to be abandoned, but their approach shows that truth can be formulated in different ways and that "true" or "false" are mere definitions with no claim to ontological validity. However, Durrell's debt to Einstein mainly concerns the notion of time. Although time is an asymmetrical concept within the frame of the theory of relativity, it is not unidirectional, and Einstein's proposition does not postulate the need for "a qualitative distinction between the two directions of time, between the 'earlier' and the 'later.'"[19] In Einstein's conception of the universe all that for each of us constitutes present, past, and future is given as a whole in which each observer, with the passing of his own time, discovers new portions of space-time, which appear to him as successive aspects of the world. In actuality, however, the whole of the events that constitute the space-time dimension existed prior to the observer's knowledge of them.[20] As Darley realizes, "it had all already happened . . . the scenario had already been devised somewhere, the actors chosen . . . in the mind of that invisible author—which perhaps would prove to be only the city itself: the Alexandria of the human estate" (*Clea*, 215).

Darley's discovery of a preexisting scenario is the discovery that any narrative is refound rather than invented and what the writer seeks to express is a ready-formed dictionary—language itself.[21] As a postmodern author, Darley renounces any claim to invention and originality. Writing becomes for him a question of assemblage in which the writing subject undoes itself and becomes dispersed and fragmented. In the recasting of space-time advanced by Einstein, Durrell finds yet another way of reaffirming what the *Quartet* has affirmed all along—the primacy of language over the speaking subject. For, as Foucault has said, "language comes to us from the depths of a night perfectly clear and indomitable to master."[22]

## NOTES

1. George Steiner, "Lawrence Durrell: The Baroque Novel," in *The World of Lawrence Durrell*, ed. Harry T. Moore (New York: Dutton, 1964), 15.

2. For a discussion of the baroque form and its relation to modern sensibility, see Umberto Eco, *Opera aperta* (Milan: Bompiani, 1962), 38–40.

3. Lawrence Durrell, *Balthazar* (New York: Pocket Books, 1975), 241. For the other volumes of the *Quartet* the following editions have been used: *Justine* (New York: Washington Square Press, 1961); *Mountolive* (New York: Dutton, 1959); *Clea* (New York: Washington Square Press, 1961). All further references to Durrell's work will appear in the text.

4. Eco, *Opera aperta*, 52. My translation.

5. John Berger, *The Success and Failure of Picasso* (New York: Pantheon Books, 1980), 59.

6. Ibid., 59–60.

7. Pierre Macherey, *A Theory of Literary Production*, trans. Geoffrey Wall (London: Henley; Boston: Routledge & Kegan Paul, 1978), 48.

8. Roland Barthes, "The Death of the Author," *Image/Music/Text*, trans. Stephen Heath (New York: Hill and Wang, 1977), 142.

9. Michel Foucault, "What's an Author?', in *Textual Strategies*, ed. Josue V. Harari (Ithaca: Cornell University Press, 1979), 147.

10. Macherey, *A Theory of Literary Production*, 48.

11. Letter to George Antheil, 3 January 1931, in Stephen Heath, "Ambiviolences: Notes for Reading Joyce," in *Post-structuralist Joyce: Essays from the French*, ed. Derek Attridge and Daniel Ferrer (Cambridge: Cambridge University Press, 1984), 40.

12. James Joyce, *Finnegans Wake* (New York: Viking, 1939), 114.

13. Roland Barthes, "From Work to Text," in *Textual Strategies*, 76.

14. Foucault, "What's an Author?, 159.

15. Niels Bohr, "Discussion with Einstein on Epistemological Problems in Atomic Physics," in *Albert Einstein: Philosopher-Scientist*, ed. Paul Arthur Schilpp (New York: Harper & Brothers Publishers, 1959), 210.

16. See, in particular, Paul M. Laporte, "The Space-Time Concept in the Work of Picasso," *Magazine of Art*, January 1948, 26–32; and "Cubism and Science," *Journal of Aesthetics and Art Criticism*, March 1949, 243–46. Edward F. Fry, *Cubism* (London: Thames and Hudson, 1966), 119, however, cautions against establishing more than a "rough metaphorical parallel" between space-time relationship in painting and the ideas of relativity in physics.

17. Berger, *Picasso*, 66–67.

18. John Dewey, *Art as Experience* (New York: Minton, Balch & Co., 1934), 183.

19. Hans Reichenbach, "The Philosophical Significance of the Theory of Relativity," in *Albert Einstein*, 305.

20. For a detailed analysis, see Louis De Broglie, "The Scientific Work of Albert Einstein," in *Albert Einstein*, 64.

21. Barthes, "The Death of the Author," 146.

22. Michel Foucault, *Raymond Roussel* (Paris: Gallimard, 1963), 54.

# The Triangle of Love, Incest, and Writing

Corinne Alexandre-Garner

A man world-weary and world-travelled,
who has spent a life-time hunting for a
philosophy and a woman to match . . .
Hum. The woman is dead.

—Lawrence Durrell, *Monsieur*

Incest is defined by the Oxford dictionary as "the crime of sexual intercourse or cohabitation between persons related within the degrees within which marriage is prohibited by law." This crime, however, is in many codes of law largely moral, state legislation interfering less in the sexual practices of consenting adults. Yet the prohibition of marriage between certain persons of uterine or agnatic relation is general, and can be found in all societies. Most societies have installed a series of prescribed and prohibited marriages, which can range from a preferential relation with uterine cousins or agnatic uncles in certain forms of endogamy, to a total interdiction of clanic women in certain forms of exogamy. If exogamy is the result of total avoidance of incest, endogamy is then a means of living with it without stopping the exchange of women, words, and life. From a purely structuralist and anthropological point of view, the prohibition of incest corresponds to the establishment of a system of exchange that allows any given society to survive. The intermarriage or choice of sexual partner between members of the same family, clan, or group has either to be strictly codified or totally forbidden in order to permit the permanence of any form of social exchange. This is a point which is summed up at once by the Sironga proverb: "A parent related by marriage is an elephant's thigh," as well as by the question of a Melanesian, quoted by Margaret Mead: "What, you do not wish to marry? But if you do not have a brother-in-law, who will go hunting with you?"[1]

Yet, at the same time, two remarks can be made. On the one hand, in psychoanalytic theory, the prohibited sexual (or marital) partner does not appear as an object of repulsion, but rather as the cause of desire: only the incapacity to fulfill this desire and the appearance of a thing forever lost can root desire and anchor it permanently in itself. Desire then becomes a reality for its own sake and its object replaceable. Yet in certain historical societies, and this will prove itself of some importance in the paragraphs to come, incest is not prohibited but prescribed. This is the case in Peru, in Hawaii, and in ancient Egypt. In the latter, from the scarce documentation that has come to our attention, the dynastic incest is restrictive: the older sister marries the younger brother, but never the contrary. All three, however, are related to power and forms of kingship in which a dynasty through incest maintains its power. Beyond these three examples, we know of incest, albeit its probable frequency, only what "collective agreement of silence has let us know about it."[2]

Perhaps literary texts, together with psychoanalysts' couches and social workers' files, are one of the privileged spaces where the collective agreement falters, and silence fissures. Yet, in terms of literary representation (as on the psychoanalyst's couch), we must transcend the purely confessional aspect and raise the question of structural pertinence. If indeed there is incest, its function within a narrative, and its importance for the continuation of the text, must be delineated. Thus, the relationship of incest to writing as graphic and communicative activity will appear.

In Lawrence Durrell's *Alexandria Quartet* and *Avignon Quintet,* we are presented with a repetitive occurrence of incestuous brother-sister relations that closely circumscribes the figure of the artist on the one hand, and questions the object of creation on the other. But whereas in *The Alexandria Quartet* the children of incest die, or their parents do, in *The Avignon Quintet* there are aborted children, missing children, but also healed children and children to be. Whereas the artist-writer is a man in the *Quartet,* she is a woman in the *Quintet.* This singular insistence upon incestuous siblings appearing as seen through a prism, as a fragmentation of an image of love, together with the appearance of an androgynous figure linked to the theme of creativity, is fundamental to Durrell's novels.

At the end of Hermann Hesse's *Glass-bead Game,* the old master, during his first day as "educator" of his friend's son, accepts the challenge of his young pupil. He dives into the cold mountain lake the young man likes to cross, and drowns. The first day of the education of the disciple becomes the last day of the master. The guilt following this death opens the possibility of an education for his student, the possibility of a *Bildung.* To a certain extent, the *Quartet* is a *Bildungsroman,* but of a higher power than the examples offered by German classicism. What is in question here is not only the becoming of a man, but the becoming of a man as writer, conscious of his power as a man who writes, who can represent reality, and willingly extract himself from this representation as narrator. He can insert himself within the text as character, or multiply himself prismatically into any number of narrators and characters.

Yet this coming of age of the artist does not go without sacrifice. In order to continue painting, Clea loses her hand. Darley can begin writing after he has lost Pursewarden, and Pursewarden commits suicide the day that he learns that he has lost his sister. The loss of the other-as-self (sister), the loss of the Other (master), or the loss of a limb indicate here more than the distance between the fragment, the reference, and the whole. They also indicate the distance between painting and writing. Whereas Clea consistently loses parts of her body (hand, fetus), and draws fragments of bodies (noses and medical sketches) before actually becoming an artist, the writer does not deal with fragmentary bodies, but with bodies that impersonate fragments of human destiny, fragments of a book perhaps never to be finished. Yet somehow this equation is thrown into question by the very existence of incest. For as much as in *The Avignon Quintet* two equals one within orgasm, this equality is established in the *Quartet* through incest. Yet while the *Quartet* represents only one incestuous couple, and a fragmentation of orgasmic encounters in which bodies are conjugated as if they were to represent the words of an unspeakable language, whose only certainty is its syntax, the *Quintet* represents a fragmentation of incestuous encounters in which the only unity between bodies, their only oneness, is represented by orgasm. The relationship between the two series of texts is here too inverted.

In the *Quartet* the incestuous pair is composed of Pursewarden and his blind sister, Liza. After having lived together and having given birth to a blind little girl, who dies in childhood, they separate. Pursewarden continues meeting other women, but he also writes to his sister until Liza meets the "dark stranger " (Mountolive), whom she will eventually marry and who will give her a child. Pursewarden commits suicide the day he learns through a letter—here compared to a death warrant—that Liza is ready to commit herself to another man. His death becomes her epithalamion. His words no longer communicate with the outside world. He orders that his letters be destroyed, but his lifeless body incorporates and signs the message that he no longer exists. For the budding writer Darley, Pursewarden represents the paradigm of the artist who has come to terms with his art:

> With an interior shock, I realized there was nothing in the whole length or breadth of our literature with which to compare them. . . . Here illusion

and reality were fused in one single *blinding vision* of a perfect incorrupti-
ble passion which hung over the writer's mind like a dark star—the star
of death.[3]

The writing of Pursewarden, the "single blinding vision," repro-
duces exactly the blindness of Liza and of their child. Their fusion of
illusion and reality corresponds to the fusion between Pursewarden
and his creation, which must die with him. Indeed, as Pursewarden
puts it himself, "there is no other." Or rather, the other is, but
Pursewarden's death and external silence are the necessary conditions
for its creation. The sentence could be rewritten as, "As long as I am
able to speak, there is no other; should I no longer be, an other may
exist."

His death here has two functions. It liberates Liza totally and allows
her to escape to the exterior world, in which words are spoken to communicate and not only to embellish silence. But it also has a function
within the text, since Darley can extract himself from the towering
shadow which Pursewarden used to cast upon him. Within the linear
series he constructs—"Arnauti, Pursewarden, Darley—like Past, Present and Future tense,"[4] the future has already begun. The four words
that close *Clea* and with which Darley, like every storyteller, stakes
his slender claim, the "Once upon a time," implies that, here and now,
a writer will re-present the past, but these words also imply that the
present will not endure.

Durrell's two series of novels express no uncertain fascination for
the androgynous body. To Scobie's toothless mouth and death in
women's clothing correspond the masculine traits of Leila. To Balthazar's unhappy homosexual encounter with Panayotis corresponds
Constance's brief love affair with Sylvie. The sexes are rarely clearly
defined, no more than languages are clearly defined in Alexandria:
"But there are more than five sexes and only Demotic Greek seems
to distinguish among them."[5] Let us, nonetheless, try in English: men,
women, children, homosexuals, and lesbians. The androgynous body
occupies here the crossroad where sexual determination meets the axis
of time: "I Tiresias, old man with wrinkled dugs," as T. S. Eliot puts
it in *The Waste Land,* "Perceived the scene, and foretold the rest."[6] The
condition of being at once man and woman, of having lived the scene
(once upon a time) and being able to predict the future, corresponded
in Greek mythology to a necessary condition in order to answer the
gods' questions.

Thus armed, Tiresias could determine who, men or women, enjoyed sexual intercourse more. The mythological Tiresias, excluded
from sexual determination, from time and from action, a mere blind

spectator, thought that it had to be women, an answer that brought the wrath of Hera upon him and deprived him of his sight. T. S. Eliot's Tiresias would probably have answered neither. But in Durrell's novels, the androgynous body becomes more than a spectator and a judge. It traces in prismatic form the outline of the writer, and it is as such that its complete figure is the incestuous couple in the *Quartet,* the orgasmic unity of the *Quintet.* The writer is no longer "an author in the cupboard,"[7] he is no longer a spectator, yet at the same time he is excluded from the thing he writes. Or rather, while having "foresuffered" the scene, the thing he writes excludes him from the act. Through incest, Pursewarden creates an androgynous double body, in which he converted Liza's blindness into poetry. Seeing with her eyes, he allowed her to see with his brain.[8] The absence of sight becomes words, the absence of words becomes vision. Yet the two are divided, two persons here embody this necessary condition of literary creation, two bodies and two sexes. In order to write, Pursewarden must assure himself of their unity, even if this unity is illusory.

Both Claude Lévi-Strauss and Émile Durkheim have sufficiently stressed that, when a man takes his sister as wife, he withdraws her from the normal flow of exchange of women that is necessary for any community to propagate itself and assure communication among its members. By keeping his sister for himself, he deprives the system of one of its components. He withdraws an essential sign from the language of customs and breaks the chain of communication. Yet the negative aspects of his choice should not overshadow its positive counterpart. By stopping the system of exchange, by breaking the chain of communication and by interrupting the flow of words, man establishes silence. Metaphorically, the Latin *silentium* does not only mean "peace," but also "muse."

But in the case of Pursewarden, the original silence of language and of communicative signs, broken only by the murmur of Plutarch's *Isis and Osiris,* which the brother would read to his sister, is at once the cause and the beginning of his artistic career, and also the harbinger of its end. Because she is committed to another man, Liza is lost to Pursewarden, and thus she loses the blindness of her eyes, which were his. We would venture that it is much more than Liza that he loses, that probably he loses through her marriage his capacity to "keep silence." The words must here be heard as man's effort not to maintain silence, nor to remain silent, but to shepherd silence in order to speak meaningfully.

For Pursewarden, Liza and his writing, *opus* or *oeuvre,* were one and the same. It was a prolonged effort to re-create the bond that united them, to re-create her within him and to express this creation. His work was to muster up a "blinding vision" of illusion and reality, thereby imitating his sister's somatic condition. The fact that she should marry Mountolive outweighs illusion, and the scales fall from his eyes. He loses his reference, the ideal blind reader, who dictates through her existence what he is to write, thereby losing the part of himself that allows him to exist and write. If Liza is to be lost, so are his letters, so is his life. It is not of the least importance that it should be someone of the opposite sex.

What did Tiresias see? According to one group of mythological accounts, he saw two snakes copulating, first killing the male, and, seven years later, the female. According to another series of accounts, he saw Athena, the virile virgin, taking a bath. Anthropologists concerned with Greek culture and civilization generally agree that what he saw was bisexuality.[9] Bisexuality is also the subject of Freud's letter to Fliess, which Durrell's *Justine* bears as an epigraph. It is precisely this aspect that underlines the *Quartet* and the *Quintet,* but they are expressed differently. The *Quartet* traces the outline of an artist-writer who can only find this *summum* of human experience through incest, through the creation of an androgynous body in incest.

For the representation of the writer within the novel, the exit from the scene of incest can only be accomplished through the loss of life. For the narrator Darley, it is no longer life that is to be lost, but the illusion of creating the past merely by assembling the different links of this past in the chain of writing. For him, the androgynous unity is no longer to be sought in incest, but in the artist's capacity for creation. Having finally become a writer, Darley says: "I had been until then like some timid girl, scared of the birth of her first child."[10] The writer is "like a girl," at once man and woman, "a real human being," according to Clea. The condition of creativity transcends sexual determination. The man must be more than a man, he must accept the female identification within himself, the woman must accept the male identification. The "real human being" becomes double.

Whereas the *Quartet* portrays only one incestuous couple and a profusion of sexual encounters, the *Quintet* concentrates almost exclusively upon descriptions of incestuous couples, all the while maintaining a representation of heterosexual and homosexual loves. All of these incestuous couples are introduced from the beginning as *ménages à trois,* three-cornered love affairs, in which the third partner is at once the lover of the man and the woman. Differing from the situation in the *Quartet,* the artist-writer in the *Quintet* has become a woman. Mad, Sylvie speaks of her dead brother, who has been her lover, as being constantly present.[11] Incest has already become a thing of the past. Death is no longer an obstacle to writing. The writer can survive both, and his (her) survival may even indicate an exit from madness. The scene of madness has replaced the scene of incest—the exit from the scene is no longer accomplished through death, but through life.

In the *Quintet,* incest has fragmented into multiple mirror images: Piers and Sylvie reappear in *Constance,* together with an anonymous lover, as paintings in the picture gallery of the Chateau de Tubain, where they watch over the love of another incestuous pair, Livia and Hilary.[12] One incestuous pair resembles another, names and places repeat and reflect each other. The very notion of character, place, and time has been decomposed by Durrell, shattered and fragmented, scattered in the novel as Osiris's limbs in the Nile. Within this constellation of fragments, it is no longer individuals or their representations that are of importance, but the syntactic repetition of situations that create a many-layered text. The Sylvie of the present and her dead brother Piers refer to another Sylvie of the past, to another Piers, absent, who was to be executed in a gnostic suicide. But Sylvie is only another facet of Sylvaine, whose brother Bruno is another impersonation of the Piers of the past, while Livia turns, in Sutcliffe's personal life and book, into the Sylvie who went mad.[13]

The list could be continued. Very much like Francis Bacon's portraits, the images of Durrell's characters flow, only momentarily arrested by the description of a scene, grasped and contained by the words that transmit a situation, already to flow into another representation that repeats and echoes the first. "The old stable outlines of the dear old novel have been sidestepped," explains Blanford, "in favour of a soft focus palimpsest which enables the actors to turn unto each other, to melt into each other's inner lifespace if they wish. Everything and everyone comes closer and closer together, moving towards the one."[14] Darley's illusion in the *Quartet,* that, by assembling the different links of the past in the chain of writing he would re-create it and heal himself from his injuries, is here completely lost. The narrators no longer try to assemble links, they merely select them, and they permit between them a flow of similarities from one into another. "After all, why not a book full of spare parts of other books, of characters left over from other times, all circulating in each other."[15] The chain of time is broken, and it is up to the reader to reconstruct it. All the brother-sister couples presented in the *Quintet* are incestuous, all are united by fragments of resemblance.

The Alexandrian unity of the androgynous body has been displaced from incest to coupling. It is with surprise that Constance, Sylvie's analyst, learns in a perfect passion with Sebastian Affad, her Egyptian lover, that the topology of the bodies mix. The gnostic vision of the division of man corrects the Platonic version, which is reduced to a biological error.

> "When the couple was created out of the original man unit, clumsily divided into male and female parts, the affective distribution did not correspond at all with the biological. The sex of the man is really the woman's property, while the breasts of the woman belong to the man. . . . In his idea of the affect link the male sex is really the woman's handbag, it hangs at her side, while her breasts belong to him with their promise of nourishment. Their souls trade sperm against milk. The female's breasts just gave him life and marked him with his ineradicable thirst for creating—Tiresias! The breasts are prophecy, are vision!"[16]

With that the androgynous body is reconstituted outside of the scene of incest, and an alternative to incest is given. Incest is no longer the cradle of writing, as it was in the *Alexandria Quartet,* but one of the objects it tries to grasp. The cradle of writing now stands in an insane asylum, in a room itself the copy of another room in a castle.[17] By a rather complex series of associations, Durrell displaces the entire scene: Liza's "Pursewarden" becomes the "handbag" constituted by the male sex and for which the woman must care. Their blind daughter becomes Sebastian's autistic boy, who the homosexual couple Constance/Sylvie will heal and bring back to living communication. Mountolive is replaced by Felix Chatto, who is also a young ambassador, thereby putting Sylvie in the place of Liza, while both Piers and Pursewarden have plaster casts made of their faces after their deaths. The dying writer Pursewarden, who only survives through his published work, is replaced by the living artist Sylvie, whose work is still unknown, while Darley/Blanford may begin to write. Change of roles, change of scenes: "People are not separate individuals as they think," says Quatrefages, "they are variations on themes outside their lives . . . just as a diamond is a variation on carbon, or a caterpillar on a butterfly."[18] What separates carbon from a diamond is, among other things, time, which here has become infinitely compressible. Time is no longer conceived as a chain of which each link constitutes an identifiable and different event, but as a stack in which the event is a layer. As in a palimpsest, the layer is written, but the written part is little more than a costume to fit an actor. As a costume, anyone can wear it.

Within this rearrangement, in which old costumes fit new actors playing similar scenes, a number of transformations are nevertheless permanent. The artist, like the child, is played in the opposite sex (Pursewarden and the blind daughter, Sylvie and the autistic boy); in-

cest, as a figure of primordial unity that engenders creativity, genera-
lizes in a concept of oneness. "Everything and everyone comes closer
and closer together, moving towards the one," says Blanford in
*Quinx*.[19] The "so-called characters" are "illustrations of a trend," since
"all people are slowly becoming the same person . . . all countries are
merging into one country."[20]

This oneness, despite its geopolitical overtones, does not refer so
much to the great melting pot of nations, as to a continuing process
in which *two* totally separate entities undergo a "mystical marriage"
and rearrange the parts that constituted their previous identity. In the
gnostic rearrangement of the biological body, the man's sex belongs
to the woman, whereas the woman's breasts belong to the man. Structurally, this is not different from the more poetic interchange that had
taken place between Pursewarden and Liza, which had allowed her
to see with his brain, and him to see with her eyes. The oneness is
not fusion, but it is the reattribution and transparency one could
imagine in a double exposure upon film, or on a palimpsest.

At the end of *Quinx*, at the moment when Blanford begins to
concentrate upon the writing of "the book," he speaks of his plan to
Constance. Already the attributive "his" and "hers" are no longer in
opposition, but in communion. What is "his," has also become
"hers":

> She felt, in fact, that the whole *oeuvre* for which he was going to try was
> *as much her work*, her responsibility, as *his*—which was indeed the case.
> To celebrate the mystical marriage of four dimensions with five skandas
> so to speak. To exemplify in the flesh the royal cobra couple, the king and
> queen of the affect, of the spiritual world. "My spinal I with her final
> she."[21]

The version of the double androgynous body carries over into the creative concerns of each, Constance's analytical work, Blanford's book,
to resolve itself finally in a marriage of western knowledge of the four
dimensions and eastern awareness of five sensibilities.

In opposition to this interchange of "spare parts" (here literally in
terms of parts that may be spared, which are not vital to the survival
of the individual, but only to the survival of the species or of culture),
which constitutes the gnostic oneness, another form of unity appears.
It is, however, no longer a marriage but an assimilation.

While waiting for the verdict of the "executive cell" which is to
judge his attachment to Constance, Sebastian's mind goes back, step
by step, to the "hard integument of Greek thought":

> It has *assimilated* and *modified* and *perhaps even betrayed* these successive
> waves of esoteric knowledge which, like a tropical fruit, were the harvest

of Indian thought, of Chinese thought, of Tibetan thought. He saw there dark waves of culture pouring into Persia, into Iran, and into Egypt, where they were churned and *manipulated* into *linguistic forms* which made them comprehensible to the inhabitants of the Middle Eastern lands.[22]

It is noteworthy that the entire process of translation and adaptation, the passage of one linguistic thought system to another, is not presented as communion of any sort, but only as assimilation, modification, manipulation, and finally as betrayal: *tradutore, trahitore!* The synthesis Plato attempted can never be more than that, a "mind-crushing synthesis," which has to do neither with marriage nor with oneness. The basic principle of oneness, and Durrell does not ignore it, is that the trace of the original alterity must persist. But at the same time, he also indicates that this mystical marriage takes place beyond language, at once *en-deça* and *au-delà*.

The path here taken is again similar to incest: coming of the Same, the Twosome can only create a unity that is double. Here too, the unity thus achieved is accomplished beyond the need of language and of communication. Here too, each takes from the other what he or she does not have—Pursewarden takes Liza's blindness, she takes his sight. And yet, one major difference remains. In the case of incest, writing is the means by which an access to the outside world can be restored, a use of language to communicate with an anonymous exterior, in which words encounter the precise degree of incomprehension that anchors their meaning and calls upon always more words to explicate them. In the case of the gnostic oneness, the mystical marriage, writing is above all the surface upon which the two antinomous elements may meet. It is no longer an exit from the scene, but the stagefloor upon which the players stand. Writing becomes the place, neither more nor less real than Alexandria or Avignon, where the betrayal of assimilation can be tried, the synthetic product decomposed, and the constituent elements divided in order to be reunited. In the same way as the pergament surface permitted the inscription of numerous texts that, through the use of time, would fade and reappear simultaneously, writing has become the stone upon which opposing thoughts may be set in a chase that neither arranges them in a linear cause-and-effect pattern, nor annuls their coexistence.

## NOTES

1. Claude Lévi-Strauss, *Les structures elementaires de la parente,* Seme ed (Paris/La Haye: Mouton, 1967), 556.

2. Ibid., 11.

3. Lawrence Durrell, *Clea* (London: Faber, 1963), 152. My italics.

4. Ibid., 154.

5. Lawrence Durrell, *Justine* (London: Faber, 1961), 14.

6. Durrell's references to Eliot are numerous. The chapter entitled "A Dying Fall" in *Monsieur* refers directly to "The Lovesong of J. Alfred Prufrock," the expression "Mr. Schwarz, he dead" to "The Hollow Men" and beyond, obviously, to Conrad's *Heart of Darkness*.

7. Personal letter from Lawrence Durrell to author.

8. *Clea*, 166.

9. Nicole Loraux, *"Ce que vit Tiresias," L'Ecrit du temps 2* (Paris: Minuit, 1982), 104–5.

10. *Clea*, 246.

11. Lawrence Durrell, *Livia* (London: Faber, 1978), 238.

12. Lawrence Durrell, *Monsieur* (London: Faber, 1974), 9.

13. Lawrence Durrell, *Constance* (London: Faber, 1982), 78; *Quinx* (London: Faber, 1985), 192; *Livia*, 19.

14. *Quinx*, 99.

15. *Constance*, 123.

16. Ibid., 284–85.

17. *Monsieur*, 25; *Livia*, 238; *Sebastian* (London: Faber, 1983), 194.

18. *Constance*, 378.

19. *Quinx*, 99.

20. Ibid., 26.

21. Ibid., 198.

22. *Sebastian*, 43.

# The Role of the Writer in Lawrence Durrell's Fiction

## CANDACE FERTILE

In *The Black Book,* Lawrence Lucifer contemplates "the age which lies beyond all this, the new dimension, the novel being a dim gnosis" (*BB,* 150).[1] In his diary, which is found by Lucifer, Death Gregory has written, "everything is plausible here, because nothing is real" (*BB,* 40). Here in this early work is one of Durrell's themes: writing as a search for knowledge, for plausibility. One of the ways he explores this theme is through increasingly complex intercalary narration. With his most recent fiction, *The Avignon Quintet,* Durrell attempts a bridging of the gulf that Lawrence Lucifer decries—"the gulf [that] has opened up between the people and their makers—the artists" (*BB,* 223). This essay will concentrate on one group of artists in Durrell's novels: the writers.

Writers create fictional worlds, and as such can be seen as gods wielding their power over their characters. When examining the role of the writer in Durrell's works, one must take into account his increasing interest in gnosticism. Although it has many sects, gnosticism holds the basic view that "the cosmos itself is intrinsically evil, and is not the work of the true God but of an opposing entity known as the demiurge, or 'creator.'"[2] The way to salvation is through knowledge that implies "an awareness of self that leads to internal harmony, to unification within, and to union with the One."[3] Lawrence Lucifer's gulf, the one created by his namesake (or even namesakes), can be eliminated through knowledge, a particular kind of knowledge that makes unification possible.

Although gnosticism is not dealt with directly in *The Black Book* as it is in the *Quintet,* suggestions of the later development exist in the pages of the former. The relationship between the novelist and his characters is evident to the reader and to them. Tarquin tells Gregory, "We do not exist; we are fictions" (*BB,* 37). Gregory accepts this idea and elaborates on it by saying that everyone has many potential

63

lives—like lines formed by railroad tracks "on which we might yet travel if only we had the strength to change." And then he self-consciously addresses the reader, saying, "You yawn? This is simply my way of saying I am lonely" (*BB,* 38). Gregory's loneliness results from his inability to put his ideas about books into practice. As G. S. Fraser points out, "emotional sterility, or occlusion of the soul, Durrell in *The Black Book* seems to see as particularly the illness of the failed artist."[4]

Gregory's failure as an artist is heightened because of the importance he places upon writing. As he notes in his diary, "The struggle is not to record experience but to record ourselves. . . . This is the ideal being we call a book. It does not exist" (*BB,* 121). Gregory exists only in a book; he is created through his writing, his diary. Once he ceases trying to write and goes to live in the suburbs, he no longer has a role in the novel. In other words, he no longer exists. Sharon Lee Brown says, "The theme of *The Black Book,* like that of the *Quartet,* is the conventional quest for self-identification."[5] In selecting his fictions, the writer is selecting himself and others. Gregory created himself for Lawrence Lucifer through his diary, and Lawrence Lucifer creates him for the reader by incorporating the diary into his book. Thus Gregory exists through the selection of Lawrence Lucifer.

In addition to the creation of particular realities in fiction, the gnostic notion of the pervasiveness of evil is also suggested in *The Black Book.* Lawrence Lucifer jokes that "In God is my hope, though the devil will have scope" (*BB,* 30). He also remarks that "Art must no longer exist to depict man, but to invoke God" (*BB,* 243). The artist calls forth God, but he is also summoning the devil. The yoking of God and the devil becomes increasingly clear in the later novels and is a basic tenet of gnosticism.

As a commentator on writing, Gregory is a precursor of Pursewarden in the *Quartet.* It is interesting to note that Pursewarden criticizes Darley in a letter to David Mountolive by saying that Darley lacks "devil" (*Quartet,* 481). Darley gets to be a writer of note after he learns about evil, after he incorporates into himself a bit of the devil. The relationship between Darley and Pursewarden, fellow writers, is similar in some respects to that of Lawrence Lucifer and Death Gregory. In each case the former must learn something the other knows, and must put it into practice. Darley also has the advice of Arnauti, who has written, "for the writer, people as psychologies are finished. The contemporary psyche has exploded like a soap-bubble under the investigations of the mystagogues. What now remains to the writer?" (*Quartet,* 95).

Darley's quest is to answer the question by finding out what

Pursewarden knows, but before he can do that he undergoes a three-fold failure, "in art, in religion, and in people" (*Quartet,* 159), which is caused by the fact that he is becoming "more and more deficient in love" (*Quartet,* 160). Darley finally learns what Pursewarden knows—that "it is only the artist who can make things really *happen*" (*Quartet,* 566), and Darley has to do the making. Once Darley resolves his difficulty with art and love, he is able to write those four important words, "Once upon a time" (*Quartet,* 877).

Writing is a process of self-discovery, Darley finds, and a process of discovering others. His search for the truth is like a gnostic's search for knowledge. Both are searches for salvation, which is a unification. For the gnostics, knowledge was gained by rejecting the material world. As a parallel, Darley removes himself from the excitement and confusion of Egypt to a small Greek island, and while there he attempts to come to an understanding of his experiences by writing about them. It is only by removing himself that he can gain any perspective, and, by doing so, he prepares the way for an eventual reconciliation and unification with Clea. James Van Dyck Card draws a parallel between Darley's personal and artistic growth: "Just as Darley moves through experience from Justine to Clea, so he moves from a reliance on the literature of others to the creation of his own."[6] Both transitions are made possible by Darley's rejection of Egypt. The rejection of the world is necessary for an understanding of the self, which in turn is necessary for the flourishing of love.

There are many references to gnosticism in the *Quartet,* particularly in *Justine.* Justine herself is viewed by Darley as being similar to "Sophia of Valentinus who died for a love as perfect as it was wrong-headed" (*Quartet,* 23). Jennifer L. Brewer says "that as Sophia was the metaphysical ground for the Gnostics' understanding of the material world, Justine is the metaphysical ground of the novel bearing her name, and, to a certain extent, a metaphysical foundation for the entire *Alexandria Quartet.*"[7] Sophia fell from the world of light into that of matter. Darley quotes Forster's *Alexandria* regarding Sophia who fell "not like Lucifer by rebelling against God, but by desiring too ardently to be united to him" (*Quartet,* 39). In the notes at the end of *Justine,* the author includes the next line in Forster's text: "She fell through love" (*Quartet,* 203). Sophia and Justine fall through love, but through a wrong kind of love.

Regarding Sophia, Darley goes on to say:

Broken from the divine harmony of herself she fell, says the tragic philosopher, and became the manifestation of matter; and the whole universe of her city, of the world, was formed out of her agony and remorse. The tragic seed from which her thoughts and actions grew was the seed of a pessimistic gnosticism. (*Quartet,* 39)

Justine tells Darley very clearly that gnosticism matters very much to her. She has learned about it from Balthazar and tries out her ideas on Darley. He recounts:

I remember her asking one night, so anxious, so pleadingly, if she had interpreted his thinking rightly: "I mean, that God neither created us nor wished us to be created, but that we are the work of an inferior deity, a Demiurge, who wrongly believed himself to be God? Heavens, how probable it seems; and this overweening *hubris* has been handed on down to our children." (*Quartet,* 39)

The fault of both Sophia and Justine is just this *hubris*. Benjamin Walker offers several reasons for Sophia's fall, but there are two main ones that have the most relevance to Justine.

Sophia falls either because she aspires to "complete knowledge of the light of the Absolute, which is denied to all," or because she desired "to create alone, like the Absolute, without the aid of a male counterpart."[8] Sophia and Justine are similar in their desire for knowledge and power, and this desire is the downfall of them both, although Justine's fall may be seen as only temporary. In a larger sense, though, Justine's demise is as permanent as Sophia's because Justine has no possibility of gaining self-knowledge. In Durrell's world, love and happiness are contingent on this self-knowledge. The importance of power to Justine can be seen when she no longer loves Nessim because he has lost his former strength. She tells Darley, "You see, when he does not act, Nessim is nothing; he is completely flavourless, not in touch with himself at any point. Then he has no real self to interest a woman, to grip her" (*Quartet,* 696). Even more important, Justine herself becomes nothing. She aligns herself so closely with Nessim that, once he is broken, so is she. When she comes to Darley in the night, he can only think of getting away as soon as possible. He has learned that what he loved was only an image, and that Justine has no substance or depth.

In addition to power, Justine also recognizes the importance of knowledge, but in many ways she is afraid of it. A possible reason for this is her realization that she is insubstantial. Justine is quite cognizant of the images or fictions that people create. She tells Darley, "Perhaps our only sickness is to desire a truth which we cannot bear rather than to rest content with the fictions we manufacture out of each other" (*Quartet,* 698). This thought shows what is wrong with

Justine and why she falls. She considers truth to be unbearable, but it is that which creates the self and, in turn, makes real love possible. While thinking about the "selected fictions" people present to one another, Darley realizes that "truth was nourishing—the cold spray of a wave which carried one always a little further towards self-realization" (*Quartet*, 694). Unlike Darley, Justine is unable to learn about herself and others from her experiences.

Self-realization is crucial to being able to love. Justine's "pessimistic gnosticism" recognizes the necessity of knowledge, but it does not contain the ability to attain such knowledge. Because she is so busy presenting her selected fictions, she is unable to become herself. When the illusion fades, as inevitably happens, nothing remains. Durrell takes this loss of the inner self and mirrors it in a loss of physical capacity. Both Justine and Nessim are physically damaged in a way that shows their damaged inner beings. Nessim loses an eye, and Justine's left eye droops because of a stroke. Eyes are the organs of sight, and in Durrell's work being fully or partially blind signifies a lack of knowledge, both of one's self and of others.

The clearest example of gnosticism in the *Quartet* is Balthazar's Cabal. Darley's knowledge of the Cabal and gnosticism shows him to be someone who is engaged in self-discovery and cognizant of the necessity of it. The information provided to Justine and Darley by Balthazar is not new to Darley, who has studied the subject and who recognizes the value of gnostic thought. He says, "I have dabbled in these matters before in Paris, conscious that in them I might find a pathway which could lead me to deeper understanding of myself—the self which seemed to be only a huge, disorganised and shapeless society of lusts and impulses" (*Quartet*, 84). Although much of what Darley hears at the Cabal is familiar, occasionally some thought has an impact on him. For example, he remembers Balthazar's saying:

> "None of the great religions has done more than exclude, throw out a long range of prohibitions. But prohibitions create the desire they are intended to cure. We of this Cabal say: *indulge but refine.* We are enlisting everything in order to make man's wholeness match the wholeness of the universe." (*Quartet*, 85)

In order to understand his disorganized and shapeless self, Darley needs to learn about himself and become whole—and through this process, he becomes a writer.

Clea carefully points out that love is the means to becoming whole, to being able to include. She says, "Love is horribly stable. . . . Its destination lies somewhere in the deepest regions of the psyche where it will come to recognise itself as self-love, the ground upon which we build the health of the psyche. I do not mean egoism or narcissism" (*Quartet,* 108). Egoism and narcissism exclude; the desired emotion is one that includes the other as he or she really is. According to Clea, neither Melissa nor Justine has the right kind of love. She explains the situation for Darley:

> "in some sense I am closer to you than either Melissa or Justine. You see, Melissa's love is too confining: it blinds her. While Justine's cowardly monomania sees one through an invented picture of one, and this forbids you to do anything except to be a demoniac like her." (*Quartet,* 109)

The lessons Darley learns about the psyche take him beyond Pursewarden's knowledge. Pursewarden believes, "We live . . . lives based on selected fictions. Our view of reality is conditioned by our position in space and time—not by our personalities as we like to think" (*Quartet,* 210). In *Balthazar,* Darley seems to agree, but he takes his theory a step further:

> And as for human characters, whether real or invented, there are no such animals. Each psyche is really an ant-hill of opposing predispositions. Personality as something with fixed attributes is an illusion—but a necessary illusion *if we are to love!* (*Quartet,* 210)

Darley's recognition of the importance of the illusion of fixed attributes shows his understanding of the fluctuations of personality through time and the human desire for security or fixity. Lisa Schwerdt remarks:

> As a result of his experiences, Darley finally achieves self-actualization. Because he has achieved this, he has developed to the full stature of which he is capable—an artist who is creative and autonomous—fulfilling himself and doing what he was meant to do.[9]

Love and creativity go hand in hand, Darley learns, and they contribute to his personal happiness.

Clea has helped Darley a great deal, and it is important to note that she and Pursewarden agree on sex. Pursewarden believes:

> very few people realize that sex is a psychic and not a physical act. The clumsy coupling of human beings is simply a biological paraphrase of this

truth—a primitive method of introducing minds to each other, engaging them. But most people are stuck in the physical aspect, unaware of the poetic *rapport* which it so clumsily tries to teach. (*Quartet,* 292)

Clea phrases it thusly:

> Paracelsus says that thoughts are acts. Of them all, I suppose, the sex act is the most important, the one in which our spirits must divulge themselves. Yet one feels it a clumsy paraphrase of the poetic, the noetic, *thought* which shapes itself into a kiss or an embrace. Sexual love *is* knowledge, both in etymology and in cold fact; "he knew her" as the Bible says! Sex is the joint or coupling which unites the male and female ends of knowledge merely—a cloud of unknowing! When a culture goes bad in its sex all knowledge is impeded. (*Quartet,* 739)

Knowledge is the desired goal for Durrell, and the goal is attained by unification of the separate strains of male and female knowledge. Without unity, knowledge is impossible.[10]

Rejection of the material world is taken to its logical end by the gnostic death pacts in the *Quintet.* The increased importance of gnosticism in the *Quintet* is mirrored by the increased complexity of the narration. Just as there are hints in *The Black Book* for the later works, so are there hints in the *Quartet, Tunc,* and *Nunquam* that shed light on the practices of the *Quintet.* First of all, in the extracts from his notebooks in *Clea,* Pursewarden talks to Darley and suggests a collaboration. In the *Quintet,* Durrell has Blanford collaborate with Sutcliffe, Blanford's fictional writer. The second hint also comes from Pursewarden, this time from his letters to Liza, which she gives to Darley, who is struck by their brilliance. He does not quote them, but he does describe their effect:

> Literature, I say! But these were life itself, not a studied representation of it in a form—life itself, the flowing undivided stream of life with all its pitiable will-intoxicated memories, its pains, terrors and submissions. Here illusion and reality were fused in one single blinding vision which hung over the writer's mind like a dark star—the star of death! (*Quartet,* 791)

The *Quintet* blends illusion and reality, and Blandford echoes Darley's view of Pursewarden when he says he is "deliberately turning the novel inside out like a sleeve" and "then back" (*S,* 124). Turning sleeves or gloves inside out can be a game, but for Durrell, unlike Pursewarden, the end of the fusion of illusion and reality in the *Quin-*

tet is not a pointless joke. The "flowing undivided stream of life" in the *Quintet* is a joke with a point, and as a writer Durrell is not the pessimist that Pursewarden is. As appalling as the material world may be in the *Quintet,* there is a way out of the darkness.

This avenue of escape is not easy, as Durrell shows by a couple of characters who move further into darkness, both literally and figuratively. Images of light and dark, archetypal symbols for knowledge and ignorance or good and evil, pervade Durrell's works. In the *Quintet* two characters who are both Nazi supporters, Livia and Von Esslin, both have damaged sight. Livia loses an eye through a self-inflicted stabbing, and Von Esslin loses most of his sight through an explosion engineered by his servant Kroc. Livia eventually succumbs to despair and, like Pursewarden, commits suicide. Von Esslin, however, makes friends with Constance who reminds him of his beloved sister Constanza, and in a way his humanity is restored, at least partially, by this friendship.

The small glimmers of humanity are not enough to eradicate the darkness—the ever-present evil in the world. Durrell's choice of World War II and Avignon as the temporal and spatial settings of most of the *Quintet* is particularly appropriate, and this complements the controlling principle of gnosticism with its emphasis on the necessity of recognizing evil as a real force in the world.

In *Monsieur,* Akkad lays out the precepts of gnosticism for Piers, who is immediately sympathetic. Piers compares his belief to "falling in love" (*M,* 94). Like Charlock and Darley, Bruce Drexel is skeptical. He says, "I had not much faith in the reality represented by such breakaway sects as gnostics, and I was on my guard against the spuriously romantic" (*M,* 108). Bruce manages to stay clear of the gnostic trap; Piers does not. Bruce survives; Piers does not. Although gnosticism is crucial to *Monsieur* and to the rest of the *Quintet,* it is not held up as the way to salvation. Gnosticism provides a way to view a world that is disintegrating, that is in the grip of evil. When Akkad is talking about his beliefs, he says that what characterizes our culture is "Monotheism, Messianism, Monogamy, and Materialism" (*M,* 141). He adds, "The cornerstone of culture then is another M—*merde*" (*M,* 141), a clear echo from *Tunc* and *Nunquam.* Gnosticism provides a way to deal with life in that it offers a way out of life through the death pacts. As Bruce says, "to be of this persuasion was to remain faithful to the fundamental despair of reality, to realize finally and completely that there was no hope unless the usurping God could be dethroned, and there seemed to be no way to do that" (*M,* 118). If there is no way to eliminate the wrong god, self-destruction is not only plausible, but it is preferable to compliance with the good god.

Durrell, in fact, calls gnosticism "a disease caused by the Christian context."[11] Both extremes are to be avoided. James R. Nichols states:

> For Durrell all religions and, I suspect, all "systems" fail because they eventually grow old, rigidify, and come to substitute abstract thought for vital energy, dogmatism for experience, rules for human contact. Such corporate structures ("Merlins" in *Tunc* and *Nunquam*) produce what Durrell and his characters fear most, forced loneliness and alienation.[12]

Nichols's point is exemplified in *Constance* when Smirgel talks about how the Judeo-Christian traditions have made the rise of the Nazis possible. One system has simply led to another. The rejection of evil as a real force has only strengthened evil's grip on the world. The obsession with the material world leads to materialism and a loss of spirituality. The importance of things that are separate from one's self furthers the disintegration of the self.

Just as the thematic concerns of the *Quintet* are brought out in *Monsieur,* so are the formal ones. The games or jokes begin near the end of the novel, when the reader discovers that Blanford the character is a writer who has created what has gone on previously. He talks about the book he has just written, *Le Monsieur,* the book the reader has just read, and is still reading. Blanford has gone so far as to have his creation Sutcliffe, as another writer, parody Blanford himself in the creation of another novelist named Bloshford. Behind all this is Durrell, and Blanford even refers to him: "Am I possibly an invention of someone like old D.—the devil at large?" (*M,* 281). Mentioning himself in his novels is not new for Durrell. In *The Black Book,* Gregory says that Tarquin has borrowed Durrell's car (*BB,* 200), and in *Nunquam* Charlock quotes a line of poetry "from the best of our modern poets" (*N,* 267), who, we are told in a footnote, is Lawrence Durrell.

Sutcliffe does more than borrow Blanford's car—he nearly takes over, and he does help Blanford with the succeeding novels. The collapsing of the barrier between illusion and reality is seen by Blanford as a new development for the novel. He calls *Le Monsieur* "this new and rather undisciplined departure from the ordinary product" (*M,* 275). The discipline erodes even further when Blanford starts having conversations with Sutcliffe and collaborating with him. At first the exchanges between the two can be dismissed as the ravings of a disordered mind—Blanford, old and infirm, has no one else to talk to but his fictions. But this theory breaks down when other characters meet Sutcliffe. Constance, for example, listens to Sutcliffe and Blanford argue about writing:

It was curious, too, to hear them discussing the interminable sequences of the "double concerto" as Blanford called their novel now. He took the concerns of form very seriously and reacted with annoyance to Sutcliffe's jocose suggestions, namely that the whole thing would be much tidier as an exchange of letters. (*S,* 123)

Constance expresses concern for the reader, and Sutcliffe counters with the statement that he and Blanford "have never been interested in the real world—[we] see it through a cloud of disbelief" (*S,* 124). The reader is also "seeing through a cloud of disbelief."

The seeing and the disbelief are generated by the two sides of the novel, or writer. Blanford tells Sutcliffe, his alter-ego or alter-writer, "Your version of our book gives the presence of events, mine the absence" (*S,* 143). Sutcliffe is cast down because he does not really exist; he is "turned on and off at will like a memory" (*S,* 144). But Sutcliffe, as the creation, gains power over his creator and does exert some autonomy. The two even tease each other—Blanford by saying that he will be glad to be rid of his creation (something that cannot happen); Sutcliffe by asking if Blanford has mistaken him for Monsieur, who is, after all, the Prince of Darkness. The other, under, world is always tied to the surface reality.

Durrell mixes up illusion and reality (even fictional reality, at that) even more, when Constance and Bruce Drexel discuss the possibility of Constance's going to Provence for Christmas. Threads of illusion and reality are so intertwined that it is impossible to tell which has precedence: "Everything is plausible here, because nothing is real" (*BB,* 40). Drexel points out to Blanford that the novelist may no longer have control: "your novel about the matter is finished: it only remains for you to see if we are going to live it according to your fiction or according to new fact, no?" (*S,* 172). Blanford's characters start to behave like real people, even whining about their treatment in the hands of Blanford and the lack of "specific and discrete identity" (*S,* 186). That the discreteness is important, that in fact that is the point of the joke, is shown when Blanford considers writing another novel. He uses the first person plural pronoun: "If we could have a summer or two of peace and quietness we might commit another novel" (*S,* 200). Sutcliffe, "his etheric double," replies, "'Why not?'" (*S,* 201). The word "commit" suggests the way in which Blanford views writing.

In *Quinx or the Ripper's Tale,* the next collaboration, the border between illusion and reality is again crossed. What Blanford says at the end of *Quinx* is what has already happened: "It was at this precise moment that reality prime rushed to the aid of fiction and the totally unpredictable began to take place" (Q, 201). For example, Sutcliffe and Sabine, who are not on the same narrative level, make love. Sutcliffe brings together the ideas of reality and love when he exclaims, "Lovers . . . are just reality—fools! And yet! How good it is, how real it is!" (Q, 83). The connection between love and reality is developed further by Sylvie whose "fearful fragility of her grasp on reality became clear—she saw herself diminishing, becoming a parody of a person, empty of all inward fruitfulness, of love" (Q, 89). No love, no being. Sylvie associates a lack of love with death—separation meaning "rejoin[ing] the ranks of the walking dead—those who were out of love!" (Q, 89–90).

In the *Quintet*, Durrell has accomplished what Blanford has attempted: "I was hoping not only to tell the truth but also to free the novel a bit from the shackles of causality with a narrative apparently dislocated and disjointed yet informed by mutually contradictory insights—love at first insight, so to speak" (Q, 165–66). As William Godshalk points out, it is necessary to distinguish between the different realities presented in the *Quintet*, or the force of the narrative is lost. He says:

> Durrell relies on our regarding the characters in his fictive reality—such characters as Blanford and Tu—as virtually real. If we fail to do this—and I believe that most readers would do this without thinking—we miss Durrell's vital distinction between the fictively real Blanford and the fictively fictional Sutcliffe.[13]

Blanford and Sutcliffe are not on the same plane of reality or fictionality. Durrell requires that the reader make an imaginative leap in accepting the narrative, just as he requires the reader to accept the duality of the world and the necessity for reconciliation. The unification of disparate elements is unlikely, perhaps even impossible, but the effort must be made.

Unification is possible only through self-knowledge and love, and "insight" and "love" are the key words to an understanding of Durrell's work. "Insight" because it is the writer's job to see. When Mnemidis asks Constance, "Where had I gone? My I? My eye?" (S, 15), he acknowledges the relationship between self and seeing. Knowledge comes through seeing, knowledge of the self and its lack of discreteness in the world. The writer must see the world to create it, not to reproduce it. The writer must also destroy the way we perceive the world, so that we can more clearly see ourselves and each other. Love is a way of seeing. The writer, therefore, is a bit of both a devil and a deity, if he does his job well.

The role of the writer, then, is to save us from the polarities of systems such as Christianity and gnosticism. Instead of looking outside ourselves, we must look within, and by doing so we will get closer to other people. Durrell expresses this idea clearly in an article written in 1960: "You get closer to your fellow man, paradoxically enough, by trying to get closer to yourself."[14] When the writer takes this knowledge and writes about it, he is engaging in a positive and necessary activity. Durrell says:

> the act of laying pen to paper, brush to canvas, is an act of mystical participation in the common world to which we all belong. . . . what emerges from the resolution of selves, if it can be called art, of whatever scale or magnitude, is a direct contribution to the health of the human psyche, a cordial which makes it better able to recuperate its forces against those of destruction. This is not, of course, to be numbered among the artist's conscious intentions. It is a by-product of the work. The artist is only concerned with the pure act of self-penetration, of self-disentanglement, when he addresses his paper or canvas.[15]

In his novels, Durrell has many characters who lack self-knowledge, who are not integrated, and who are finally destroyed. There are many instances of love, but very often the love is destructive, or at least counterproductive because of the damaged psyches involved.

Healthy psyches are fundamental to healthy love, which in turn is fundamental to a healthier world. In the *Quintet*, the culmination of his formal and thematic efforts, Durrell smashes the barrier between illusion and reality to force us to look differently at a "fictional" and a "real" world. As we watch the barrier being removed, Durrell shows us that new ways of seeing can help to create a coming together, a unity. Love unites and melts the boundaries, and it is through love that we will save ourselves. It is the role of the writer to facilitate the process. Lee Lemon notes:

> From *The Black Book* on, Durrell has kept reminding us that, if anything, the creative person is charged with the difficult responsibility of being more human than others; only when he is able to be more sympathetic, more sensitive, more understanding, is the creativity meaningful.[16]

With sympathy, sensitivity, and understanding, the writer creates a world in which these qualities are promoted.

In *The Dark Labyrinth*, Ruth Adams tells the Trumans:

> I remembered how life was before . . . I was outside everything in a certain way. Now I participate *with* everything. I feel joined to everything in a

new kind of way. Before I lived by moral precepts—for morality is an at-tempt to unite ourselves to people. Now I don't feel the need for religion, or faith in the old sense. In my own mind, inside (not as something I think or feel, but as something I *am*) inside there I no longer prohibit and select. I include. It's the *purely scientific* meaning of the word "love." (*DL*, 244–45)

Love includes and closes the gap—bridges the gulf—because it blurs the boundaries. The influence of gnosticism is to avoid the barrier of the material world. Schwarz tells Constance, "Our whole civilization is enacting the fall of Lucifer" (*S*, 21). One of Lucifer's sins was envy, whose opposite is love. Lucifer separated; love can bring together. As Akkad says, "We can make amends by loving correctly" (*M*, 143).

## NOTES

1. Quotations from Durrell's works are cited in the text using the following ab-breviations:

*BB: The Black Book* (London: Faber, 1977).

*Quartet: The Alexandria Quartet* (London: Faber, 1977).

*T: Tunc* (London: Faber, 1980).

*N: Nunquam* (London: Faber, 1978).

*DL: The Dark Labyrinth* (London: Faber, 1979).

*M: Monsieur* (London: Faber, 1981).

*L: Livia* (London: Faber, 1978).

*C: Constance* (London: Faber, 1982).

*S: Sebastian* (New York: Viking, 1983).

*Q: Quinx* (London: Faber, 1985).

2. Benjamin Walker, *Gnosticism: Its History and Influence* (Wellingborough: The Aquarian Press, 1983), 12.

3. Ibid., 99–100.

4. G. S. Fraser, *Lawrence Durrell: A Study* (London: Faber, 1973), 56.

5. Sharon Lee Brown, "*The Black Book:* A Search for Method," *Modern Fiction Studies* 13 (Autumn 1967): 320.

6. James Van Dyck Card, "'Tell Me, Tell Me': The Writer as Spellbinder in Law-rence Durrell's *Alexandria Quartet*," *Modern British Literature* 1 (1976): 80.

7. Jennifer L. Brewer, "Character and Psychological Place: The Justine/Sophia Relation," *Deus Loci* 5 (Fall 1981): 237.

8. Walker, *Gnosticism*, 40.

9. Lisa Schwerdt, "Coming of Age in Alexandria: The Narrator," *Deus Loci* 5 (Fall 1981): 219–220.

10. Ann Gossman says, "Indeed, for Durrell the only valid modes of knowing are art and love," in her "Love's Alchemy in *The Alexandria Quartet*," *Critique* 13 (1971–72): 83. Alan Warren Friedman also explores the relationship between art, love, and knowledge in *Lawrence Durrell and The Alexandria Quartet: Art for Love's Sake* (Norman: University of Oklahoma Press, 1970).

11. James P. Carley, "An Interview with Lawrence Durrell on the Background to

*Monsieur* and Its Sequels," *Malahat Review* 51 (1979): See also Carley's "Lawrence Durrell and the Gnostics," *Deus Loci* 2 (September 1978): 3–10, and "Lawrence Durrell's Avignon Quincunx and Gnostic Heresy," *Deus Loci* 5 (Fall 1981): 284–304.

12. James R. Nichols, "Sunshine Dialogues: Christianity and Paganism in the Works of Lawrence Durrell," *On Miracle Ground III: Second International Lawrence Durrell Conference Proceedings* (Baltimore: University of Baltimore Press, 1984), 132.

13. William L. Godshalk, "Commentary," *On Miracle Ground: II,* 109.

14. Lawrence Durrell, "No Clue to Living," *Times Literary Supplement,* 27 May 1960, 339.

15. Ibid.

16. Lee Lemon, *Portraits of the Artist in Contemporary Fiction* (Lincoln: University of Nebraska Press, 1985), 10.

# Part 2
# Portraits of the Artist in Fiction

# That "one book there, a Plutarch": Of *Isis and Osiris* in *The Alexandria Quartet*

## CAROL PEIRCE

All blessings, Clea, should be sought of the gods by the intelligent, and we especially pray that in our search we may receive direct from them an understanding of their own nature, as far as that is possible to men; for nothing greater is attainable by man, and nothing nobler can be granted by God, than truth.[1]

So begins the book that Liza Pursewarden describes to Darley, the narrator, in *Clea,* the fourth volume of *The Alexandria Quartet.* Explaining her childhood with her brother "in an old rambling farm-house among the frozen lakes, among the mists and rains of Ireland," she says:

"There was only one book there, a Plutarch, which we knew by heart. Everything else he invented. This was how I became the strange mythological queen of his life, living in a vast palace of sighs—as he used to say. Sometimes it was Egypt, sometimes Peru, sometimes Byzantium."[2]

A little later she adds that when Pursewarden "started looking for justifications for our love instead of just simply being proud of it, he read me a quotation from a book":

"'In the African burial rites it is the sister who brings the dead king back to life. In Egypt as well as Peru the king, who was considered as God, took his sister to wife. But the motive was ritual and not sexual, for they symbolized the moon and the sun in their conjunction. The king marries his sister because he, as God the star, wandering on earth, is immortal and may therefore not propagate himself in the children of a strange woman, any more than he is allowed to die a natural death.' That is why he was pleased to come there to Egypt, because he felt, he said, an interior poetic link with Osiris and Isis, with Ptolemy and Arsinoe—the race of the sun and the moon!" (*C,* 191)

Obviously, as the brother-sister gods and lovers of both ancient and

Ptolemaic Egypt, Isis and Osiris form a deeply symbolic link with the past of Alexandria in the *Quartet*. The very name Clea, as well, may relate to Clea Montis of the *Quartet*. And, finally, it is possible that Plutarch's "one book there" has a larger relationship to Durrell's *Quartet*, especially the last volume.

What Liza is talking about is Plutarch's *Isis and Osiris,* one of the two main classical works from which we derive knowledge of the god and goddess, the other being *The Golden Ass* of Apuleius, which treats solely, and in fiction, of Isis. Although numerous references to parts of the story exist in ancient Egyptian sources, such as the *Coffin Texts,* the *Pyramid Texts,* and the *Book of the Dead* (which was Durrell's original title for the *Quartet*),[3] the Egyptian scribes seem to have assumed that their audience knew the myths. It is only with large assumptions that Egyptologists can begin to piece the stories together. Plutarch, however, who learned them in Egypt, and who may possibly himself have been a priest of Osiris, as we know he was of Dionysus, considers both the story and its symbolic and philosophic implications in his work. He dedicated it to his young friend Clea, a priestess of Isis, described as "a leader of the Thyiades [The Bacchantes] at Delphi." It is known that she had been "consecrated in the Osirian rites by father and mother," in addition to serving Dionysus at Delphi (*P,* 95). Indeed, it may have been because of his deep friendship with Clea, along with the wide popularity of the old mystery cult, still alive in his time (ca. A.D. 120), that Plutarch wrote the volume.

Briefly, the story is that Osiris and Isis, brother and sister gods, children of sky and earth, "being in love with each other even before they were born, were united in the darkness of the womb" (*P,* 137). They later wed, Osiris bringing knowledge and civilization to the world as king and Isis bringing the arts of love and cultivation as queen. Typhon (as Plutarch calls him) or Set (in the Egyptian texts), another brother god, being jealous, tricked Osiris into lying in a coffin, closed its lid, suffocating him, and cast it into the Nile. The first to learn of Set's deed were "the Pans and Satyrs"; because of this such moments "of sudden disturbance and excitement" are still called "panic," Plutarch adds (*P,* 139). Isis eventually found the coffin lodged in a tree, had intercourse with Osiris, revived for a moment by her breath, and brought it back. While she watched her son Horus, born of this brief reunion, Typhon refound the coffin, cut Osiris's body into pieces, and scattered them throughout Egypt. Isis again set out and found and buried all but the phallus, to the life-giving power of which she raised a monument. When Horus grew older, he fought Typhon to avenge his father and defeated and bound him. Isis, however, sorry for her brother, or perhaps in love with him now (as suggested in older texts), freed him, whereupon Horus tore off his mother's head-dress (Plutarch) or her head (Egyptian texts). Hermes, her father, re-stored it in the shape of a cow's head. As Osiris called to Horus from the grave, Horus set out for the underworld to free him and his pow-ers from death. Having accomplished this, Horus returned to reign over the living, and Osiris ruled the dead or, indeed, all the quick and the dead as the sun, while Isis reflected his glory as the moon.

After telling the story, Plutarch speculates on its possible meanings; for he feels no myths stand alone, but all have symbolic and philo-sophic meanings. As he puts it:

Just as the scientists tell us that the rainbow is an image of the sun made brilliant by the reflection of its appearance into a cloud, so the present myth is the image of a reality which turns the mind back to other thoughts. (P, 149)

The first theory he discusses is tied to nature and to the nature of Isis and Osiris. The Dog-star, Sirius, is connected to Isis and the con-stellation Orion to Horus. Osiris himself rides in the star vessel of the Argo (P, 151). When Sirius and Orion appear over the horizon, the time of the inundation of the Nile is near. Plutarch considers vari-ous possible meanings but concludes that the likeliest is the one that suggests that Osiris represents moisture and the generation of seed through Isis, the earth. Typhon is the dry, scorching element that burns it up to desert (P, 169). While Osiris is in the coffin, water has disappeared from the Nile delta.

But somehow another story has been woven in; for Plutarch ex-plains that Osiris and Isis may have been demons or demigods, crea-tures born between gods and men, like Heracles and Dionysus, who were later changed to gods (P, 159). One modern theory, discussed by Frazer in *The Golden Bough*, holds that Osiris was an actual early king of Egypt who died the sacrificial death of "the king who must die," his limbs scattered to bring fresh life to the land.[4] He would have been followed by his son (Horus), who in ascending the throne needed the strength and power of his father behind him, until he too grew old to become Osiris in death. So each king, marrying his sister, finally sacrificed himself, helping to bring strength to his land and suc-cessor.

In another even more pervasive symbolic identification, Plutarch says, Osiris is the sun and Isis the moon, and:

Further, on the first day of the month of Phamenoth they hold a festival, which they call "The Entry of Osiris into the Moon," for it is the beginning of spring. Thus they locate the power of Osiris in the moon and say that Isis, as the creative principle, had had intercourse with him. (*P,* 187)

Finally, philosophically, the myth can be seen as a sort of perfected triangle of Plato. Osiris represents the spiritually intelligible idea, origin, word, Isis the material, or receptive, element, and Horus, the creation or perfected achievement (*P,* 207–8).

Plutarch concludes that the myth is not just Egyptian but a common heritage: "But Isis and the gods related to her belong to all men and are known to them . . ." (*P,* 223). In fact, although this myth was bound deeply into Egyptian and then Ptolemaic Greek legend and history, it eventually moved on into all the Greek and even the Roman worlds. Truly Isis, the myriad-named, as Plutarch calls her and as Apuleius represents her, with Ceres, Venus, Artemis, Athena, and Proserpine as only her varied manifestations, became a goddess worshiped in herself throughout the Classical period and lived on, merging into the Virgin Mary, an enduring force and symbol. She is forever the great White Goddess described in Robert Graves's monumental work.

In many ways the whole movement of *Clea* relates to the myth of Isis and Osiris, beginning with the de Sade epigraph, "The Primary and most beautiful of Nature's qualities is motion, which agitates her at all times . . ." (*C,* 8). And, of course, a central motion in *Clea* is that of time, though Darley makes clear near the beginning that he has begun to develop understanding as well, "learning at last to inhabit those deserted spaces which time misses—beginning to live between the ticks of the clock, so to speak" (*C,* 14). Plutarch puts it at the end of his invocation to Clea:

> For the divine is not made blessed with silver and gold, nor strong with thunder and lightning, but is blessed and strong through understanding and insight. . . . for if one took away knowledge of what really exists, and insight, immortality would be a matter not of life but merely of the passage of time. (*P,* 119)

Isis herself is closely related to the concept of the soulful and intelligent motion of nature. Plutarch states that her name comes from *epistêmê,* or "understanding," and *kinêsis,* or "movement" (*P,* 215), and says that the sistrum she often carries "indicates that the things which exist should be shaken . . . and should never stop moving, but should be awaked and disturbed, as it were, when they are sleepy and sluggish" (*P,* 219).

In *Clea* too, Durrell at last sounds his deepest mythic resonances as Darley reaches the conclusion of his long initiatory journey. The theme of Antony and Cleopatra is closing; Cavafy's recessional music is beginning. But, as *Clea* begins, Darley must still come really to know Pursewarden who speaks to him in "My Conversations with Brother Ass" from beyond the grave. He must with Liza piece together and then destroy Pursewarden's poetic letters. He must descend, led by Pursewarden, into the deepest mysteries of initiation culminating in his final trial of death with Clea beneath the sea.

Thus, one of the most beautiful and profound shifts of meaning deep in the *Quartet* comes in the symbolic identification of Liza and Pursewarden with Isis and Osiris. Durrell touches detail after detail and symbol after symbol to make it theirs. Of course we have met both characters earlier. Pursewarden is central to the whole *Quartet*, though he dies in *Justine* and appears thereafter only "through the distorting mirror of anecdote or the dusty spectrum of memory."[5] Liza enters in only a few episodes, primarily in the few pages in which, with her brother, she meets David Mountolive in *Mountolive* and in the longer and more important section in *Clea* in which, in Alexandria after her brother's death, she consults Darley on the disposition of Pursewarden's love letters.

Liza then begins to tell her story to Darley, how from orphaned childhood on they lived and loved in incest in their palace of sighs: "We used to sit like this as children with our playbox between us, before the fire, in the winter" (*C,* 190). She speaks of their parents:

> "All we knew of our parents, the sum of our knowledge, was an old oak cupboard full of their clothes. They seemed enormous to us when we were small—the clothes of giants, the shoes of giants. One day he said they oppressed him, these clothes. We did not need parents. And we took them out into the yard and made a bonfire of them in the snow. We both wept bitterly, I do not know why. We danced round the bonfire singing an old hunting song with savage triumph and yet weeping." (*C,* 191–92)

It is an episode straight from myth, fairy tale, Frazer, or Jung—the succession of the old gods, the old kings, by the new.

A fascinating series of details in *Mountolive* begins to unfold. Plutarch says that Isis was the inventor of weaving and describes her clothes as "variegated in colour" (*P,* 241). Apuleius, in his transcendent vision of her rising from the night sea becomes inspired:

> Her many-coloured robe was of finest linen; part was glistening white, part crocus-yellow, part glowing red and along the entire hem a woven bordure of flowers and fruit clung swaying in the breeze. But what caught

and held my eye more than anything else was the deep black luster of her mantle. She wore it slung across her body from the right hip to the left shoulder, where it was caught in a knot resembling the boss of a shield; but part of it hung in innumerable folds, the tasselled fringe quivering. It was embroidered with glittering stars on the hem and everywhere else, and in the middle beamed a full and fiery moon.[6]

Her hair is most vividly described in the translation of William Adlington of 1566:

First, she had a great abundance of hair, flowing and curling, dispersed and scattered about her divine neck; on the crown of her head she bare many garlands interlaced with flowers, and in the middle of her forehead was a plain circlet in fashion of a mirror, or rather resembling the moon by the light it gave forth; and this was borne up on either side by serpents that seemed to rise from the furrows of the earth, and above it were blades of corn set out.[7]

In his own description of the White Goddess, Graves writes that her "broad high brow was white as any leper's."[8]

When Liza appears in *Mountolive*, she can be immediately seen to possess several of the attributes and accoutrements of Isis. In the very first sentence describing her, she is wearing "a brilliant tartan shawl with a great white brooch."[9] The second sentence mentions "her broad pale face with its helmet of dark curling hair" (*M*, 59). Another tells us she is blind; a little further along,

It was the head of a Medusa, its blindness was that of a Greek statue—a blindness perhaps brought about by intense concentration through centuries upon sunlight and blue water? (*M*, 60)

She, indeed, calls to mind *"Greek statues with their bullet holes for eyes"* (*M*, 66). This blindness may also point to the reflected light (and not her own) she gives to Pursewarden, as Isis the moon reflects Osiris the sun.

Liza has prophetic vision as well to go with her blindness. Mountolive recounts the episode:

"Only once, when he [Pursewarden] had gone out for a second, she turned to me and said, 'He shouldn't concern himself with these matters really. His one job is to learn how to submit to despair.' I was very much struck by this oracular phrase which fell so naturally from her lips and did not know what to reply." (*M*, 63)

On a lighter note, when asked her drinking preference, Liza mentions brandy and soda but in a voice, Durrell says, that should be calling for "Honey and nectar" (*M*, 61). And as the evening moves on, in one of the most charming of all the scenes of the *Quartet*, the brother and sister dance round Trafalgar Square to celebrate William Blake's birthday; Durrell adds, "Snowflakes like dissolving jewels in her dark hair" (*M*, 65), surely a reflection of Isis with her dazzling headdress, the White Goddess of the ancient world.

Durrell's description of Liza's "helmet of dark curling hair" corresponds well to that of a goddess twice seen by Plutarch as also being Athena. To carry that helmet image a little further, it might be recalled that Plutarch writes about Horus that "laying hands on his mother he ripped off the crown from her head. Hermes, however, put on her instead a cow-headed helmet" (*P*, 147). Plutarch also sees Isis as the Titaness, Tethys, and her husband, Oceanus, as Osiris (*P*, 171). The Greeks considered them "the parents of all Waters."[10]

Thus, Pursewarden, now in Alexandria, thinks of his sister:

Her saw her—the marble whiteness of the sea-goddess' face, hair combed back upon her shoulders, staring out across the park where the dead autumn leaves and branches flared and smoked; a Medusa among the snows, dressed in her old tartan shawl. (*M*, 161)

Finally, the name *Liza* itself, if not an anagram, certainly recalls *Isis* in sound.

The name Pursewarden, totally different from Osiris, has some fascinating aspects to its meaning. It is closely allied through Durrell's use of Tarot symbolism to the Fool, who himself symbolizes Osiris, Horus, Dionysus, and Zeus together, and who is pictured as the bearer of the purse of wisdom, stepping toward the edge of a cliff into eternity, both fallible, despairing man and laughing god. In some versions of the card a crocodile (one of Set's symbols) waits in a pool below, symbolizing sacrificial death and rebirth and reflecting Osiris's death and rebirth in the Nile.[11] As we have seen, Plutarch presents a Platonic version of the meaning behind the myth. Isis is to him, although material, a goddess of wisdom, and "her mysteries lead to *gnô-sis* of the highest being, that is, Osiris," the creative Logos (*P*, 51). If Isis is matter, Osiris is spirit and mind that she reflects. Just so Pursewarden, and just so his reflection by the dark moon, Liza.

There are only a few direct references to Isis and Osiris in the *Quartet*. One occurs as Mountolive, who may be in some sense Typhon, returns to Egypt triumphantly as ambassador and stands looking out at the Nile. He hears music, laughter, and,

> . . . the harsh thrilling rattle of the sistrum. "I had forgotten," he said with a pang. "The tears of Isis! It is the Night of the Drop, isn't it?". . . . Isis-Diana would be bright in the heavens. . . . He gazed vaguely round searching for the constellations. (*M*, 135)

With the final drop of the Nile, Isis laments Osiris' fate; but the star of Isis, Sirius, and the constellation of Orion rising in the sky foretell his resurrection. A brief mention, but it suggests the myth. It is, of course, Mountolive's return and his and Liza's love that lead directly to Pursewarden's suicide.

Thus Osiris was the god of poetry, of inspiration, of divination, but he was even more the god of the dead and the spirit of becoming, "the personification of the coming into being of all things."[12] Like Isis he was often associated with the stars—of life and death. In fact, Graves tells us he was a Star-son. In processional his fifty-yard-long phallus was crowned with a golden star.[13] He was, however, always portrayed swathed in mummy wrappings, speaking from beyond the grave. It is as if his own story begins with his death. So it is with Pursewarden, whose suicide is retold in each book but who continues to live and speak both through his writings and through memory:

> . . . he has simply stepped into the quicksilver of a mirror as we all must— to leave our illnesses, our evil acts, the hornets' nest of our desires, still operative for good or evil in the real world—which is the memory of our friends. (*J*, 118)

And while Plutarch shows Osiris as killed by Typhon, older stories and later theories, as mentioned before, suggest the vegetation god on the one hand and the historical king on the other who, in royal martyrdom, sacrificed himself for the good of his people. Pursewarden's suicide—to die rather than to betray his friend or country and even more to release Liza to love and marry Mountolive—was such a death. Durrell, talking about it himself in "The Kneller Tape," said, with gnostic symbolism involved as well, "Pursewarden's suicide is the sacrificial suicide of a true cathar."[14]

Pursewarden comes like a Dionysiac god, of wine, of song, of poetry, laughing at all of life, in joy, in tenderness disguised as irony, and with phallic symbolism galore, like ". . . Osiris with erect phallus because of his procreative and nourishing nature" (*P*, 210). He is able to break Justine's check with laughter, to inspire Clea to understanding, to make the sacrificial gift of love to Liza and Mountolive, and to initiate Darley into true artisthood. All this from beyond the grave, so to speak, for in the middle of the first volume he commits suicide.

Darley comments later: "The best retorts always come from beyond the grave."[15]

In contrast to Durrell's very descriptive and detailed identification of Liza with Isis, only a few short passages in the *Quartet,* and those only loosely relevant, seem to connect Pursewarden to Osiris. His symbolic relationship with Osiris, more than that of Liza with Isis, is deeply interfused within the heart and meaning of the novel.

During the first episode with Liza, he laughs:

"What am I, Pursewarden, doing here among people who live in a frenzy of propriety? Let me wander where people have come to terms with their own human obscenity, safe in the poet's cloak of invisibility. I want to learn to respect nothing while despising nothing—crooked is the path of the initiate!" (*M,* 63)

Just before he kills himself, he calls Nessim, and his parting chuckle has to Nessim "a sound of some resurrected Pan" (*M,* 214). One also recalls that Osiris originally as a man came to Egypt where he became a king and "showed them how to grow crops, established laws for them, and taught them to worship gods." Plutarch continues:

Later he civilized the whole world as he traversed through it, having very little need of arms, but winning over most of the peoples by beguiling them with persuasive speech together with all manner of song and poetry. That is why the Greeks thought he was the same as Dionysus. (*P,* 137)

Thus, Pursewarden is quoted by Clea on what he hoped to achieve in his last book, *God Is a Humorist:*

"Yet I must in this last book insist that there is hope for man, scope for man, within the boundaries of a simple law; and I seem to see mankind as gradually appropriating to itself the necessary information through mere attention, *not reason,* which may one day enable it to live within the terms of such an idea—the true meaning of 'joy unconfined.'" (*B,* 238–39)

And almost immediately afterward he continues:

"Now in my life I am somewhat irresolute and shabby, but in my art I am free to be what I most desire to seem—someone who might bring resolution and harmony into the dying lives around me." (*B,* 239)

There could hardly be a clearer statement of the god's central function in ancient mythology. Clark says that he is "a messenger with good news, the essential good news that chaos has been put down and life and order revived."[16] Osiris is the real man who died, the mummy with its green-gold death mask—the symbol of death, the lord of the dead. But he is also the resurrected life-spirit who inspires and gives hope of eternal life or eternal memory. He is both Hades and Dionysus, and to dying men he becomes God himself, the symbol of living and growing beyond life into the universal. As Clark puts it, "Osiris has been transformed into a 'living soul.'"[17] Darley comments after Pursewarden's death:

> It was amazing how quickly the human image was dissolving into the mythical image he had created for himself in his trilogy GOD IS A HUMORIST. . . . for after all the fallible human being had belonged to *us*, the myth belonged to the world. (*J*, 168)

In his art as well as his life, Pursewarden seems cast in the mold of Osiris.

Of closer connection to the myth itself, however, are two passages in *Clea*. Clea tells Darley about Liza's coming to Alexandria to find Pursewarden's papers and manuscripts and to arrange his effects. This undertaking parallels Isis's searching for the remains of Osiris to bless and bury, especially in one strange, affecting scene. Clea recounts how Liza came to her studio to find the plaster negative of Pursewarden's death mask. After feeling it carefully with her fingers, "She held it to her breast for a moment as if to suckle it, with an expression of intense pain . . ." (*C*, 115).

Later, as Liza, now in love with Mountolive, prepares to relate their childhood story with its mythic nuances to Darley, she says, "It would be inexpressibly painful to me if anything got out which harmed my brother's memory" (*C*, 170). Immediately,

> Somewhere to the east I heard a grumble of thunder. She stood up with an air of panic and after a moment's hesitation crossed to the grand piano and struck a chord. Then she banged the cover down and turned once more to me, saying: "I am afraid of thunder. Please may I hold your hand in a firm grip." Her own was deathly cold. (*C*, 170)

It is a strange passage, loaded with mythic reference to the east, the thunder, and the very word *panic*, which Plutarch says derives from the response to Osiris's fate. The possible references all unite in a sort of revelation: "The power in charge of the wind is called by some Osiris . . ." (*P*, 217). And Liza becomes "deathly cold," as of course Osiris and Pursewarden now are and as she, in the role of the White Goddess, a "Medusa of the snows," also appears. One is reminded of

Graves's characterization of the White Goddess's "cruelty and past betrayal."[18] And one thinks of her relationship to both Osiris and the ancient version of Typhon, Set:

> . . . the love-hate that Osiris and Set feel for each other on her account is a tribute to her divinity. She tries to satisfy both, but can only do so by alternate murder, and man tries to regard this as evidence of her fundamental falsity, not of his own irreconcilable demands on her.[19]

In the end Liza burns Pursewarden's brilliant letters as he had requested. Darley comments:

> . . . I realized that there was nothing in the whole length and breadth of our literature with which to compare them! . . . Here illusion and reality were fused in one single blinding vision of a perfect incorruptible passion which hung over the writer's mind like a dark star—the star of death! (C, 175)

Darley now, at last, begins to perceive, to understand "the true Pursewarden—the man who had always eluded me" (C, 176). He begins through him to know himself and to find himself, as Horus came to find adulthood and gain his kingship after listening to the voice of Osiris, speaking to him from beyond the grave. ". . . I realized that poetic or transcendental knowledge somehow cancels out purely relative knowledge," says Darley:

> Blind as a mole, I had been digging about in the graveyard of relative fact piling up data, more information, and completely missing the mythopoeic reference which underlies fact. I had called this searching for truth! (C, 176)

Horus, however, must still journey to the Underworld to free Osiris from death to take his true place among the gods before he, Horus, can finally rise to become king of his own life and the world. In one of the *Coffin Texts*, which relates to the Osirian mystery rites, the initiate, playing the role of Horus, comes to Osiris's "house of the dead":

> "Tell him that I have come hither to save myself . . .
> to sit in the room of Father Osiris
>     and to dispel the sickness of the suffering god, so that I
>     can appear an Osiris in strength,
> that I may be reborn with him in his renewed vigour. . . ."[20]

In many ways this situation is comparable to that of the Grail

Knight and the Fisher King, as is, of course, the "matter" of the last book of the *Quartet*. As Clark points out, "He, too, is the monarch of a palace of the lifeless until the hero comes to restore him." The poem "assumes the soul's visit to Osiris at the end of a journey or a series of initiations during which the Horus soul-figure has acquired the superlative qualities of a hero—might, glory, strength, power and divinity."[21] In order to save Osiris, Horus must have the strength to go to him and to help and understand him; for he is the inheritor of the eternal king who must die and only through this final trial can he at last learn "the secret of the renewal of the seasons and human redemption" that the god keeps hidden.[22] Clark concludes: "As an imaginative exercise it is also a journey into the inner reaches of the mind and an attempt to penetrate to the reality which underlies phenomena."[23]

This is just the heritage that Darley must claim from Pursewarden in order to rise above his old self and find his inner being and ability. Pursewarden writes to him directly in "My Conversations with Brother Ass": "Force the lock, batter down the door. Outface, defy, disprove the Oracle in order to become the poet, the darer!" (*C,* 154).

Pursewarden, then, a seeker for truth beyond "realism," finally transmits his secrets of life and artisthood to Darley, who in his own journey to the depths to free Clea comes to know what tenderness is and asks the right question at last: "It was as if I were for the first time confronting myself—or perhaps an alter ego shaped after a man of action I had never realized, recognized" (*C,* 249). To save Clea becomes more important than life itself. And he also begins to understand the true relationship of life to art, as Pursewarden puts it, "that a civilization is simply a great metaphor which describes the aspiration of the individual soul in collective form—as perhaps a novel or a poem might do" (*C,* 143). As he comes to recognize with Pursewarden—and Durrell—that, "A novel should be an act of divination by entrails" (*C,* 73), he finally begins to make his own "enigmatic leap into the heraldic reality of the poetic life" (*C,* 153). Eventually he too will assume the artist and know that magnificent epiphany of transition in which man becomes god, even as god, created by man's mythmaking, can become man. It is this vision of love, of artisthood, of the mythopoeic relationship of man to god, that sets Pursewarden most certainly apart in *The Alexandria Quartet,* a man living both in and out of relative time, but always in the "heraldic universe" to be reached and achieved only through the creative imagination.

In the course of the last novel, Clea herself clearly becomes Darley's "grey-eyed Muse," as the original Clea was Plutarch's. It is curious, but seems not coincidental, that the search for truth that Plutarch inaugurates is one of the key quests of the *Quartet* and that Clea plays a significant role in resolving the search. Many of the most important statements are transmitted by her, and many central moments of understanding are connected to her. It is through her that Durrell sounds the last notes of the Antony and Cleopatra theme and achieves the saving grace at the end of the Grail journey. Indeed, the volume *Clea*, with its final symbolic rendering of Plutarch's *Isis and Osiris*, can be seen as Durrell's own Book of Myth.

Most profoundly of all, the myth begins to pluck out the heart of Pursewarden's mystery, so much the center of the whole *Quartet*, "the real secret which lay hidden under the enigma of his behavior." He had once given a clue—and himself—away. Clea quotes him:

"You see, Justine, I believe that Gods are men and men Gods: they intrude on each other's lives, trying to express themselves through each other— hence such apparent confusion in our human states of mind, our intimations of powers within or beyond us. . . ." (*B*, 124)

And Clea again, talking about Pursewarden's strange suicide, muses, "They are his own secrets, after all, for what we actually saw in him was only the human disguise the artist wore" (*B*, 241)—the life mask that he took off when he put on the death mask, and both masks for the deeper being, the creative artist, who exists behind his own work like a god. Thus Durrell creates a deep and powerful symbol for connecting the artist with the god. Clea concludes:

"In much the same sort of way, Pursewarden carried the secret of his everyday life over into the grave with him, leaving us only his books to marvel at and his epitaph to puzzle over: 'Here lies an intruder from the East.'" (*B*, 241)

One path toward the solution of his mystery leads us back in myth beyond the Fisher King, beyond Dionysus, to the splendor of that ancient name, Osiris.

## NOTES

1. *Plutarch's De Iside et Osiride*, ed. and trans. John Gwyn Griffiths (Cardiff: University of Wales Press, 1970), 119. All further references to this work appear in the text as *P*.
2. Lawrence Durrell, *Clea* (New York: E. P. Dutton, 1960), 190. All further references to this work appear in the text as *C*.

3. Durrell speaks of his "Book of the Dead" as early as 1937 in a letter to Henry Miller, and he refers to it several times thereafter, writing Miller in 1946: "I have done a little bit of the Book of the Dead, from the beginning this time. I am using Alexandria as a locale, and it comes out bold and strong in bright colors." See *Lawrence Durrell and Henry Miller: A Private Correspondence,* ed. George Wickes (New York: E. P. Dutton, 1963), 105, 224.

*The Egyptian Book of the Dead* is also known as "The Book of the Great Awakening," as might be *The Alexandria Quartet.* On another level Durrell was drawing on *The Tibetan Book of the Dead* as well. Both books follow patterns of guidance to death, rebirth, and a way of living—which is also a pattern to be found in the mythic identification of Pursewarden with Osiris. See *The Book of the Dead: The Papyrus of Ani,* ed. E. A. Wallis Budge (New York: Dover, 1967), and *The Tibetan Book of the Dead,* ed. W. Y. Evans-Wentz (London: Oxford University Press, 1960).

4. Sir James George Frazer, *The New Golden Bough,* ed. Theodor H. Gaster (New York: S. G. Phillips, 1959), 347, 349–50.

5. Lawrence Durrell, *Justine* (New York: E. P. Dutton, 1957), 168. All further references to this work appear in the text as *J.*

6. Apuleius, *The Golden Ass,* trans. Robert Graves (New York: Farrar, Straus and Giroux, 1951), 263–64.

7. Robert Graves, *The White Goddess* (New York: Vintage, 1960), 63.

8. Ibid., 2.

9. Lawrence Durrell, *Mountolive* (New York: E. P. Dutton, 1959), 59. All further references to this work appear in the text as *M.*

10. H. J. Rose, *Gods and Heroes of the Greeks* (New York: Meridian Books, 1958), 65.

11. Richard Cavendish, *The Tarot* (New York: Harper and Row, 1975), 64–65. Tarot interpreters identify the Fool with both Osiris and Horus, though some emphasize one and some the other. Cavendish writes:

> Horus eventually vanquished Seth and succeeded to the throne of his murdered father, Osiris. He was lord of the sky and the sun, and each pharaoh of Egypt was Horus in his lifetime and Osiris after his death.

12. R. T. Rundle Clark, *Myth and Symbol in Ancient Egypt* (London: Thames and Hudson, 1959, repr. 1978), 165.

13. Graves, *White Goddess,* 430.

14. Lawrence Durrell, "The Kneller Tape" (Hamburg), in *The World of Lawrence Durrell,* ed. Harry T. Moore (New York: E. P. Dutton, 1964), 168.

15. Lawrence Durrell, *Balthazar* (New York: E. P. Dutton, 1958), 20. All further references to this work appear in the Text as *B.*

16. Clark, *Myth and Symbol,* 154.

17. Ibid., 122.

18. Graves, *White Goddess,* 2.

19. Ibid., 107.

20. Clark, *Myth and Symbol,* 160.

21. Ibid., 161.

22. Ibid., 162.

23. Ibid., 166.

# Love and Meaning in *The Alexandria Quartet:* Some Tantric Perspectives

## David M. Woods

It has been nearly thirty years since the publication of *The Alexandria Quartet,* and today it has achieved widespread recognition, chiefly as a stylistic masterwork. But one hears with some frequency, sometimes even from those who grant its stylistic powers, vague expressions of distaste. Efforts to discover the bases of these complaints reveal that a couple of the central charges in the early criticism still linger, namely that the *Quartet* is not profound or meaningful, or that its view of love is shallow or perverse.

On the issue of substance, John Mortimer wrote that the *Quartet* deals with "essentially unimportant ideas."[1] John Coleman protested "the absurd cancelling confrontation with previous knowledge."[2] R. T. Chapman complained that the narrative moved him "no nearer to absolute truth . . . all attempts to come to grips with experience are confounded . . . the reader cannot find a stable foothold."[3] And Walter Creed called the novels "no more than an overlong prelude to a rather uninspiring discovery."[4] Concerning the view of love, Mortimer wrote: "although there is a good deal of copulation of various sorts we do not feel we are learning much about love."[5] V. S. Pritchett asked, "And are they talking about love? Not really; only about Narcissism and desire. Sterile, they are talking about its perversity, its sadness, its anecdotage, its variety, its passing."[6] And Lionel Trilling wrote: "no one is going to find it easy to believe that what he is investigating is really modern love."[7]

A key factor, I suspect, behind those complaints is that the novels are strongly animated by a deeply Eastern metaphysical disposition. Thus critics with narrowly Occidental ideas and sensibilities may not know quite what to make of the *Quartet,* and often dismiss it as meaningless, shallow, or perverse. I believe that the *Quartet* has something profound to say about love and meaning—something complex, elusive, and foreign. Durrell's influences are extremely diverse and his creative process amalgamative, so I do not propose that he incorporated, in a strict or exclusive or even fully conscious fashion, the ideas of any single Eastern religion. But I would like to discuss how the mysterious metaphysical animus of the *Quartet* can be exposed, enhanced, and considered coherent when viewed from the perspective of Eastern metaphysics in general and Tantric Buddhism in particular.

Durrell has discussed the important influence of Buddhism on his life in general and on the *Alexandria Quartet* specifically, calling the *Quartet* a "Tibetan-type novel."[8] He was, we remind ourselves, born in the Himalayas, the center of Tantric Buddhism—and lived there for 11 years. His interest in and familiarity with various Eastern metaphysical systems is well documented. In *A Key to Modern British Poetry,* Durrell discusses the Buddhist and Taoist influence in the work of several British writers.[9] In various interviews, he makes general references to Hinduism and, in some cases, to his borrowing of certain Hindu notions and their incorporation in the *Quartet.*[10] As early as 1939, Durrell had published an article, "Tao and Its Glozes," in which he displays a fundamental grasp of Taoism.[11] In a letter of 1955 to Henry Miller, Durrell writes: "I'm deep in Zen Buddhist treatises these days—Suzuki!"[12]

There is a specific link between the *Quartet* and Buddhism. The title *Justine,* as Durrell mentions in his correspondence,[13] was originally to have been *Book of the Dead,* which is a title shared by two ancient works: One is Egyptian; the other is the central Tibetan Buddhist scripture that deals with death and rebirth. In his *A Smile in the Mind's Eye,* Durrell writes of "Milarepa, whose poems and teachings I have known since I was sixteen."[14] Milarepa was a Tibetan saint and early exponent of a strain of Buddhism that would eventually evolve into Tantric Buddhism, or Tantra, as I shall refer to it hereafter. In several passages in *A Smile in the Mind's Eye,* Durrell makes direct reference to Tantra; of his wife Claude, he writes: "she had carried the *tantric* look with her, right into the midst of her death, like a standard."[15] Before undertaking a closer analysis of Eastern ideas and attitudes in the *Quartet,* we first need to explore the antagonistic presence therein of a Western center of meaning.

1

The notion of "the English Death" had been a central preoccupation with Durrell for some twenty years prior to the publication of the *Quartet.* He has said that *The Black Book* is "a chronicle of 'the English Death',"[16] and that it could also be considered "a confused sketch for the *Quartet.*"[17] My view is that "the English Death" should not be regarded as a clearly definable label, but as the central phrase to which are connected, in a very loose and ambiguous manner, a number of related ideas and attitudes. "The English Death" is so important in Durrell's work that it deserves a more thorough treatment than space allows here, but a brief outline of its general shape should serve our purposes.

In *A Key to Modern British Poetry,* Durrell discusses the term *gentleman* as a descriptor of the English. The qualities of gentleness, he says, have degenerated into *gentility*.[18] This word, *gentility,* and its implications are worth stressing and elaborating because they provide a springboard to a better understanding of "the English Death." *Gentility* connotes social refinement (and, sometimes, priggery), social poise (or social pose), and social respectability (degenerating, at times, into social conformity).

If one examines Durrell's books, letters, and interviews, it becomes clear that he does believe that the drive toward social respectability often degenerates into conformity. The particular vision of conformity he finds so repugnant is characterized by boredom and habit in a suburban setting. In a letter of 1937 to Henry Miller, Durrell writes sarcastically, "I want a good steady job with a little house, lots of children, a lawn mower, a bank account, a little car, and the respect of the man next door."[19]

Linked to his dislike of conformity is his view of English life as lifelessly stable and comfortable. In the *Quartet* the narrator makes this observation about David Mountolive: "He had been formally educated in England, educated not to wish to feel . . . towards personal emotions he could only oppose the nervous silence of a national sensibility almost anesthetized into clumsy taciturnity."[20] And in 1938 Durrell complains to Miller of "that terrible English numbness, the English death infecting . . . my soul."[21]

That numbness is related to another quality, visible in the *Quartet's* Maskelyne, a British military intelligence officer. The Maskelyne/Pursewarden nomenclature and conflict seem symbolic. "Maskelyne" is obviously a sound-alike of "masculine"; "Pursewarden" combines the feminine "purse" with "warden" (guard), which adds up to something like "guard of the feminine." A masculine/feminine opposition seems clear. Maskelyne is the model of rationality and objectivity. (Further, Justine is repeatedly described as masculine—and also as obsessively mental). So Durrell intends, I think, a linkage between masculinity and excessive ratiocination. Pursewarden, on the other hand, is highly imaginative and intuitive. The masculine vs. feminine opposition in the *Quartet* extends, then, into a homologous ratiocinative vs. intuitive polarity. The English overemphasis upon the detached, "objective," ratiocinative aspect of human nature is articulated by Pursewarden: "We Anglo-Saxons are incapable of thinking for ourselves; about ourselves yes . . . there we excel, for we see ourselves at one remove from reality, as a subject under a microscope. This objectivity is a really flattering extension of our sense of humbug."[22]

What I am attempting to show is that "the English Death" is broader and deeper in its implications than the related ideas of priggishness, respectability, conformity, stability, suburban boredom, and so on. "The English Death" generally implies an exaggerated ratiocinative aspect of consciousness, a numbing of the emotional and intuitive aspects, and a misplaced security in so-called objective truth.

An experience in Durrell's youth has bearing upon "the English Death." When Durrell was seven or eight in Darjiling (as he spells it), India, he was placed in a Jesuit school. He describes his shock when he sneaked into the chapel:

> So this is what those austere and bearded priests worshipped in this dense gloom among the flowers and candles! The horror remains with me always; and later on, when my father decreed that I must go to England for education, I felt he was delivering me into the hands of these sadists and cannibals, men who could worship this brutal and savage effigy on the Christian cross . . . this doom-laden symbol of unhappiness.[23]

So here, England, Father, and Christianity are all fused. This fusion becomes even more significant when we consider that outside of the Jesuit chapel in India, after that traumatic experience, young Durrell watched the "Tibetan lamas setting off on their long pilgrimage to the distant plains of India. . . . Smiling . . . they whirled their prayer wheels." "The English Death," then, encompasses aspects of Christianity that Durrell experienced as dark and cruel—in dramatic contrast to his fond memories of the Buddhist lamas. Thus, a fundamental East-West, India-England, Buddhist-Christian, mother-father psychological dichotomy took root in Durrell at a very early age.

I would like to carry this analysis of the link between Christianity and "the English Death" a bit further. In an interview of 1960 Durrell says, "the thing I have never marched well with is all the hebraic gibber we have incorporated into our view of Christianity."[24] Balthazar describes his own weakness as "the bloodthirsty rationality of the Jews";[25] so an aspect of "the English Death"—overemphasis on the ratiocinative—is linked to the Jews. Pursewarden says of the Jews:

> For this gifted and troublesome race which *has never known art,* but has *exhausted its creative processes* purely in the *construction of ethical systems* . . .

we have had our *testicles pinched* for centuries by the Mosaic Law . . . hence the *mincing effrontery* of adults willed to *perpetual adolescence!* (*C*, 132, my italics)

A great deal is contained in that quotation: there is the specification of the Jewish aspect of Christianity as the dangerous aspect; there is also the notion that an overemphasis on "ethical systems" causes sexual repression ("pinched testicles"), incomplete maturation ("perpetual adolescence"), priggery ("mincing effrontery"), and depletion of imagination ("has never known art," "exhausted its creative processes").

In interviews during the late 1950s, Durrell said that "In England . . . what is killing is the spineless and revolting life they have built up around themselves, the habits, the boredom, the lack of *bonne chere*. No belly worship!"[26] and "I very much hoped England was going to be . . . something with its vulgar roots in food, sex, and good living. By which I don't mean fine living or refinement . . . because these are just top-dressing. It is at the roots that something is wrong."[27] The result of that sensual/sexual constriction—what Durrell calls "no belly worship," evoking the classical model of belly/heart/head consciousness—is an imblance in man between the sensual/sexual/emotional aspect and the ratiocinative aspect. Further, Durrell complains that "In England everyone is worried so about moral uplift and moral downfall, and they never seem to get beyond that problem, simply because they feel separated from the arts."[28] If we keep in mind that Pursewarden says "religion is art bastardized out of recognition," we might sum up by stating that what Durrell objects to is a morality of the rational, codified, absolute sort, which is rigidly imposed by an overgrown and arrogant ratiocinative aspect of man, resulting in the repression of the sensual/sexual/emotional aspect. Such a morality is disconnected from a deeper, nonrational spiritual source—from the artistic impulse. ("Artist" is synonymous with "spiritual seeker" in the *Quartet*. I will have more to say on this later.)

Durrell's "English Death" is not without ancestry. One could trace the lineage back at least as far as Matthew Arnold's concept of "Hebraism." Arnold's criticism of his countrymen was that "they have thought that their real and only important homage was owed to a power concerned with obedience . . . [to] the moral side of their nature exclusively. Thus they have been led to regard in themselves, as the one thing needful, strictness of conscience, the staunch adherence to some fixed law."[29]

It is interesting to observe that, as Arnold located the main source of Hebraism in the Jewish influence, Durrell likewise traces elements of "the English Death" to the Jews. And Arnold opposed his Hebra-ism to "Hellenism," setting up a broad cultural, metaphysical polarity. I would suggest that it is useful to view the *Quartet* in the light of a similarly broad polarity: "the English Death" forms one pole of such a system—a pole I will refer to as the "Western Pole" for reasons that will be clarified later, when I will also discuss the nature of the second pole.

2

A fundamental, distinguishing feature of Tantric Buddhism has to do with its unique attitude toward life's duality. Most of us are famil-iar with the Indian terms that classify life's dual nature: *Nirvana* (the essential, unchanging, complete, and perfect state) and *Maya* (the earthly state of transience, soullessness, and suffering). In Tantra those two aspects of life are seen as proceeding from the same supernal source. Reality is considered to be nondual. Indologist Heinrich Zimmer writes:

> Maya, the world illusion, is not to be rejected but embraced. . . . the candi-date for wisdom does not seek a detour by which to circumvent the sphere of passions—crushing them within himself and shutting his eyes to their manifestations without, until, made clean as an angel, he may safely open his eyes again to regard the cyclone [of earthly life and passion] with the untroubled gaze of a disembodied apparition. Quite the contrary: the Tan-tric hero goes directly *through* the sphere of greatest danger. . . . It is an essential principle of the Tantric idea that man, in general, must rise *through* and by means of nature, not by the rejection of nature.[30]

The gist then, in the Tantric method, is to embrace the fleshly, passio-nal Mayan aspect of life—not to stand aloof from it or repress it. By this method the Tantric pupil hopes to move beyond the boundaries of ego-consciousness. In Tantra, romantic/sexual love and desire have a highly symbolic role, because that sphere of life contains the most active essences and vivid displays of Maya.

This principle of Mayan embrace does not mean that Tantra en-dorses wholesale, drunken debauchery and hedonism, or that there are no codes of conduct. Quite the contrary. The first stage of Tantric practice, called *Samatha,* requires a very precise sober effort. In *Dawn of the Tantra,* Chogyam Trungpa writes that, "It is in relation to the world of projections that the precision of Samatha is extremely power-ful. It is a kind of scientific research."[31] This Samathic practice is char-acterized by a general intensification of cognitive functions, including memory and reflection upon remembered events. However, this sober examination does not necessitate ascetic withdrawal, but is, rather, conducted through an honest engagement with life's carnal, sensual, emotional dimension.

In the *Quartet*, something very close to those basic Tantric attitudes mentioned above—the embrace of Maya and the symbolic primacy of romantic/sexual love as foundations for spiritual growth—seems to animate the thought and behavior of several central characters. And Darley is, throughout the novels, engaged in what is, essentially, Samathic practice. Through his writing of the original *Justine* draft and his study of Balthazar's revision (the "Interlinear"), through his reading of Arnauti's novel *Moeurs* and his perusal of Justine's notebook, through his own memory and the memories of others, and through his own intimate relation with Justine—Darley is conducting a precise, sober examination of the object of his passion as well as the nature and workings of this passion itself.

Consider also, as consistent with Samathic practice, Pursewarden's attitude while seducing Melissa: "As usual, at a level far below the probings of self-disgust or humiliation, he was writing, swiftly and smoothly in his clear mind" (*M*, 173). The sobriety and precision of observation and analysis while immersed in passion are perfectly Samathic as are many other comments: Balthazar's insistently repeated dictum, "indulge but refine";[32] Pursewarden's motto for artists, "Reflect and weep" (*C*, 141); the narrator's observation about Mountolive, "he was learning the two most important lessons in life: to make love honestly and to reflect" (*M*, 33). And in the "Consequential Data" appended to *Balthazar*, Durrell writes: "'My object in the novel? To interrogate human values through an honest representation of the human passions'" (*B*, 247).

If we take this Tantric notion—spiritual growth through the embrace and examination of one's passional, carnal nature—and combine it with the ideas of psychologist Georg Groddeck (one of Durrell's strong influences), we can shed some light on a strange view of love that lies at the heart of the *Quartet*. The central idea of Groddeck's I wish to draw upon here is his view of disease as the expression of what he calls "the It"—a powerful, hidden intelligence often at odds with the rational, conscious mind. Disease, to Groddeck, is always a symptom of schism between the inflated and repressive consciousness and the irrepressible "It." In *A Key to Modern British Poetry*, Durrell writes:

"The It" then antedates all our intellectual apparatus, our conceptual mechanism. It is later, with the growth of the ego, that we persuade ourselves that our reasoning powers belong to our personality as private property. . . . With Groddeck we learn the mystery of participation with a world of which we are a part and from which the pretentions of the ego have sought to amputate us.[33]

Durrell notes that disease for Groddeck is "something like bad metaphysics,"[34] and that disease should be viewed enlightenedly and positively—as a clue to self-revelation and spiritual healing. So with these Tantric and Groddeckian ideas stewing in his mind, it is easy to see how Durrell could have come up with this notion: *love is a potentially therapeutic disease.*

The *Quartet* is filled with expressions of that paradoxical attitude toward love. Arnauti writes in *Moeurs:* "It [love] may be defined as a cancerous growth of unknown origin," (*C,* 106), and Pursewarden calls love "the point *foible* of the human psyche . . . the carcinoma maxima." (*C,* 131). In *Mountolive,* Nessim's and Justine's relationship is described: "They had found each other's inmost weakness, the true site of love" (*M,* 50). Pursewarden writes in his notebook: "Possession of a human heart—disease without remedy" (*C,* 165). Of her painful affair with Amaril, Clea says: "What wounded me most as a woman nourished me most as an artist (*C,* 112). The word "wound" appears over and over again in the *Quartet.* Darley recalls Nessim saying that "Alexandria was the great winepress of love; those who emerged from it were the sick men, the solitaries, the prophets—I mean all who have been deeply wounded in their sex" (*J,* 14). Clea cries to Darley: "I am sure if you analyze your feelings, you will find you love Justine *better* because she betrayed you! . . . we are born to love those who most wound us" (*B,* 236). And Clea tells Darley, concerning a love affair: "It is curious that an experience so wounding can also be recognized as good, as positively nourishing" (*C,* 111). In the *Quartet,* love and sex are frequently linked with disease and wounds, but when viewed from the Tantric/Groddeckian perspective, these wounds and disease can be seen as conditions of health.

This strategic view of love permeates the heart of the *Quartet* (its "investigation of modern love" [*B,* i]) and baffles many critics. Consider the following remarks made by Lionel Trilling in 1961:

> . . . if the subject of his investigation is indeed to be described as "modern love" . . . then he is certainly telling us something new and strange. No one who has formed an idea of love from contemporary American and British fiction is likely to take for granted what Durrell is writing about; no one is going to find it easy to believe that what he is investigating is really modern love. For none of Durrell's lovers has the slightest interest

in *maturity* or in *adult behavior* or in *mutuality of interest* or in *building a life together* or in many of the characteristics of *healthy relationship* which we suppose modern love to be. Tenderness plays some part in the feeling of some of the lovers, and on some occasions it is highly praised, but the lovers do not expect from each other *emotional support* or *confirmation* or a *sense of security* . . . none of them . . . enters into one of those *therapeutic alliances* which, under the name of marriage, passes with us for the connection of love.[35] (My italics)

Trilling's reaction sharply displayed (and still *displays*, I would say; but part of the motive of this essay is to update and reassess) a predominant, modern Western picture of romantic love. The case for a charge of cultural insularity seems quite strong. In order to understand the extensive foreign animus in *The Alexandria Quartet*, we should continue to examine the principles and phases of Tantric spiritual growth.

### 3

In the second phase of Tantric spiritual work, called *Vipassana* meditation and practice, "one begins," says Chogyan Trungpa, "to realize that spending one's whole time on the details of life, as in Samatha meditation [the first phase], does not work. . . . It is necessary to begin to have a sense of totality."[36] The rationally assembled constructions of the Samatha phase begin to weaken and crumble, and this crumbling contributes to an "unfreezing" or letting go of those constructs.

Consider two characters—Darley and Justine—in light of this Tantric Vipassana stage. Darley clearly reaches a point at which confidence in his Samathic analysis, as manifested in his original draft of "Justine" and his study of Balthazar's "Interlinear," crumbles away. He comments upon this breakdown at the beginning of *Clea:* "Yet if I had been enriched by the experience of this island interlude, it was perhaps because of this total failure to record the inner truth of the city" (*C,* 12). Here we see a qualified positive attitude toward failure, which is also expressed in *Balthazar:* "Perhaps then the destruction of my private Alexandria was necessary; perhaps buried in all this there lies the germ substance of a truth—time's usufruct—which, if I can accommodate it, will carry me a little further in what is really a search for my proper self" (*B,* 226).

Justine, on the other hand, does not seem able to move beyond the level of Samathic, intellectual self-examination and self-questioning, into the Vipassana stage of growth; her ratiocinative, analytical effort to make sense of things does not crumble, "unfreeze." Arnauti describes Justine in his novel *Moeurs:* "I see a sort of composite Justine, concealing a ravenous hunger for information, for power through self-knowledge, under a pretense of feeling" (*J,* 71). Significantly, in connection with "the English Death," Justine is often described as essentially masculine in nature. In my discussion of "the English Death," I showed the connection between masculinity and rationality in the *Quartet.*

The general point here is that a frozenness in the rational or Samathic mode is part of "the English Death," and is, in terms of Tantric principles of spiritual growth, an obstruction. Also, we can see— in Darley's comments expressing a paradoxical sounding inherence of success in failure, of truth in destruction of truth—a strange notion of knowing, which seems strongly analogous to the previously discussed Tantric/Groddeckian notion of therapeutic disease. The connection to stress here is that in Tantra love and sex are, as I said earlier, highly symbolic, because the displays of Maya are most vivid and intense in that sphere. But Maya exerts itself in all earthly life, so notions of reality, truth, and meaning are subject to the same Mayan nature revealed in the realm of love and sex.

The failure of analysis and rationality is not, in the Tantric system, seen as a final collapse of meaning and purpose in life, but rather as part of an ongoing process of knowing and not knowing—an oscillation or flux. This oscillation is part of a fundamental view in Tantric Buddhism called the "Middle Path." It is along this Middle Path, through an oscillation between a sense of knowing and not knowing, that truth is approached.[37] Out of that Middle Path oscillation evolves the central Tantric experience called *Shunyata.* Chogyam Trungpa describes the emergence and nature of Shunyata:

> . . . having established the precision of details [through the first phase, Samathic practice], one begins to experience the *space around them.* . . . When we perceive, we usually attend to the *delimited forms* of objects. But these objects are within a field. Attention can be directed either to the concrete, limited forms or *to the field* in which these forms are situated.[38] (My italics)

The Shunyata experience involves an attention to the field. In this mode of perception discrete forms blur and fade, and as a result an "open dimension" arises. There is no finality in the shift in perspective; one is free to shift back and forth between the mode of perceiving limited forms, and the mode of perceiving the field. But the freedom to shift is based on the ability to perceive this "open dimension," which is actually the essential meaning of Shunyata.

To bring these abstract principles, Middle Path oscillation and Shunyata, into clearer focus, perhaps it would be helpful to set them in a Western context. In "The Critic as Host," J. Hillis Miller discusses nihilism and makes some broad observations on the nature of meaning and cultural differences in the making of meaning. Miller describes Western metaphysics as logocentric, by which he means a metaphysical outlook that obsessively attempts to find in life or literature a univocal, unified, "totalitarian" interpretation, and does so by "attempting to cover over the unhealable by annihilating the nothingness within itself."[39] Nihilism, according to Miller, is actually generated by logocentric metaphysics, and he cites Nietzsche in locating the core of that nihilism-generating logocentrism in "Christian-moral"[40] interpretation, though more generally we could say that in "Western logocentric metaphysics" Miller refers to traditional, Western, Christian humanist values and attitudes. Of his own critical approach, deconstruction, Miller writes that it

> encounters always, if it is carried far enough, some mode of *oscillation*. In this oscillation two genuine insights . . . inhibit, subvert, and undercut one another. This inhibition makes it impossible for neither insight to function as a firm resting place, the end point of analysis.[41]

Miller's critical oscillation is closely analogous to the Tantric Buddhist oscillation. Both principles resist mastery of meaning, resist totalizing, univocal interpretation. And Miller's vision of "Western logocentric metaphysics" suggests some possible insights into "The English Death." Both are linked to traditional Christian morals and values. I would argue that the English Death is a manifestation of Western logocentric metaphysics (thus my suggestion, at the end of section one, that we view "The English Death" as a "Western pole"). At the core of "The English Death" is the obsessive attempt to cover up or repress nothingness (or Shunyata), and thereby possess univocal meaning, certainty. Those afflicted with "The English Death," Justine, Mountolive, Maskelyne, and others, cannot permit themselves to be wounded—in the sense of being *opened* at the fleshly, passional level. Nor can they open themselves in the Shunyata sense: open to the oscillation of knowing and not knowing, which dissolves treasured (but spiritually obstructive) stabilities and certainties, and which allow (in the Tantric sense discussed earlier) the spiritual seeker to move beyond the boundaries of ego-consciousness.

The gist of this comparison of Tantric principles with Miller's critical concepts is this: in Tantra, the Shunyata experience is considered highly positive, denotes openness and freedom, and forms the foundation for spiritual growth and meaning. The "equivalent" experience in Occidental metaphysics is called nihilism, is considered distinctly negative, is feared and repressed, and describes a state of spiritual desolation and meaninglessness. These broad cultural insights provide a commentary on the complaints concerning the *Quartet*'s substantiality, some of which I mentioned at the outset. The detractors exhibit the tendencies of Western logocentric metaphysics in their frustrated attempts to find some final resting place of analysis, some univocal interpretation. They see nihilism, no Shunyata. And it is not just the vision of Shunyata those critics fail to understand. Shunyata is only the foundation for spiritual growth. As in Tantra, the *Quartet*'s spiritual seekers go beyond Shunyata's oscillation and openness and enter a higher phase, wherein meaning is reconstituted.

In Tantra, that higher phase is called the *Mandala* experience. In this Mandala phase, one begins—not to put one's hands upon some rational, absolute body of knowledge that is the Truth—to be capable of entering into a different, enlightened mode of perception. The characteristics of this mode are: an accent on direct attention or experience (as opposed to conceptual analysis); the development of the intuitive faculties; the perception of a synchronic time (or one could say a "timelessness" or an "eternal Present"); and the use of symbols (mandalas are symbols) as devices for breaking free from illusions and preconceptions and entering into the original, primordial unity.[42]

There is a close parallel to this Tantric Mandala stage of growth present in the *Quartet*. It becomes clear in the tetralogy that what is meant by the idea of becoming an artist is not merely the ability to create an expression or product. The art product is portrayed as only the physical trace of an inner spiritual development. In *Balthazar*, Pursewarden discusses art and writing: "'What is the purpose of writing?' His answer was this: 'The object of writing is to grow a personality which in the end enables one to transcend art'" (*B*, 141); and "In my art, indeed, through my art, I really want to achieve myself shedding the work, which is of no importance" (*B*, 239). Darley, Clea, and Pursewarden are all artists or aspiring artists, and their development should be viewed as a spiritual growth. Durrell, in a recent talk, discussed his philosophical equation (which evolved during the time he was working on the *Quartet*) of Buddhist spiritual growth and artistic growth: "In some curious way I made the conjunction between what was taking place in the yoga world and what was taking place in myself as somebody evolving towards a nature of poetry."[43]

To appreciate the presence in the *Quartet* of a mode of meaning parallel to the mode involved in the Mandala stage of Tantra, we need to examine an important term. Pursewarden uses the term "the Heraldic Universe" frequently. Its meaning is highly ambiguous, and in function and form it resembles another frequently repeated term in the *Quartet*—"the English Death." It also resembles "the English Death" in that it, too, is used repeatedly throughout *The Black Book,* Durrell's novel of 1936, which, as I have mentioned, Durrell has called a "confused sketch for the *Quartet.*" Like "the English Death," "the Heraldic Universe" has been discussed by Durrell in interviews, correspondence, and in at least one of his other books. In *A Smile in the Mind's Eye,* Durrell discusses the meaning of his term "the Heraldic Universe": "I note also the use of the word 'heraldic' for which I have often had to answer the critics. It means simply the 'mandala' of the poet or of the poem."[44] There is then, in Durrell's comment, the clear connection between "the Heraldic Universe" and "mandala," which is, as we recall, the name of the third stage of Tantric spiritual development. The connection is also made between "the Heraldic Universe" and art (poetry, in this case).

As is the case in the Tantric Mandala experience, "the Heraldic Universe" represents a dimension or mode of perception highly attuned to symbolic modes of meaning. Pursewarden, purveyor of the term "the Heraldic Universe" in the *Quartet,* says in *Clea:* "Symbolism! The abbreviation of language into poem. The heraldic aspect of reality. Symbolism is the great repair-outfit of the psyche, Brother Ass, the *fond du pouvoir* [fundamental power] of the soul" (*C,* 137). Here again we can see a link between the Mandala experience and "the Heraldic Universe" (a mandala, remember, is a symbol), and a connection between "the Heraldic Universe" and art (poetry) is also expressed.

"The Heraldic Universe" is related to a concept of synchronic time (another characteristic of the Tantric Mandala experience). In a 1936 letter to Henry Miller, Durrell writes, "I chose the word 'heraldic' for a double reason. . . . what I am trying to isolate is the exact moment of creation in which the maker seems to exist *heraldically.* That is to say, time as a concept does not exist, but only as an attribute of matter—decay, growth, etc."[45]

The attitude of accentuation on direct experience versus conceptual thinking connects "the Heraldic Universe" with the Tantric Mandala experience. In a correspondence of 1936 to Miller, Durrell writes, "What I propose to do . . . is to create my Heraldic Universe quite alone. I am very carefully and without conscious thought destroying time."[46] Though not explicitly connected with "the Heraldic Universe," similar attitudes toward experience are present throughout the *Quartet.* In *Balthazar* Pursewarden writes to Clea, "I see mankind as gradually appropriating to itself the necessary information through mere attention, not reason. . . . Truth is a matter of direct apprehension—you can't climb a ladder of mental concepts to it" (*B*, 142). And in *Justine*, Darley muses, "Somewhere in the heart of experience there is an order and coherence which we might surprise if we were attentive enough" (*J*, 221). The emphasis in those quotations is upon attention, awarenesss, and direct experience, rather than conceptual, analytical thinking.

So by examining some of the explicit philosophizing in the *Quartet*, and with the help of some commentary by Durrell exterior to the text, it is possible to indicate with some clarity the general contours of "the Heraldic Universe": it is closely related to artistry, which in the *Quartet* is a cover word for spiritual growth; it is related to symbolic language; it is tied to the concept of synchronic time; and it is connected to an accentuation of direct experience over conceptual, analytical thinking. For the spiritual seekers in the *Quartet*, meaning is dissolved in the Vispassana and Shunyata phases, but is reconstituted in the Mandala phase. Meaning-making enters a new mode or higher dimension: "the Heraldic Universe." Darley's "heraldic" realization is perfectly Tantric: "I realized that poetic or transcendental knowledge somehow cancels out purely relative knowledge . . . [is] above, beyond that of the relative fact-finding sort" (*C*, 176).

So far I have attempted to enhance the meaning of "the Heraldic Universe" by presenting explicit evidence from the *Quartet* and some outside sources, and by making comparisons with the Tantric Mandala experience. There is enough of that explicit evidence to indicate the presence of "the Heraldic Universe." But there is a simple reason why an attempt to define the meaning of "the Heraldic Universe" by analysis of explicit evidence must fall short. In the *Quartet*, "the Heraldic Universe" operates according to its own principles—symbolic and poetic meaning-making, direct experience, and timelessness or synchronic time. It is through exertions of that nature that the *Quartet* attempts to draw the reader into a direct experience of "the Heraldic Universe." It invites the operation in the reader of a "heraldic" mode of perception. In fact, I would go so far as to suggest that the *Quartet* operates as a coach to the reader, urging him through what generally resembles the stages of Tantric spiritual growth: (1) the reader "participates" with the various characters' subjective points of view in a process of examination and analysis; (2) the reader begins to feel, along with those characters' subjective viewpoints (centrally Darley's), the crumbling away of a sense of "objective" certainty; and (3) the reader is invited to enter into a perception of the Mandala experience, or "the Heraldic Universe."

"The Heraldic Universe" is the other pole—the "Eastern Pole"—in the dipolar scheme ("the English Death" is the "Western pole") I proposed at the end of the first section. We should next examine more carefully the workings of the "heraldic" mode of meaning-making in *The Alexandria Quartet*.

4

At this point I would like to focus upon one highly significant event at the end of the *Quartet*, Darley's rescue of Clea, in an attempt to throw some light on this "heraldic" mode of meaning formation in the novels. The difficulty inherent in this kind of approach is the meaningful extraction of one element of a whole interwoven symbolic network. But I believe that sort of extractive approach can succeed if I might sketch in some crucial elements of that larger symbolic, "heraldic" presence.

We should return for a moment to the basic Tantric notion of embracing Maya—the earthly, passional, carnal aspect of life—and rising *through* that sphere to divinity. This principle is elaborated through two key Tantric notions, both of which express unique attitudes toward carnality in general, and especially sexuality. The first is the principle of transmutation—of the carnal into the divine. Some verses of an ancient Tantric poem vividly express this concept:

> The mystics, pure of mind
> >   Dally with lovely girls,
> Infatuated with the poisonous flame of passion,
> >   That they may be set free from desire
>
> The mystic duly dwells
> >   On the manifold merits of his divinity,
> He delights in thoughts of passion,
> >   And by the enjoyment of passion is set free.
> As a washerman uses dirt
> >   To wash clean a garment,
> So, with impurity,
> >   The wise man makes himself pure.[47]

Implicit and explicit linkage of the carnal with the divine occurs with great frequency in the *Quartet*, as does expression of the principle of transmutation of the carnal into the divine. Alexandria is described as a "princess and whore" (*C*, 63), "a city at once sacred and profane" (*B*, 183). Pursewarden writes that "the sexual and the creative energy go hand in hand. . . . the truth is only to be found in our own entrails" (*C*, 141). The narrator of *Mountolive* describes

Pursewarden in a café at night, "purged by the darkness and the alcohol" (*M,* 163). Justine declares, "I must work through the dross in my own character and burn it up" (*J,* 72). Durrell discusses these ideas in several interviews, saying in one, "It's only with great vulgarity that you can achieve real refinement, only out of the bawdy that you can get tenderness."[48]

Tantra also contains the concept of *chakras,* which are centers of energy located from the base of the spine to the top of the head. The chakra at the lowest level is associated with the most carnal energy. With each step upward the chakras are linked with energy of increasing spiritual purity. Durrell was familiar with the notion of chakras before the *Quartet* was published. In a 1956 interview, responding to a question concerning D. H. Lawrence, Durrell replied:

> I feel that to cut off the head and exclude the reason in order to locate the affective nature of man in the abdomen, as Lawrence did, is to make the river flow backwards. Underneath it I discern another attempt to foist on us Rousseau's "Noble Savage." My notion of the affective flow is upwards, a notion I have borrowed from the Hindus.[49]

At the base of the spine at the lowest chakra (associated with the extremely carnal aspects of lust and sexuality), there resides what is known as the *Kundalini.* The following passage is taken from M. P. Pandit's study of Tantra, *Kundalini Yoga:*

> In the lowest bodily centre at the base of the spine, there lies a fundamental Power due to the presence of which the entire organism is enlivened. This Power is described as lying *coiled* in the Muladhara; it is the . . *Kundalini* . . [it] is spoken of as *coiled,* because [it] is likened to a *serpent* . . . which, when resting and *sleeping, lies coiled.*[50] (My italics)

Kundalini is, then, the basic energy of life. Its energy is regarded as undifferentiated in terms of good or bad, holy or unholy. The degree to which this energy is manifested as carnal or divine is determined by the chakratic level to which it rises. This Kundalini energy is, I stress, symbolically represented as a *serpent—coiled and sleeping.* That central Tantric symbol—the coiled, sleeping serpent—is highly and significantly visible in the *Quartet.* The object most frequently described in serpent imagery is Alexandria: "Alexandria, basking like some old reptile" (*C,* 14); "Alexandria, unrolling once more on either side of me"; "The city . . . coils about the sleeping lives like some great anaconda digesting a meal" (*C,* 64).

Durrell has said in an interview, "I had strict historical references to Alexandria, and the important factor was that Alexandria was the *source* of our entire culture"[51] (my emphasis). The crucial word, as I have indicated, is "source." The Kundalini serpent is, similarly, the source of human energy—undifferentiated, at once carnal and divine. Throughout the novels Alexandria is described by linked opposites—carnal and divine: "impossible city of love and obscenity" (*B*, 183); "a city at once sacred and profane" (*B*, 183); "Alexandria, princess and whore" (*C*, 63); "The royal city and anus mundi" (*C*, 63). In the *Quartet*, Alexandria functions symbolically as a giant, cultural Kundalini; the Tantric view of human essence is presented macrocosmically.

The perversely sexual character Capodistria, as well as the subject of prayer, are both frequently described with serpent images. Of Capodistria, Durrell writes: "Women feel like birds confronted by a viper when they gaze into that narrow, flat face" (*J*, 39). Darley describes prayer as follows: "The great prayer wound its way into my sleeping consciousness like a serpent, coil after shining coil of words" (*J*, 25). This association of serpent symbolism with *prayer* on the one hand, and with *carnal sexuality* on the other, is perfectly consonant with Tantric Kundalini principles, as the Kundalini energy is not limited to carnal sensual spheres: it *originates* in the carnal but *rises through the carnal* to energize the highest spiritual levels (or chakras).

Narouz and his whip are often described in snake images: for example, "Nessim heard the great whip [Narouz's] slither along the dry boards like a cobra" (*M*, 228). And: "as he [Narouz] rode, his pulse slowed and his anger emptied itself into loathsome disgust which folded up into his mind like a venomous snake" (*M*, 229). Nessim has this realization about his brother: "Narouz was right in his desire to inflame the *sleeping* will. . . To awaken not merely the impulses of the forebrain with its limited formulations, but the *sleeping* beauty underneath—the *poetic consciousness* which lay, *coiled* like in a spring, in the heart of everyone" (*M*, 231; my italics). The "poetic consciousness" is clearly analogous to the Kundalini serpent energy—coiled and sleeping.

Narouz's association with serpent imagery is crucial when we consider the final climactic scene of *The Alexandria Quartet*: Darley's underwater rescue of Clea. Recall these crucial bits of information: Clea won't go to carnivals—a festival of demonic, chaotic, Dionysian, carnal energy. She is repulsed by the atmosphere of lust and war in Alexandria and complains that her virginity constitutes an obstacle to her growth as an artist. In regard to Narouz, she expresses extreme disgust when Narouz kisses her *hand*. Clea is pinned to the underwater wreck through her *hand* by the late Narouz's spear gun, which, as it discharges, makes a "cobra-like hiss" and trails a "long green line" (*C*, 247).

With all these pieces of information in mind, I would like to suggest this Tantric, "heraldic" interpretation of the final scene: Narouz represents the basic Kundalini serpent energy—carnal and violent. The fair, artistic, refined Clea embodies the higher and purer spiritual forces, but she is unable to come to terms with life's carnality. Clea is speared below Narouz's island, by Narouz's harpoon, through her hand (perhaps the one Narouz earlier kissed, to her disgust). The "cobra-like-hiss" of the gun and "long, green line" of the harpoon line extend and sharpen the symbolic linkage. The gist of the symbolic meaning is, I believe, that Clea has been painfully connected to the carnality of life. Her resuscitation by Darley, which takes the form of a "pitiful simulacrum of the sexual act—life-saving, life-giving" (*C*, 251), reinforces the basic Tantric notion of spiritual growth through an enlightened acceptance of one's carnal, sexual nature. Clea says:

> The sex act is the most important, the one in which our spirits most divulge themselves. Yet one feels it is a sort of clumsy paraphrase of the poetic, the noetic, *thought*. . . . Sexual love is knowledge, both in etymology and in cold fact. (*C*, 113)

## 5

From opposite ends of the *Quartet*'s cosmos, two poles radiate profoundly different ideas and attitudes about love, meaning, and life in general. To the west lies "the English Death," a nexus for destructive Occidental concepts and dispositions. To the east hovers "the Heraldic Universe," the center of a complex of Eastern metaphysical views and sensibilities. The unfamiliarity and difficulty of meaning in the novels puzzle and threaten many critics. Over twenty years ago, Trilling, in his refreshingly candid exposure of critical perplexity, half-complained and half-exclaimed that in the *Quartet* Durrell "is certainly telling us something *new and strange* about modern love" (my italics). Newness and strangeness should not be qualities that, of themselves, cause us to value a book. At the same time, those qualities should not prevent us from valuing it. But I suspect, unfortunately, that a general critical complacence and cultural insularity have led some critics casually to classify (and dismiss) the *Quartet* as a stylistically majestic but substantially empty or perverse work. Pursewarden put his finger on the problem when he speculated: "Perhaps at the bottom of the Anglo-Saxon soul there is a still small voice forever whispering "'Is this Quaite Naice?' and my books never seem to pass the test" (*B*, 247).

## NOTES

1. John Mortimer, "Comus, Durrell, Wain and Kavan," *Encounter* 57 (1958): 84.

2. John Coleman, "Mr. Durrell's Dimensions," *The Spectator* 204 (19 February 1960): 256.

3. R. T. Chapman, "'Dead or Just Pretending?' Reality in the *Alexandria Quartet*," *Centennial Review* 4 (Fall 1972): 411.

4. Walter G. Creed, "'The Whole Pointless Joke'? Darley's Search for Truth in *The Alexandria Quartet*," *Etudes Anglaises* 27, no. 2 (April–June 1975): 173.

5. Mortimer, "Comus, Durrell," 84.

6. V. S. Pritchett, "The Sun and the Sunless," *New Statesman,* 13 February 1960, 223.

7. Lionel Trilling, "Lawrence Durrell: Two Reviews," in *The World of Lawrence Durrell,* ed. Harry Moore (Carbondale: Southern Illinois University Press, 1962), 52.

8. Lawrence Durrell, *On Miracle Ground: The Fourth International Lawrence Durrell Conference,* Pennsylvania State University, State College, Pennsylvania, Apr. 11–13, 1986.

9. Lawrence Durrell, *A Key to Modern British Poetry* (Norman: University of Oklahoma Press, 1952), 83.

10. Kenneth Young, "A Dialgoue with Durrell," *Encounter* 13 (1959): 5.

11. Lawrence Durrell, *A Smile in the Mind's Eye* (London: Wildwood House, 1980), 53.

12. George Wickes, *Lawrence Durrell–Henry Miller: A Private Correspondence* (New York: E. P. Dutton, 1963), 301.

13. Alan G. Thomas, *Spirit of Place: Letters and Essays on Travel* (New York: E. P. Dutton, 1969), 83.

14. Durrell, *Smile,* 33.

15. Ibid., 29.

16. Wickes, *Durrell-Miller,* 49.

17. Young, "A Dialogue with Durrell," 67.

18. Durrell, *Key,* 95.

19. Wickes, *Durrell-Miller,* p. 8.

20. Lawrence Durrell, *Mountolive* (New York: E. P. Dutton, 1958), 18. Further references will be included in the text.

21. Wickes, *Durrell-Miller,* 91.

22. Lawrence Durrell, *Clea* (New York: E. P. Dutton, 1960), 35. Further references will be included in the text.

23. Durrell, *Smile,* 19.

24. Young, "A Dialogue with Durrell," 3.

25. Lawrence Durrell, *Balthazar* (New York: E. P. Dutton, 1958), 93. Further references will be included in the text.

26. Wickes, *Durrell-Miller,* 349.

27. Gene Andrewski and Julian Mitchell, "Lawrence Durrell: The Art of Fiction XXIII: An Interview with Lawrence Durrell," *Paris Review* 22 (Autumn–Winter 1959–1960): 37.

28. Ibid., 40.

29. Matthew Arnold, *Culture and Anarchy* (Cambridge: Cambridge University Press, 1932), 142.

30. Heinrich Zimmer, *Philosophies of India* (New York: Meridian Books, 1956), 576.

31. Herbert V. Guenther and Chogyam Trungpa, *The Dawn of the Tantra* (Berkeley and London: Shambhala, 1975), 59.

32. Lawrence Durrell, *Justine* (New York: E. P. Dutton, 1957), 100. Further references will be included in the text.

33. Durrell, *Key*, 78.

34. Ibid., 79.

35. Trilling, "Lawrence Durrell: Two Reviews," 52.

36. Guenther and Trungpa, *Dawn of the Tantra*, 24.

37. Ibid., 27.

38. Ibid.

39. J. Hillis Miller, "The Critic as Host," in *Deconstruction and Criticism* (New York: Seabury Press, 1979), 228.

40. Ibid., 230.

41. Ibid., 252.

42. Guenther and Trungpa, *Dawn of the Tantra*, 43.

43. Durrell, *On Miracle Ground*.

44. Durrell, *Smile*, 53.

45. Wickes, *Durrell-Miller*, 23.

46. Ibid., 19.

47. William Theodore de Bary, *The Buddhist in India, China, and Japan* (New York: Random House, 1969), 119.

48. Andrewski and Mitchell, "Lawrence Durrell . . . Interview . . . ," 60.

49. Young, "A Dialogue with Durrell," 2.

50. M. P. Pandit, *Kundalini Yoga* (India: All India Press, 1970), 9.

51. Harry T. Antrim and Eugene Lyons, "An Interview with Lawrence Durrell," *Shenandoah* 2 (Winter 1971): 47.

# Who Wrote *Mountolive?* The Same One Who Wrote "Swann in Love"

## Eugene Hollahan

Most critical discussions of Lawrence Durrell's daring tetralogy *The Alexandria Quartet* (1957–60) focus on a portentous array of difficult modern ideas. Thus we encounter serious, frequently literal-minded, discussions of Durrell's masterpiece in terms of Einsteinian relativity, space-time continuum, dimorphism, cyclism, and indeterminacy. Some of Durrell's own utterances invite such arcane commentary. But we normally read these books as novels, and, as Durrell's best critic G. S. Fraser has noted, such ideas have no privileged place "other than as elements in a composition."[1] It seems better to approach this admittedly problematical sequence in more familiar terms of theme and form.

Deliberate literary obscurity, as A. K. Moore makes clear, has its justification in that it stimulates and challenges the reader's mind.[2] The general problem of obscurities resulting from Durrell's compositional strategies can be glimpsed by referring to John Unterecker's summary of Durrell's technical problem and his varied solutions:

> Durrell's solution is a little like Gide's in *The Counterfeiters* or Faulkner's in *Absalom, Absalom!:* a storyteller finds variant accounts of what ought to be a single story. In *The Alexandria Quartet,* Darley's initial version of a set of events is corrected by Arnauti's *Moeurs* and by the diaries of Nessim and the false diaries of Justine; these versions are in turn corrected by Balthazar's interlinear; that interlinear is corrected by the objective history of events in *Mountolive* and by a number of sets of letters, most significant of which are those between Leila and Mountolive, Pursewarden and Mountolive, and Pursewarden and Liza. Finally, time itself offers a shifted perspective; and in *Clea,* the one novel that moves forward in time, each of the central characters is allowed the opportunity to re-examine and re-evaluate his past and the pasts of the group of wounded survivors from the first three books.[3]

It is within this set of deliberate confusions and their accompanying

113

obscurities that the present interpretation of *Mountolive,* the third part of *The Alexandria Quartet,* situates itself.

Naturalism is the main threat to modern novelists.[4] I take this to mean that realism and its ever-present intensification, naturalism, being allied with the lowest common denominators of quotidian life and literature, the human bedrock so to speak, tend to militate against individual experimentation in subjective content and form. Durrell faced this problem head-on in *The Alexandria Quartet.* He explicitly announced as much to fellow artist Henry Miller with a statement that represents the starting point for any critical examination of *Mountolive.* Durrell's letter is of January 1958.

> Just sent off the huge *Mountolive* MS. They want it set up now so I should have a proof in a while which I'll route via you as a curiosity. I wanted you to read *Balthazar* as it was countersprung and have a clue as to the form. This big novel is as tame and naturalistic in *form* as a Hardy; yet it is the fulcrum of the quartet and the rationale of the thing. With the fourth I can plunge back into the time-stream again as per *Justine.* You may yawn your head off over *Mountolive* and whisper, "Shucks."[5]

Durrell's critical intelligence shines brightly in this statement as he shows himself aware of one of the dangers of naturalism, i.e., simple boredom. He was well aware that the objective mode could cause readerly problems. Unterecker has commented upon Durrell's general awareness of certain problems involving subjectivity; he notes simply that if we are part of a whole, we cannot easily objectify that whole.[6] I intend to explain how, as Durrell asserts but does not explain, the objective *Mountolive* is the "rationale of the thing."

In a passage of remarkable beauty, Durrell uses the opening lines of chapter 12 of *Mountolive* to express his grasp of the philosophical principles of literary naturalism (determinism and its attendant constraints upon human freedom).

> Indeed, now the masters were beginning to find that they were, after all, the servants of the very forces which they had set in play, and that nature is inherently ungovernable. They were soon to be drawn along ways not of their choosing, trapped in a magnetic field, as it were, by the same forces which unwind the tides at the moon's bidding, or propel the glittering forces of salmon up a crowded river—actions curving and swelling into futurity beyond the powers of mortals to harness or divert. . . . Beyond the connivance of the will they knew it, and felt the portents gathering around them—the paradigms of powers unleashed which must fulfill themselves. But how? In what manner? That was not as yet compellingly clear.[7]

On the basis of such a naturalistic assumption Durrell builds his firm yet precarious world.

That we should think of Durrell's general project in terms of ontology—i.e., the nature of its existence—is urged by Kruppa. He says that Durrell's emphasis upon indeterminacy placed the novelist in the vanguard of modern thought and "demands a new ontology of the novel."[8] I believe that Darley does not "narrate" *Mountolive* in the same sense that he narrates the other three books but rather "composes" or "writes" it. Thus, ontologically, within the admitted fiction of *The Alexandria Quartet,* it has the peculiar status of a fiction within the context of a set of facts, i.e., Darley's actual life as narrated in *Justine, Balthazar,* and *Clea.*

The question "who wrote *Mountolive?*" was first posed in 1963 by Howard L. Shainheit. His own answer: "everybody and nobody." *Mountolive* is thus said to constitute the "public view of the situation . . . that common body of knowledge." Shainheit dogmatically adds: "If it is considered otherwise, it has no rationale in the *Quartet.*" He bolsters his argument by citing Richard Haven's theory that the "information" in *Mountolive* should be considered as the "ordering facts" and explanations that most people assume to exist: "In this view it doesn't matter who is supposed to present the material." Interestingly, Shainheit goes on to speculate that "the novel might have been better off being written from a particular person's point of view"; he suggests Mnemjian the barber.[9] Thus Shainheit laid down the essential groundwork for this crucial problem.

Shainheit's question, if not his provocative answer, was picked up by Alan Friedman, whose own initial answer is provocatively to suggest that the "particular person's point of view" is that of the putative main character, David Mountolive. Surprisingly, Friedman says that *Mountolive* is like the first person narrative of *Great Expectations* in being "written from the point of view of its protagonist as he relives the events he narrates." But after an intelligent discussion of - *Mountolive,* Friedman changes his mind. Next he argues thus: because we cannot quite believe that Mountolive could treat his own "spiritual decline and defeat" with such objectivity, we should not insist that Mountolive "literally" wrote the novel. Friedman then decides that an equally good answer is simply that the book gives us the object truth of an old fashioned realistic novel with its omniscient narrator. Friedman finally hopes that Darley's subjectivity will not be invalidated by the objectivity in *Mountolive.* His final opinion that - *Mountolive* presents a reliable omniscient narrator's objective/realistic account is by and large the standard opinion, echoed by Weatherhead, Levitt, Fraser, and Unterecker.[10]

The nearest any critic comes to the ontological premise I am urging is Wedin's argument that Durrell shows Darley's artistic growth by having Darley "narrate" each of the four novels. He sees a steady growth in Darley, throughout the first to the third book, from immature subjectivity toward mature objectivity in *Mountolive*. Thus, when Darley begins *Clea*, narrative continuity smoothly merges into Darley's "final breakthrough": Darley's realization of a "mythic or archetypic" meaning underlying life's multitudinous data. Wedin sees a smooth pattern by which Darley translates each stage of his artistic development into the form of the novel he writes.[11] The only general problem with Wedin's neat interpretation is that no reader anywhere—even having read Wedin—would ever read *The Alexandria Quartet* in the seamless way Wedin describes. Taylor is much more on target when he objects that the growth-of-the-artist theme must be urged with caution because Durrell's style from book to book does not easily adapt itself to Darley's presumed "growing awareness."[12] Durrell himself, as we have seen, said that *Clea* would "plunge back into the time-stream again as *per* Justine [sic]," and surely all readers experience a shock—not a smooth transition—at the beginning and end of *Mountolive*.

Even if I can partially grant Wedin's hypothesis that Darley "narrates" all four novels, I wish to amend Wedin's opinion by taking account of the ontological differences between *Mountolive* and the other three books. My own hypothesis is more radical than Wedin's. I believe that Darley does in one sense "narrate" *Justine, Balthazar,* and *Clea*, but in a very different sense he "writes" or "composes" - *Mountolive*. I am contending that the "particular person's point of view" that Shainheit originally sought to identify has been in front of readers' eyes since the beginning, and only a failure of sensibility has kept us from seeing it.[13]

Critics have generally agreed that Durrell developed some single major theme in *The Alexandria Quartet,* but in general they have disagreed as to its exact nature. One of the more appealing formulations holds that Durrell's unifying theme celebrates the ability of the human will to function in the real world.[14] Another formulation, by Fraser, has it that the unifying idea is provided by the dynamics between love, death, art, and power.[15] Burns thinks that the tetralogy develops a four-stage Plotinian ascent to the knowledge of God.[16] One further example emphasizes a congeries of major themes: Personality, Causality, Rational and Moral Consciousness, Time, and Society.[17] These widely differing critical views represent but a sampling.

Another set of critics agrees in finding one theme and the same: the growth of the literary artist. Pinchin asserts that the theme of *The*

*Alexandria Quartet* viewed as a *Bildungsroman* is Darley's "coming of age" as a person and a writer.[18] Godshalk uses almost exactly the same terms.[19] Levitt emphasizes the relationship between art and life, and he focuses on Darley's maturing as a person and artist.[20] Unterecker broadens the idea a bit to embrace the "emotional education of a hero and his friends." Even so, despite his partial consensus, Unterecker notes that no critic has explained *how* Darley arrives at the "tender acceptance of things."[21] Likewise, Taylor points out that Durrell's main point ("the nature of Darley's triumph of awareness as dominant narrative viewpoint character") has eluded critical understanding and contributes to the confusion over Durrell's thematic intention.[22] My hypothesis will be that this growth toward the "tender acceptance of things" is accomplished in large part by an implicit decision on the part of Darley the would-be writer to become Darley the accomplished writer by virtue of his first extended piece of realistic prose fiction (on the subject of David Mountolive).

Given the strenuous demands made upon readers by the shifting, subjective *Justine* and *Balthazar,* readers understandably feel relieved—albeit puzzled—to encounter the objective-seeming world of *Mountolive.* The rationale for such relief has been perfectly expressed by Burns: "This is the novel of reason and when it comes to a close we feel comfortably sure that the answers given are the true answers."[23] My argument is that, yes, *Mountolive* gives us "true answers" but the true answers of objective factuality and not of imaginative realistic fictionality.[24]

*Mountolive* is a medium-length fiction of sixteen chapters containing powerful symbols (trap, whip) and strong themes (memory, entrapment, futility). It begins with an unforgettable "fish drive" on Lake Mareotis, in which David Mountolive participates, and it ends with an equally memorable Coptic wake, from which Mountolive is absent. In between these vivid episodes, we are presented with a detailed account of the experiences of Mountolive, the English ambassador to Egypt. In order briefly to summarize the story, we can usefully divide it into two basic parts. In one part, we are shown a complicated set of personages and circumstances that make up Egyptian politics just prior to the Second World War. Egypt has its independence from England, and a difficult transfer of power is underway. The Arab majority threaten to obliterate a Coptic-Christian minority, and the Copts scheme in various ways to ensure their future safety. Hoping to protect themselves by aiding other Mediterranean minorities, they have secretly shipped guns to the Jews in Palestine. These guns are used to kill British soldiers.

Even though a junior diplomatic officer, Mountolive is romantically drawn toward a mysterious Coptic group, the Hosnani family. He is seduced into a love affair by Leila Hosnani, mother of his friend Nessim. Posted away to Prague and other capitals, he corresponds with Leila, who tries unsuccessfully to broaden his education with poetry, art, and the like. Returned to Egypt as ambassador (chap. 6), he is vexed by the sequestered Leila's refusal to see him and also by rumors of a Coptic conspiracy involving his friend Nessim Hosnani. At the crisis or turning point (p. 180) he must cope with Pursewarden's revelation that Nessim smuggles guns to Palestine. Mountolive's dilatory behavior prevents his carrying out any official action until a British intelligence officer in Palestine confronts him with incontrovertible evidence.

By this time, chaos reigns. The Coptic community is scattering to Kenya and other refuges. Mountolive is summoned to a final confrontation with the secluded Leila, now a hideously pock-marked, grotesque, "fattish Egyptian lady with all the marks of eccentricity and age written upon her appearance." When she begged him to protect her son Nessim, he curtly dismissed her plea and "took to his heels" (p. 280). The book closes with a detailed account of a Coptic wake for the fanatical Narouz Hosnani, Nessim's brother, who had been assassinated by less rabid Copts.

David Mountolive appears in nine of the sixteen chapters. Major episodes not directly dealing with him include a visit to the Arab quarter by Pursewarden, an embassy employee and writer, during which he inadvertently discovers Nessim's secret arms buildup (chap. 8); Pursewarden's suicide (chap. 9); a flashback that recounts Nessim's courtship of a Jewess, Justine Arnauti (chap. 10); Nessim's discussion of the Coptic scheme with Justine (chap. 11); Nessim's violent confrontation with his whip-wielding brother Narouz (chap. 13); Nessim's meeting with the Egyptian minister of the interior to stave off official reprisal against the Copts (chap. 14); and Narouz's murder and funeral (chap. 16). Anyone who has read Durrell's daring experiment in narratorial strategy, language, and form will recognize the inadequacy of this summary.

Since I intend to show that Durrell modeled *Mountolive* on Proust's "Swann in Love," thus making a kind of intertextual reference back to Proust's text, I should note the presence in *Mountolive* of a considerable number of other kinds of allusions. Given Durrell's unmistakable ambition of producing a large fiction that would be evaluated in the context of a main tradition, we should not be surprised to discover numerous allusions to earlier authors and texts in that tradition. A few of these allusions consist of explicit namings of authors, e.g., Schopenhauer, Hume, and Spengler (231), which help to establish a philosophical basis for Durrell's skepticism. Both William Blake and Henry James are referred to by name, the latter disparagingly by Pombal—"Henry James was a pussy" (156)—but the former admiringly by Pursewarden as a champion of personal freedom (64–65).

At deeper levels and more obliquely, a variety of prior texts supply Durrell-Darley with literary comparisons. Greek mythology supplies several telling allusions (e.g., Aphrodite, 205; Pygmalion, 153). Shakespearean allusions to Othello (285), Hamlet (242), and Antony and Cleopatra (249) deepen the cultural background of Durrell's narrative action, and a dream of Mountolive's (291) includes his visualizing his assault by child prostitutes as a humiliation comparable to Swift's Gulliver being poked and prodded by the Lilliputians.

Novelists provide the most compelling allusions. Two French novelists (Flaubert and Gide) supply materials for reference. *Madame Bovary* is alluded to during a rendezvous, a horse-drawn cab ride taken by the two lovers, Mountolive and Leila Hosnani (278–82); *L'Immoraliste* is brought to mind by the idea of a respectable young man, Darley, engaging in nocturnal poaching (12). Even so, English novelists are most richly brought to mind. The disfiguring smallpox that sends Leila deep into seclusion (57) recalls similar tragic occurrences in both Thackeray's *Henry Esmond* and Dicken's *Bleak House.* Then, too, Leila's crippled husband Faltaus rides in a rubber-tired wheelchair (37) reminiscent of the one utilized by Sir Clifford Chatterley in D. H. Lawrence's *Lady Chatterley's Lover.*[25] A bizarre policeman named Scobie "who spends his time dressed as a woman walking about the harbor at Alexandria" (139) recalls and satirizes Henry Scobie, the main character in Graham Greene's *The Heart of the Matter.*[26] Also, at the beginning of chapter 8, the repartee between roommates Pombal and Pursewarden as they perform their toilet alludes to Joyce's opening scene in *Ulysses* ("A hundred times I've asked you not to use my razor"), with cynical novelist Pursewarden being cast as an unlikely substitute for that other prickly writer, Stephen Dedalus. Finally, when Nessim Hosnani begins to court Justine, he offers her "a large sum of money" so that she can be free, be "a wholly independent person" (197); this episode clearly recalls Henry James's construction of Isabel Archer's predicament vis-á-vis Ralph Touchett's problematical generosity in *The Portrait of a Lady.* In these allusions, Durrell's intention is clearly satirical, as he presumably clears a place for himself in a great tradition by echoing and parodying great predecessors.

Given the relatively moderate length of *Mountolive,* I want to approach it by invoking Howard Nemerov's 1963 definition of the short novel. Nemerov thinks that the short novel is itself the primary form of prose fiction. He links the form with the tragic dimension of our fictional tradition. The short novel takes a stark form comparable to a scientific demonstration; thus it has vital links with abstract thought.

Nemerov bases his model of the short novel on his study of more than a dozen classic texts: e.g., *Notes from the Underground, Billy Budd, Death in Venice,* and *The Death of Ivan Ilyich.* He extracts from these texts a predominant theme and a characteristic action essential to the genre. The theme of identity represents the conceptual basis, and the action can be reduced to the following pattern: two people become attached to and dependent upon each other to the extreme of some life-or-death predicament, so that only a difficult decision (choice, crisis) can dissolve their bond and at least one can be saved. Life itself depends upon this decision. The author of the short novel composes a story that develops the theme of identity and character interdependence. The story takes the following shape:

> . . . the man of the middle class, rational, worldly, either rather stupid or of a somewhat dry intelligence and limited vision, plunged into the domain of the forbidden, extravagant, and illicit, the life of the impulses beneath or the life of compulsive and punitive authority above, both of them equally regions in which every detail gains fatal significance, every perception is excruciatingly intensified, and every decision for salvation or doom . . .

Surprisingly, Nemerov goes on to assert that the protagonist of the short novel (e.g., Ivan Ilyich or Gustave Aschenbach) though seemingly the victim of "fate" should be regarded as also a victim of a literary style or of the principles of composition itself.[27]

Nemerov's striking theory is convincingly argued. Moreover, its application to *Mountolive* seems direct and cogent. Durrell's novel does both pose and answer the question "who is David Mountolive?" Likewise, the main plot does display, like a ruthless demonstration, how Mountolive and Leila Hosnani become dangerously dependent upon each other. Somewhat like Aschenbach in Mann's Venice, as if to illustrate Nemerov's theory, Mountolive the cautious English diplomat in Alexandria plunges feverishly into the intricacies of Coptic-Arabic intrigues and finds himself out of his depth in a culture where "salvation or doom" depend upon his own actions.

Nemerov does not discuss "Swann in Love," but in 1979 I applied his provocative theory to Proust's text. In "Nemerov's Definition and Proust's Example: A Model for the Short Novel," I argued that "Swann in Love," the third part of the four-part *Swann's Way,* calls for unique responses from the reader. My enterprise then (as now) was to determine what story this is and who tells this story.[28]

After a Barthesian deconstruction of *Swann's Way* (163–67), I established the puzzling rhetorical-ontological status of "Swann in Love" by suggesting that it be regarded as both a "short novel in itself and as Marcel's first effort to produce an extended piece of prose fiction," The other three sections of *Swann's Way* ("Overture," "Combray," "Place-Names: The Name") are autobiographical (hence historical), whereas "Swann in Love" itself "takes the form, *within* the fictive world, of an autotelic fiction":

> One's feeling that "Swann in Love" does not quite fit results, obviously, less from its subject matter than from its form, tone, and narrational perspective. One solution to this problem (if indeed it is a problem) would be simply to ignore the technical problems implied here and simply to accept the story of Swann and Odette as having the same ontological status as the rest of the novel. A more challenging solution, which sacrifices none of the advantages of the first possible solution and which adds to our sense of Proust's experimental boldness and mastery would be to imagine that young Marcel, having decided to become a writer, and having rejected the perverse life style represented by the Meseglise way for the disciplined creativity represented by the Guermantes way, has taken the trouble to try his hand at a short novel and, with no explicit fanfare, has presented it to his reader, or, in other terms, has inserted it in his private journal.

Thus I suggested how the third part of *Swann's Way* that has pleased and baffled readers is shown to be "a remarkable gathering up of and concentration of problems and themes of Marcel's own personal life, as well as a stunning first fruit of a fictive literary career." Finally, I noted that "Swann in Love," with its distasteful contents, displays the signs of "serious realistic fiction" but that after its closure *Swann's Way* reverts back to its basic mode, i.e., Marcel's subjective account of his own life.[29]

Proust looms large as a presence in Durrell's cosmopolitan imagination and in our perceptions of Durrell himself. Durrell has said in an interview that Proust is one of the modernist writers with whom he has felt most naturally in sympathy.[30] He pays tribute to Richard Aldington as the first writer he encountered who gave "serious praise" to Eliot, Joyce, and Proust as the "true creative spirits of our time."[31] Victor Brombert notes that when Durrell became famous in the 1950s the example of Proust was regularly evoked: early French critics "quite exuberantly compared Durrell's fiction with the haunting edifice of Proust."[32]

Moreover, critics looked closely at Durrell and Proust side by side. Asserting that Durrell does not merely imitate Proust, Brombert explains that Durrell's multifaceted fictions, with their fourth dimension of Time, make it difficult not to evoke the themes and techniques of

*A la recherche du temps perdu,* yet Durrell's peculiar notion of time emphasizes action rather than memory and hence is "not at all Proustian."[33] Also, George Steiner cites the widespread view in the 1960s that *The Alexandria Quartet* is "the highest performance in the modern novel since Proust and Joyce." He praised *Clea* as presenting a "tragedy of homosexual passion" worthy of Proust's deep understanding. But Steiner praises Proust by complaining that Durrell's "severing his imagined world from the intrusions of political and social fact" compares badly with Proust, who "buttressed his narrow and even perverse view of human conduct with a close, technical awareness of social, political, and military affairs."[34] Then, too, Weigel notes that Proust constitutes a source for Durrell's lovers who are acutely "aware of the polyvalences of love." But he too asserts that Durrell's methods are not truly Proustian. Rather, Durrell, although not attempting to out-do Proust's "deep research into the springs of memory," nevertheless goes beyond Proust by intensifying the elements of confusion, indeterminacy, and relativity. Unlike Proust, Durrell implies that the truth is never to be known.[35] Another distinction between the two authors is offered by Fraser, who thinks that Durrell, in retaining action as a human possibility, is unlike Proust, who wishes "to dissolve the experience of living and loving into pure reflection."[36]

Of Durrell's relation to Proust, the novelist himself has stated: "I hoped by this ["paper construct"; i.e., *The Alexandria Quartet*] to restore action to the novel, for since Proust the novelist has become a ruminant where he isn't a mere pictographer."[37] Among critics, Alan Friedman has had the most to say about Durrell's complex response to Proust. He places Durrell and Proust among the "supreme novelists of this century" (Conrad, Lawrence, Faulkner, Mann) who seek to create art of lasting significance and to offer "new modes of thought, new ways of viewing" a world that they themselves have been instrumental in bringing into existence. Friedman assesses Durrell as being, at his best *(The Alexandria Quartet),* the "conscious heir to the dual tradition of Ford-Conrad impressionism and Proust-Joyce stream of consciousness." At a more specific level, Friedman focuses on *Swann's Way* when he examines Durrell and Proust. The earlier novelist demonstrated that Charles Swann selectively revealed several faces to the world; Durrell literalizes this phenomenon by having Justine sit enigmatically before mirrors showing five profiles. In discussing *Balthazar,* Friedman cites *Swann's Way* to the effect that we can only know other people's passions, not our own. In addition, in discussing the theory of the multifaceted personality, Friedman distinguishes between Durrell (broadminded) and his narrator Darley (narrowminded) by saying that Darley, like Charles Swann, "contradictorily expects people to be unequivocal, monolithic, readily comprehensible."[38] On the whole, then, it is not surprising that Proust constitutes a presence in *The Alexandria Quartet.*[39]

Richard M. Eastman describes "Swann in Love" as having enough internal coherence to be read as an independent novel offering Proust's best writing and few of his special difficulties.[40] Milton Hindus goes even farther, calling it Proust's "most brilliant gem."[41] "Swann in Love" depicts in realistic prose fiction an account of Charles Swann's obsessive, self-destructive passion for Odette de Crecy. Following an abrupt beginning, which introduces the dilettantish Verdurin household, we are given an exhaustive treatment of Swann's degradation, culminating in his final cry of painful awareness: "To think that I wasted years of my life, that I have longed for death, that the greatest love that I have ever known has been for a woman who did not please me, who was not in my style!"[42]

Briefly, Proust characterizes Swann as follows. He womanizes among lower-class women; he is a failed writer; he is a man of the middle class with aristocratic connections; he is an obsessive pleasure seeker who uses art as diversion; he compromises his mind and morals in order to enjoy Odette; he is a jealous lover.

Briefly, Proust constructs a story line as follows. Swann becomes infatuated with Odette; he seeks out her friends the Verdurins; he is obsequious toward them though despising them; he defies convention by pursuing Odette; he initiates a correspondence with her; he follows her through the streets of Paris; he becomes her regular lover; he praises the Verdurins as "magnanimous creatures"; he torments himself with jealous fantasies; he alternates between a desire for dominance and a desire for self-abasement; he becomes unbalanced when he is excluded from gatherings at the Verdurins; he projects his own feelings of worthlessness onto Odette herself; at the crisis of the plot, he retreats from his decision not to give money to Odette—"his case was past operation" (*SW,* p. 237); he relives in memory his entire affair; he investigates her past life and is shocked by her sexual history; at the end, as he is about to take up with another woman, he utters his piteous cry of regret over his wasted life.

Key structural points figure in Durrell's modeling of *Mountolive* upon Proust's story. Swann's ultimate ignominy is to seek out prostitutes in a brothel so as to ferret out information about Odette's sexual history. Durrell matches (and overmatches!) Swann's humiliation by exposing Mountolive to a gross humiliation after his rejection of a desperate Leila Hosnani. Fraser describes it this way: "He has his moment, anyway, of terrible shock and punishment, when, after rejecting Leila, he disguises himself as a Syrian merchant and is lured into a child brothel, where the children rend his clothes" (159–60). The general effect of Mountolive's story, as of Swann's, is bleak indeed. The crisis of the Mountolive plot itself resembles the crisis in "Swann in Love," as Mountolive, because of his residual desire for the sequestered Leila, procrastinates (183ff) rather than act upon Pursewarden's revelation that Nessim Hosnani was involved in an arms buildup intended for the Jews in Palestine.

Other details fill out the resemblance. Both Swann and Mountolive engage in detective work; both are willing to deny the evidence they uncover. Mountolive takes notes on people (31) and even imagines himself a writer (159), but he never writes anything of substance. He has compromised his official role in order to enjoy the Hosnanis. He is jealous of Leila's husband. He is obsessive concerning his affair with Leila, "as if vicariously to provoke and master the whole new range of emotions which Leila had liberated in him" (27). In general, the bulk of the story, from his first departure from Leila's arms (48) up to his shocking reunion with her (278), provides an excruciatingly drawn-out period of emotional and sexual deprivation during which he obsessively broods about her to the detriment of other aspects of his life.

In summary, we might simply note that just as Durrell took over from "Swann in Love" the idea of having Darley begin his novelistic career by "writing" a novel about David Mountolive, he also took over from Proust's short novel a theme—"sexual obsession is a main source of error and illusion—" that, according to Fraser, informs much of *The Alexandria Quartet*.[43]

In *The Alexandria Quartet* as a whole, L. G. Darley plays a role that is central to all of Durrell's work to that point. Friedman characterizes that central role with its attendant theme as "the *Kunstlerroman* treatment of the frustrated, isolated individual maturing into someone capable of meaningful human involvement." In this maturation process, the individual achieves his potential in both art and life via a "total, active commitment to the creative process."[44] In *The Alexandria Quartet,* Darley enacts this peculiarly modern role. At the same time as he undergoes this thematic pattern of experiences, he must also carry the burden of being, in a sense, Durrell's hero. As Read puts it, Darley "persistently functions as a kind of savior or healer."[45] But what are the facts of Darley's characterization in the tetralogy as a whole?

A part of Durrell's Proustian problematic involves the question of how Darley would inscribe himself into his "fiction" about David Mountolive. The "real" Lawrence George Darley, an Anglo-Irish schoolteacher who lives in Alexandria just prior to and during the Second World War, has retired to a small island in the Cyclades. In this seclusion, he plans to reconstruct in his imagination and on paper the places, people, and problems he experienced in Egypt. With no ostensible background before his Alexandrian experiences, he makes himself the subject and protagonist of his imaginative reconstruction. He structures his account by means of three love affairs, with Melissa Artemis, a dancer and prostitute; Justine Hosnani, a Jewess married to a wealthy Copt; and Clea Montis, an artist. He meets and learns about numerous other people, Egyptian and English, in the city. He attempts to render the sights, sounds, and smells of Alexandria, where flesh and spirit violently collide. He undergoes a war-time self-examination and purification. At the end of the fourth volume, *Clea,* he is ready to begin his life as an artist, taking up his pen to write "Once upon a time. . . ."

Friedman thinks that Darley, being of no political importance, is mentioned only rarely in *Mountolive* and in fact "has almost no place in *Mountolive.*"[46] But Darley does have a place, and qualitatively no mean place, in this novel that, as I am asserting, he himself composes. Specifically, Darley is mentioned in chapters 5, 8, 9, 10, and 11. In order to achieve a fresh perspective on Durrell's peculiar rhetoric of fiction and puzzling ontology in *Mountolive,* I wish to distinguish heuristically from this point on in my argument between two personae, whom (for the sake of convenience) I will designate "Darley-Writer" and "Darley-Character."

We first encounter Darley-Character in *Mountolive* when he is mentioned several times in Pursewarden's twenty-eight-page letter to Ambassador Mountolive. Thus, at the outset, Darley-Writer links Darley-Character with a writer and a literary form (epistolary). He shows an ironical but affectionate Pursewarden introducing Darley-Character as a "vaguely amiable bespectacled creature" who sometimes lives with Pombal, teaches for a living, and plans to write novels. Pursewarden describes this Darley as follows: a babyish cultural type, stooped, fair, with a "shyness that goes with Great Emotions imperfectly kept under control" (110). Pursewarden notes that Darley had introduced him to Arnauti's *Moeurs* (an Alexandrian *succes de scandale* about nymphomania and psychic impotence). Thus Darley-Character is linked with a second literary form, one in fact with decided Proustian overtones.

Pursewarden's epistolary view of Darley-Character embraces several features. Darley is a "modest British" type, and Pursewarden admits his own puzzlement over Justine's choice of lover: "poor fellow flutters on a slab like a skate at her approach" (111). A victim of his own "fine sentiment," Darley-Character is also said to be entangled with the dancer-prostitute Melissa Artemis. Because of this connection (Melissa had been mistress to one Cohen, an arms dealer), Darley is being watched by British Intelligence. As if to emphasize Darley-Character's literary aspirations, Pursewarden mentions that he has read one of Darley's short stories.

Unaware that Justine makes love to Darley-Character in order to spy on him (re Melissa), Pursewater continually wonders what the passionate Jewess sees in his compatriot, so "snobbish and parochial at once." Pursewarden says: "He lacks devil." Ironically (if my premise holds up), just as we seem to learn the most convincing facts about Mountolive from Darley's putative "fiction" about the ambassador, *within* the framework of that fiction we learn the most reliable seeming facts about Darley-Character from Darley's own invention of Pursewater's letter to Mountolive.

When Pursewarden sees Darley-Character at a café, Darley excitedly discusses art, even though Pursewarden objects to such talk as appropriate for critics but not for the artist, who must "surrender" himself to his discipline (114). Pursewarden's letter informs Mountolive that Darley goes with Justine to Nessim's secret Coptic meetings so as "to suck up hermetical lore" (115). However, when Pursewarden had suggested to Meskalyne of British Intelligence that Darley should be used as a spy on Nessim, he is told that Darley would not be reliable in such a role (121–37).

Darley-Writer filters most of his references to Darley-Character in *Mountolive,* even oblique ones, through the literary lens of Pursewarden. During Pursewarden's adventurous walk through the "evening promise of Alexandria" (open sores, sex, money, perfumes), he bumps into a preoccupied Darley who quickly excuses himself to go home. Later, Pursewarden meditates upon his social neglect of the young Irishman. He consoles himself by enigmatically recalling: "But the poor bastard is still interested in *literature*" (163). This sarcastic remark seems to reiterate Darley-Writer's belief that only gradually did he develop the readiness to become a committed artist.

But Darley-Character also surfaces in the consciousness of other characters. When Pursewarden makes love to the impoverished Melissa so as to pay her one thousand piasters, she refuses to discuss her lover Darley, even though during their coupling she thinks of Darley's bed (171). Pursewarden resolves to give Darley five hundred pounds so that he can take Melissa away for a rest (168). In this crucial episode, when Pursewarden deliberately reminds Melissa of Darley, she thinks of her lover's dalliance with Justine and in a pet she blurts out the terrible truth about Nessim's transactions with the arms dealer Cohen (176–77). Thus, Darley-Writer uses Darley-Character to trigger three important plot developments: Pursewarden's suicide, Nessim's downfall, and Mountolive's own crisis.

Darley-Writer uses other characters to fill out details of the sketchy characterization of Darley-Character in *Mountolive*. An embassy employee (Telford) reports to Ambassador Mountolive that "Darley, the schoolteacher" was the last person to see Pursewarden alive (181). Other characters discuss him: Nessim tells Justine early on that Darley's liaison with Melissa could be dangerous to them (203); Justine tells Nessim that Darley is merely fascinated by her "diary"— notes left over from her husband Arnauti's *Moeurs* (207); and Justine replies to Nessim's warning about Darley to the effect that Darley would not inform upon them but instead would "bury" information potentially damaging to the Hosnanis (209). And, in fact, Darley-Writer does subtly "bury" such information in his fictive account of David Mountolive.

Durrell's modeling of *Mountolive* upon "Swann in Love" extends beyond the basic rhetoric/ontological dimension to include numerous details and structural elements of characterization, plot, and theme. *Mutatis mutandis,* what Friedman labels David Mountolive's "spiritual decline and defeat,"[47] strongly resembles the unhappy decline of Charles Swann.

Darley-Writer's characterization of David Mountolive illustrates a formulaic conception of the kind employed by Proust and described by Nemerov. He is a mother's boy who develops earaches under stress (99, 191). By contrast with Leila Hosnani's impassioned acceptance of her English lover, he can offer nothing but "the nervous silence of a national sensibility almost anaesthetized into clumsy taciturnity: an education in selected reticences and shames" (18). At the outset, Mountolive is shown with the Hosnani family at their estate and "rambling old-fashioned house built upon a network of lakes and embankments near Alexandria" (11). He has ingratiated himself with this exotic crew, and, at her husband's suggestion, he has been taken as Leila's lover (30). From the opening descriptions of an exciting fish drive, characterized by the "barbaric blitheness" of the Arabs (16), the Egypt that Mountolive sees is exotic, erotic, exciting, forbidden, forbidding.

He is attracted to the "world of anomalies" (20) enacted in the old rambling house full of magnificent carpets and "weird Second Empire furniture of a Turkish cast." Much of the story depicts Mountolive obsessed with the lover he left behind when he followed his ambitions to various capitals of the world. *Mountolive* effects a spectacular closure by presenting the elaborate, codalike funeral of Narouz Hosnani (chap. 16). But the book in a sense closes one page earlier with

Mountolive's own story, which itself ends, almost exactly like Swann's sad tale, with the ambassador's realization that he had wasted his life, as it were, on a woman not in his style. His muted cry at seeing "a fattish Egyptian lady" moaning in a carriage fills him with "self-pity and disgust": "He was suddenly face to face with the meaning of love and time. They had lost forever the power to fecundate each other's minds" (281). As if to literalize Mountolive's degradation, Darley concludes Mountolive's story by showing him reduced to taking care of an unwanted dog (297).

Fraser's analysis of David Mountolive is germane. Hapless Mountolive lives all of his life near centers of power, yet "he will never be able to initiate anything, only to check or delay." Mountolive is a well-bred Englishman but suffers from a "rawness of inner sensibility, a lack of emotional self-knowledge." He cultivates art only to impress Leila. For sentimental reasons, he begins his ambassadorship with the blunder of ignoring official advice to get rid of Pursewarden. We can admire Mountolive's rectitude but must wonder at his "immature heart."[48] One way to judge Mountolive's character would be to assume, with Taylor, that Mountolive arrived in Egypt with approximately the same handicaps and potentials as Darley, but, as Taylor thinks, "Mountolive moves to the opposite pole; he is a man whose potential for awareness, and thus for valid action premised on this awareness, is to be defeated."[49]

*The Alexandria Quartet* is an archaeological excavation of motives and motifs, but there are advantages to seeing *Mountolive* in the ontological/rhetorical way I am suggesting. By interrupting his subjective work with an objective-seeming structure, Durrell-Darley dramatizes several related principles essential to Durrell's general view of life: no ultimate certainty can ever come into perfectly clear focus, but humans will persist in making the attempt; objectivity and subjectivity are not stages in a process but rather dialectical functions of each other; in Durrell's neo-Hegelian epistemology, there is neither absolute error nor absolute truth;[50] and so on. In broad terms, we may subsume all such ideas under the generalization that in literature as in life realism will always constitute the basis for perceptions, expressions, and existence (ontology) itself. My hypothesis is quite simple. We should yield to our innate desire for aesthetic unity by extending the Proustian education-of-Darley-as-a-writer theme to include the most puzzling piece of *The Alexandria Quartet* as the only piece that could be construed as "written" in the usual novelistic sense. When we posit that Darley "wrote" *Mountolive*, we grant a specificity to the Proustian model that undoubtedly is so important to Durrell's oeuvre.

Darley-Writer coopts Pursewarden's artistic ideals for himself, but

Pursewarden kills himself, thus taking what Mountolive calls a "plunge into anonymity" (158). Darley himself foregoes any actual suicide, but his temporary sacrifice of his own precious subjectivity and daring plunge into the stark objectivity necessitated by the composition of *Mountolive* is an artistic act comparable to but more admirable than Pursewarden's literal suicide. Like Oedipus, who gains in stature by not taking Jocasta's suicidal way out of trouble, Darley continues to make a quantum leap forward in humane development by writing *Mountolive*. The entrapment motif announced in the opening episode, the fish drive, receives its subtlest development in Durrell's own use of Proust's daring experiment in shifting perspective. Houdini-like, Darley traps himself in a boxed-in form of brute objectivity, but he escapes and thus lives and grows.[51] Thus, and only thus, as Durrell asserted in his letter to Henry Miller, *Mountolive* proves indeed to function as the "rationale of the whole thing."

Like Marcel, Darley begins his novelistic career just as one is enjoined to do by writers of how-to writing manuals; he writes a detailed, realistic prose fiction about familiar things and persons, firm materials that nonetheless allow working room for the imagination. *The Alexandria Quartet* deals with love, politics, art, and other aspects of human experience, but Durrell's main concern is arguably not with any such content but with "writing" itself.[52] Durrell never forgets that he is writing, and the reader who forgets that he reads Durrell's writing does so at his own risk. Fraser notes: "Durrell the joker is always there, who likes his little mystifications, who enjoys pulling our legs."[53] Durrell himself was generously pleased with the technical discoveries made by one of his pioneer interpreters, the poet Christopher Middleton. He noted admiringly: "This is really excellent . . . he's twigged what I'm up to."[54] Surely it makes better sense than heretofore of the splendid, vexing *Alexandria Quartet* to imagine that by seeing Durrell's close Proustian modeling we have once again "twigged" this playful author at his astonishing games.

## NOTES

1. G. S. Fraser, *Lawrence Durrell: A Critical Study* (New York: Dutton, 1968), 162

2. Arthur K. Moore, *Contestable Concepts of Literary Theory* (Baton Rouge: Louisiana State University Press, 1973), 98.

3. John Unterecker, *Lawrence Durrell* (New York: Columbia University Press, 1964), 39

4. Chet Taylor, "Dissonance and Digression: The Ill-Fitting Fusion of Philosophy and Form in Lawrence Durrell's *Alexandria Quartet,*" *Modern Fiction Studies* 17 (Summer 1971): 169.

5. Lawrence Durrell, *Lawrence Durrell and Henry Miller: A Private Correspondence,* ed. George Wickes (New York: Dutton, 1963), 327.

6. Unterecker, *Lawrence Durrell,* 19

7. Lawrence Durrell, *Mountolive* (New York: Dutton, 1959), 213. All subsequent references to this text will be given parenthetically in the body of the essay.

8. Joseph E. Kruppa, "Durrell's *Alexandria Quartet* and the 'Implosion' of the Modern Consciousness," *Modern Fiction Studies* 13 (Autumn 1967): 416.

9. Howard L. Shainheit, "Who Wrote *Mountolive?:* An Investigation of the Relativity-Aesthetic of Lawrence Durrell's *The Alexandria Quartet.*" Cited in Alan Warren Friedman, *Lawrence Durrell and "The Alexandria Quartet": Art for Love's Sake* (Norman: University of Oklahoma Press, 1970), 127–28.

10. Friedman, *Lawrence Durrell,* 128.

11. Warren Wedin, "The Artist as Narrator in *The Alexandria Quartet,*" *Twentieth Century Literature* 18 (July 1972): 179–80.

12. Taylor, "Dissonance and Digression," 179.

13. In a sense, the puzzling rhetorical status of *Mountolive* vis-á-vis the other three novels can be understood in terms of what Michel Foucault describes as the modern episteme, i.e., a system of analysis based on categories of identity and difference. See *The Order of Things* (New York: Vintage-Random, 1973), chap. 1. The modern outlook involves not so much an interaction *with* the world (such as we see in *Justine, Balthazar,* and *Clea*) as rather a reasoned, objective analysis *of* the world. See Timothy J. Reiss, *The Discourse of Modernism* (Ithaca: Cornell University Press, 1982), 30.

14. A. K. Weatherhead, "Romantic Anachronism in *The Alexandria Quartet,*" *Modern Fiction Studies* 11 (Summer 1964): 128–36.

15. Fraser, *Lawrence Durrell,* 141.

16. J. Christopher Burns, "Durrell's Heraldic Universe," *Modern Fiction Studies* 13 (Autumn 1967): 375–88.

17. Stanley G. Eskin, "Durrell's Themes in the *Alexandria Quartet,*" *Texas Quarterly* (Winter 1962): 43–60.

18. Jane Lagoudis Pinchin, *Alexandria Still: Forster, Durrell, and Cafavy* (Princeton: Princeton University Press, 1977): 196.

19. William Leigh Godshalk, "Some Sources of Durrell's *Alexandria Quartet,*" *Modern Fiction Studies* 13 (Autumn 1967): 361.

20. Morton P. Levitt, "Art and Correspondence: Durrell, Miller, and *The Alexandria Quartet,*" *Modern Fiction Studies* 13 (Autumn 1967): 316.

21. Unterecker, *Lawrence Durrell,* 36–46.

22. Taylor, "Dissonance and Digression," 168.

23. Burns, "Durrell's Heraldic Universe," 385.

24. Throughout my study of Durrell I worked under the influence of a stimulating discussion of fictionality by Floyd Merrell. His main idea: "What makes us *as free as we are* is our penchant for intrinsically conceiving/perceiving-imagining fictions from *inside* in order somehow to get *outside.*" See his *Pararealities: The Nature of Our Fictions and How We Know Them* (Philadelphia: John Benjamins, 1983). Several of Merrell's propositions explain the curious ontological status of *Mountolive* in the context of the other three novels: a totally autonomous fictional world is impossible (3); fictions are determined by their capacity to function outside of a "real" world (21); creative imaginary fictions are the product of foregrounding from an intrinsic background (52); fiction creating is necessarily an incomplete project (89); the literary fiction can be adequately intelligible only with respect to a "real" world (118).

25. George Steiner notes that the presence of Lawrence is felt throughout *The Al-*

exandria Quartet. "Lawrence Durrell: The Baroque Novel," in *The World of Lawrence Durrell,* ed., Harry T. Moore, (New York: Dutton, 1964), 17. In addition, in an appendix to *Balthazar,* Durrell himself offered the following opinion concerning Lawrence's novel: "In order to secure the lifelong devotion of an Anglo-Saxon woman one has only to get one's leg cut off above the waist. I've always thought Lady Chatterley weak in symbolism from this point of view. Nothing should have earned the devotion of his wife more surely than Clifford's illness" (*Balthazar* [New York: Dutton, 1960], 245).

26. Another view of Scobie's original, based upon historical research, is as follows: "his only original would appear to be that elderly and repulsive pederast Tarquin, so lovingly depicted by Mr. Durrell in *The Black Book.*" Captain H. Dare, M.C., "The Quest for Durrell's Scobie," *Modern Fiction Studies* 10 (Winter 1964–65): 383. George Steiner thinks that Scobie is "the finest comic invention in English fiction since *Tristram Shandy*" (Moore, *World,* 22).

27. Howard Nemerov, "Composition and Fate in the Short Novel," in *Perspective in Contemporary Criticism,* ed. Sheldon Norman Grebstein (New York: Harper & Row, 1968), 124–31.

28. Eugene Hollahan, "Nemerov's Definition and Proust's Example: A Model for the Short Novel," *Studies in the Novel* 11 (Summer 1979): 162.

29. Ibid., 163–73.

30. Moore, *World,* 153.

31. Alister Kershaw and Frederic-Jacques Temple, ed., *Richard Aldington: An Intimate Portrait* (Carbondale: Southern Illinois University Press, 1965), 19.

32. "Lawrence Durrell and His French Reputation" in Moore, *World,* 172–73.

33. Ibid., 173.

34. Ibid., 21.

35. John Weigel, *Lawrence Durrell* (New York: Twayne, 1965), 98–148.

36. Fraser, *Lawrence Durrell,* 136.

37. Moore, *World,* 163.

38. Friedman, *Lawrence Durrell,* 79ff.

39. Another place to see Durrell's constant use of Proust as a medium through which to pass raw materials is in the celebrated correspondence between Durrell and Henry Miller. On 8 February 1944, Durrell wrote to Miller from Alexandria: "The Alexandrian way of death is very Proustian and slow, a decomposition in greys and greens" (Durrell, *Correspondence,* 181). On 23 May 1944, he complains that because of war-time shortages he cannot find the "wonderful half-crown editions" of Proust available in prewar Alexandria. As if to validate that he was aware of the importance of being acquainted with the totality of *A la recherche du demps perdu,* in June 1947, from Bournemouth, England, he wrote: "I am in the position of someone trying to write about Proust who has seen only three of the seven volumes." Finally, in June 1957, from Villa Louis he reminds Miller of the impressive fact that their mutual friend Richard Aldington had served a valuable literary apprenticeship: "Imagine, as a young man he was corresponding with de Gourmont and Proust."

40. Richard M. Eastman, *A Guide to the Novel* (San Francisco: Chandler, 1965), 219.

41. Milton Hindus, *A Reader's Guide to Marcel Proust* (New York: Noonday, 1962), 17.

42. Marcel Proust, *Swann's Way* (New York: Vintage Books, 1970), p. 292. Further quotations will be drawn from this edition and included in the text as *SW*).

43. Fraser, *Lawrence Durrell,* 20.

44. Friedman, *Lawrence Durrell,* xv.

45. Phyllis J. Read, "The Illusion of Personality: Cyclical Time in Durrell's *Alexandria Quartet*," *Modern Fiction Studies* 13 (Autumn 1967): 398.

46. Friedman, *Lawrence Durrell*, 129, n. 15.

47. Ibid., 132.

48. Fraser, *Lawrence Durrell*, 158–59.

49. Taylor, "Dissonance and Digression," 174.

50. Fraser, *Lawrence Durrell*, 135.

51. The peculiarly complex status of objective facts (things) in Durrell's world has been commented upon by Lionel Trilling (Moore, *World*, 58ff).

52. Jane Lagoudis Pinchin, "Durrell's Fatal Cleopatria," *Modern Fiction Studies* 28 (Summer 1982): 231.

53. Fraser, *Lawrence Durrell*, 141.

54. Ibid., 135.

# Authorial Conscience in *Tunc* and *Nunquam*

## Frank Kersnowski

Lawrence Durrell's novels *Tunc* and *Nunquam* form a two-decker he called *The Revolt of Aphrodite*. As is the case with *The Alexandria Quartet* (and afterward with *The Avignon Quintet*), reality is no more than a point of view; events are of little consequence compared with the ways they are understood by the characters, the readers, and Durrell himself. The story narrated by Felix Charlock moves as steadily as if it were on rails, and we are at first stunned to find a madman at the throttle. As Charlock condemns and exonerates people involved with his psychosis and his recovery, his narratives reflect his illnesses. Each book develops to illustrate how Charlock reached the point that he could begin the narrative we have just read. As such, the novels are what Steve Kellman has called "self-begetting."[1] Except that Charlock is not a writer, and he even has an "abhorrence for ink and paper." He does not tell a tale but offers evidence by which he can be judged. Though he addresses the "gentlemen of the jury," he never specifically mentions his crime.[2]

Understandably, Charlock's narratives reflect on past events. *Tunc* is essentially a complex flashback as he recalls his early days in Athens with the prostitute Io and the seemingly random events that led to his marriage to the daughter of Merlin, founder of an international cartel. The sole purpose of the account is for his own understanding of the circumstances that contributed to his breakdown. *Nunquam* begins with Charlock's awakening in a private sanitarium belonging to the firm and proceeds through his recovery. His marriage is healthy, his foe (also his wife's brother) makes peace, and Charlock heads the Firm. Since all is told by Charlock, we know a great deal about him. But we do not know when he recorded his observations.

Clearly, Charlock narrated *Tunc* between the ending of the action it delineates and the beginning of *Nunquam*. So it had to have been written at one of two times: during Charlock's travels, which seems unlikely since he was on the run from the Firm's agents, or after they found him and checked him into a rubber room. The latter is likely, making *Tunc* the record of Charlock's therapy, his psychiatrist's investigation into the causes of his schizophrenia. *Tunc,* then, is actually a double novel: one purports to be an objective account of events and characters by Charlock and the other a totally subjective account of the development of a psychosis. If we remember Durrell's use of the "great interlinear" commentary of Balthazar to Darley's account of events and characters in *The Alexandria Quartet,* the view here presented of *The Revolt of Aphrodite* makes sense.

My critical self is almost completely gratified and convinced by this reading. However, I sought critical expiation. Talking with Lawrence Durrell in Paris during October of 1984, I found him to be so generous that with scarcely a gritted tooth I told him my theory of the double structure of *Tunc:*

> *Me.* "Well. Is that what you did? Am I right?"
> *LD.* "No. But I like it."

This reaction by Durrell is consistent with the rhetoric he has developed in his fiction. As Durrell said to Marc Alyn, he wanted the reader to read himself in these two novels. Ray Morrison delineated the complex value of such self-knowledge when he examined the gathering cultural darkness in the works:

> Into the mirrored world of *The Revolt of Aphrodite* the reader stares. The ape within stares back. With fright we realize how sleep-ridden and earthbound we have become. Such reminders, Durrell seems to hope, will awaken to a new consciousness of the self. Vision is meant to be exorcism, as it is in all his novels. What verdict the reader delivers about himself is up to him. Whatever the case, it is *"aut tunc aut nunquam"* all over again.[3]

That Ray Morrison finds "exorcism" indicates his interaction with the novels. For him, they heal. Though another reader may have a very different view, such interaction as Morrison's is necessary for a serious reading of Durrell. In fact, the narrators Durrell creates necessitate such interaction. At the end of *The Alexandria Quartet,* we are left to decide if Darley's "Once upon a time . . ." is to become the four novels we have just read. In *Quinx,* with a Sterne-like touch, Durrell gives us five pages to write our own ending to the five novels. Such offers of interaction to readers, however, do not mean that Lawrence Durrell, author, has removed himiself aesthetically, philosophically, and morally from the novels. He is present.

The indicators of Durrell's presence in the novels are so pervasive that one might even refer to them as overcoding, repetition in a vari-

ety of ways for emphasis. Simply in terms of structure, Durrell is present in *Nunquam,* for instance. Since Charlock must act before he can
record, he knows what happens after he departs on a most symbolical
Christmas Eve to destroy the microfilm records of the Firm; he knows
if chaos occurs or if human trust returns to consecrate business deals.
Yet he does not tell us, and we simply know he leaves his house on
his mission. The ending is left open to create suspense and to involve
the reader in the idea of the novel. Yet by leaving the ending open,
Durrell has made his presence as author important because he is
clearly manipulating the plot. Durrell, not Charlock, has a reason to
end *Nunquam* without bringing the plot to closure.

In keeping with the most enduring value of art, Durrell has made
idea—not action—the most important element of his fiction. By the
time *The Revolt of Aphrodite* ends, we should be prepared to examine
the concepts that provide the motives for the characters and that drive
the plot. As is the case with Darley in *The Alexandria Quartet,* so
Charlock compounds the difficulty for the reader working to construct the basic concept. Each narrator convinces us that his sins are
largely ones of omission: an emotionally tepid nature resulting in a
lack of passionate response to others. In the case of Charlock, especially, this emotional reticence has its basis in an attempt to conceal
the inner self, the unconscious, from becoming the subject of conscious inquiry. Charlock has withdrawn from involvement in life by
opting for scientific and sexual dabblings rather than extending himself intellectually and emotionally. The Firm and Benedicta involve
him so intensely in the complexity of life that he becomes very anxious, perhaps paranoid. The process is slow, though, as we realize at
the end of *Tunc* with the death of his son, who seems to be about
ten. As do most of us, Charlock accommodates as long as he can.[4]

Our sympathy with Charlock (and identification with him) increases as he comes to view Julian Pehlevi, Benedicta's brother, as the
cause of all his troubles with his wife. Julian drained Benedicta emotionally during their childhood affair, which for him was an expression of sadism. Castrated by his father because of the affair, Julian's
need to control women increased. Benedicta became the extension of
his will. Enigmatic, changeable, and dangerous, Benedicta literally
lured men to their deaths and found sustenance in an arrogant dismis-
sal of pity, sympathy, and compassion. When she raises the whip to
the representative modern man, Charlock, we flinch and blame Julian
the perverse. By the end of *Tunc,* we understand that Charlock's initial
uneasiness with Benedicta originates not only from his accurate sens-
ing of danger: Julian wants to drain and discard the inventor. Of
equal, perhaps more, importance is Charlock's own uneasiness with

a humanly complex woman. Soon after meeting Benedicta, he finds
her in his dream with the voice of a great bird, "at once tender and
obscene" (*Tunc*, 140). She is a frightening animal from heraldry, a
mixture of odd parts able to mesmerize and wound. In the dream,
Benedicta is the quintessential Great Mother: the seducer of the son
for Freud, the anima for Jung. She has the power of life and death,
being mother, lover, and destroyer. To a very great extent, Charlock
projects this complex and paradoxical role on Benedicta.[5]

Unwilling to consider Benedicta as having an identity and a reality
perhaps different from his projections and his desires, Charlock ap-
proaches her as had Julian: an entity whose reality is only a reflection
of his own. For both men, woman must be malleable and passive or
else she is, as Julian said, a "monstrous androgyne."[6] After years of
therapy, Charlock's Benedicta is completed: a complacent housewife
who passes around the cheese. In response to a friend's concern that
he might not like this quieter version, Felix replies that he is pleased:
"Besides, she's exactly how I wanted her, always imagined her. I almost invented her" (*Nunquam*, 237).[7] Felix, the inventor, follows the
course of Julian. So heavily is Felix's perverse need for control im-
printed that he loses the reader's sympathy. Even when Julian reveals
in *Nunquam* that he had tried to kill Charlock, we cannot respond
with our previous sympathy for a Charlock who can comment about
Julian: "I badly felt the need to insult him, I loved him so much"
(*Nunquam*, 110). As was true for Julian, so is it for Charlock: both
must debase what they love and can only love what they debase. Understandably, both men find fulfillment in carrying their need to shape
and control women to its logical excess: the creation of a robot Io
after the death of the original. Their desire to supplant the creative
power of women with their own mimetic ability dominates their exis-
tences.

Neither man discriminates between the robot and the living Io—or
between her and any other women. When Charlock shows Benedicta
Io recumbent, the robot repeats her original: "'Kiss, Kiss,' she said.
'Felix.' And pursed her red smiling mouth for a kiss which I gave her
while Benedicta looked on in a kind of scandalized amusement mixed
with loathing" (*Nunquam*, 188). The act seems natural to Felix, con-
fusingly so for him as he reveals later on returning home to Benedicta
after a day of working on the new Io:

> It was so natural—Benedicta before the fire reading, with a sleeping kit-
> ten beside her, it was so familiar and so *reliably real* that I was suddenly
> afflicted by almost the same sense of unreality I had had in talking to
> Iolanthe. (*Nunquam*, 284)

Not only does Charlock equate the realities of Io past and present, he equates his wife's reality with theirs: all being reflections of what he believes.

The distinction between Charlock the obtuse and Lawrence Durrell the author is clear from the punishment dealt out in the novels, from the title, from this comment to Marc Alyn, and from his comment to me when I asked about his intent in the two novels: "I wanted to show the terrible treatment women have received in this culture." G. S. Fraser was, also, aware that Durrell used Charlock as a device through which to inform the reader, yet having only *Tunc* to work with, since *Nunquam* was not yet published, he could not estimate the distance Durrell would create between himself and his narrator.[8] Considered as a representative of the culture, Charlock loses the sympathy he had elicited from us when he seemed only the object of Julian's malevolence. The men reflect each other's fears. Terror of a world that does not recognize human constructs impels both men to extreme efforts to control as much of their experience as possible.

The development of character and the unfolding of events that harm the body and humiliate the spirit indicate Durrell's disapproval of the industrial-technical elite that substitutes logic for understanding, innovation for empathy. The death of Julian, locked in the arms of the new Io, serves as a warning to those who would supplant the good that can be with a malevolence approaching pure evil. Yet Durrell is not content to rely solely on character and plot to direct our attention, but provides as well codes that by reference and allusion enforce the view implied.

His most telling references are to the Third Reich. Charlock and his colleague Marchant have their laboratory at Toybrook, which has a striking resemblance to Belsen, as Marchant noted when he saw a picture in a newspaper of the death camp: "a long terrain of old-fashioned potting sheds with the two funnels, like a liner or a soap factory." The resemblance is so incongruous to the two scientists that they laugh loudly at the irony and fail to see the greater irony in Charlock's description of Toybrook:

> But reassuringly enough Toybrook was not in the least like Belsen—quite the contrary, despite the two stout brick towers exuding a lick of white smoke from the ovens in the experimental section. (*Nunquam*, 140–42)

In the experimental section of Toybrook, new methods of embalming are being developed by men for whom humanity is only a mass to be used in furthering the cause of the Firm. In their laboratory, Charlock and Marchant build the *perfect* woman. In *The Avignon Quintet*,

Durrell will continue his censure of the mentality that created the Third Reich, but he will not exceed the intensity of the condemnation expressed here. In fact, the use of Belsen as a code has greater effect than Durrell's depiction of the Third Reich. Human perversity itself is censured, not merely a particular manifestation of it.

We see what happens in *The Revolt of Aphrodite* through the eyes of Charlock, yet that should not restrict our understanding of the characters and events. As Wayne C. Booth said in so many ways, readers have an obligation to evaluate literature as a process that begins with the author and is communicated through a narrator to a reader: "To pass judgment where the author intends neutrality is to misread. But to be neutral where the author requires commitment is equally to misread; though the effect is likely to be less obvious and may even be overlooked except as a fleeting boredom."[9] Durrell, in general, is present in his writings, and we abrogate responsibility if we do not become active participants with him in a moral and aesthetic evaluation of the conditions about which he writes—as expressed in the writings themselves.

In the case at hand, that of Felix Charlock, Durrell has provided us with ample evidence to indicate his own view of the characters and events. Further, he has placed us as readers in a position in which we must evaluate what we are told. Charlock as narrator speaks directly to us, but not as "dear reader," the traditional term for the audience as confidant. Instead, we are addressed as "gentlemen of the jury." In our role as *men* representative of the traditions of western culture, we must decide on Charlock's guilt or innocence. Unfortunately, his crime remains unstated and must be inferred from the evidence he has given in two volumes. We know that he has willfully constricted nature and that he, like Marchant and Julian, regards women as characterized by a "bottomless masochism," needing to be beaten and even raped. This observation Charlock makes directly to us as "gentlemen of the jury" (*Tunc,* 189). Charlock in both novels is driven by a need to control the process of existence to relieve his own anxiety and to make dominant his own view of reality. As insane as that view is, in trying to suborn the process of nature itself, it is the view of his society. Charlock is guilty for reasons of insanity.

## NOTES

1. Steve Kellman, *The Self-Begetting Novel* (New York: Columbia University Press, 19), is largely concerned with the narrator as author preparing to write the novel we are reading. Both Kellman's approach and his examination of Darley in *The Alexandria Quartet* are instructive in explaining Durrell's development of Felix Charlock.

2. Lawrence Durnell, *Tunc* (New York: Penguin Books, 1979), p. 19. Further references will be included in the text.

3. Ray Morrison, "Memory and Light in Lawrence Durrell's *The Revolt of Aphrodite, Labyrs* 5 (July 19): 153.

4. The concurrence of concerns between Jung and Durrell about the psyche are pervasive in *Tunc* and *Nunquam,* as I discussed in my "Paradox and Resolution in Durrell's *Tunc* and *Nunquam,*" *Deus Loci* 7, no. 1 (September 1983): 1–13.

5. Eric Neumann in "Leonardo and the Mother Archetype," *Art and the Creative Unconscious* (New York: Harper and Row, 1966), 3–80, discusses Freud's view of the effect of what both regard as the quintessential woman and his disagreement with Freud's view. Jung's discussion of the "anima" pervades his work, but in *Memories, Dreams, Reflections,* he presents her very much in terms of the traditional Great Mother: he is in awe of her powers.

6. Lawrence Durrell, *Nunquam* (New York: Penguin Books, 1979), p. 46. Further references will be included in the text.

7. As James R. Nichols noted, Durrell presents all "corporate structures," religious or secular, as forcing life to atrophy into static infertility, as happens with Benedicta. See Nichols's "Sunshine Dialogues: Christianity and Paganism in the Works of Lawrence Durrell," in *On Miracle Ground II: Second International Lawrence Durrell Conference Proceedings,* ed. Lawrence W. Markert and Carol Peirce (Baltimore: University of Baltimore Press, 1984), 129–33.

8. G. S. Fraser, *Lawrence Durrell: A Critical Study* (New York: Dutton, 1968), 172.

9. Wayne C. Booth, *The Rhetoric of Fiction* (Chicago: University of Chicago Press, 1983), 152.

# "The True Birth of Free Man": Culture and Civilization in *Tunc-Nunquam*

## Donald P. Kaczvinsky

G. S. Fraser, in his revised edition of *Lawrence Durrell: A Study,* justifies his disappointing explication of *Tunc-Nunquam* in his earlier edition by openly admitting his confusion over the "real problem" with these companion novels: "I had, as it were, various bits of the jigsaw in my hand but could not quite fit them together. I fell back on plot summary, summarizing, as Rayner Heppenstall noted, at inordinate length: fell back on this because I had not solved the real problem about *Tunc-Nunquam,* which is not a problem about its themes, but about the kind of book it is."[1] Fraser suggests that he originally thought *Tunc-Nunquam* was a "philosophic romance, like Mary Shelley's *Frankenstein* or Godwin's *Adventures of Caleb Williams,* in which an improbable but thrilling story is used for the expression of important ideas, and in which, though the characters are in some sense simplified, we are meant to share their fears and their passions."[2] In the revised edition, he is not quite so sure that the novels are a philosophic romance and makes a case for the novels as comic satire. At the end of his discourse, however, he admits to his uncertainty about this theory as well and, by the end, throws up his hands, condemning *Tunc-Nunquam* as "not a failure," but also not a work he will read again often.[3] But Fraser already had the answer to the "real problem" of *Tunc-Nunquam;* he simply chose the wrong books for comparison.

In *Clea,* the fourth book of *The Alexandria Quartet,* there is a chapter entitled "My Conversations with Brother Ass (being extracts from Pursewarden's Notebook)." Here Pursewarden speaks of his profession of writing and of his relationship with Darley, a fellow writer and the narrator of the novel. More important, he talks of the possibilities for civilization in the twentieth century, especially as heirs to the vision set forth in D. H. Lawrence's own philosophic romance, "The Man Who Died":

Yet in "The Man Who Died" he tells us plainly what must be, what the reawakening of Jesus should have meant—the true birth of free man. Where is he? What has happened to him? Will he ever come?[4]

Although these questions are never fully answered in the *Quartet,* they provide a helpful context—in E. D. Hirsch's terms, "a structure of expectations"[5]—by which we can interpret and understand *Tunc-Nunquam.* In fact, *Tunc-Nunquam* is an extension and expansion of Lawrence's short story and attempts to give Durrell's answer to what happened to "the true birth of free man."

1

To begin, we should clarify the difference between "culture" and "civilization," which we will use in the following argument. A discussion in *Nunquam* between Felix and Julian on just this subject can help. We must be wary, however, for Julian as head of the Firm is trying to persuade Felix of the validity of contractual relationships for modern man. Julian's terms later in the discussion, his metaphors for culture and civilization, change in order to suit his purposes. Yet his early remarks as he works out his theory provide a useful path to our goal if we tread carefully:

"The firm itself, Merlin's firm," he uttered the proper name with a profound, a sad bitterness, "what is it exactly? It isn't just a loosely linked association of enterprises coordinated under one name; its very size (like a blown-up photograph) enables us to see that it is the reflection of something, the copy of something. Though on one plane you might consider it a money-making contrivance, the very terms under which it operates reflect the basic predispositions of the culture of which it is only an offshoot. . . .

"It doesn't seem possible to break either the mold of the firm or the mold of ourselves as associates or even hirelings (you might think) of the thing."[6]

From these few hints a definition of "culture" and "civilization" may be formulated. Culture is the "mold of ourselves" as understood by a particular people or nation. Civilization, on the other hand, is the "offshoot" of culture as manifested in the association of human beings in the society. Every civilization springs forth organically from the culture peculiar to it. D. H. Lawrence and Lawrence Durrell conceive of man as essentially instinctual and sexual in nature. Therefore, for both authors, in a "healthy" civilization, social relationship should be based on man's physical and sexual life.

D. H. Lawrence's two "psychoanalytic" studies, *Fantasia of the Unconscious* and *Psychoanalysis and the Unconscious,* attempt to work out theoretically (rather than imaginatively) what has gone wrong with modern civilization. Sometimes inconsistent, Lawrence's two books explore the growth and development of the human psyche from conception to death. Basically, for Lawrence, maturation comes through the constant interaction of vital forces within the individual and the outside world, the self and the other. Before adolescence the child's life forces are concentrated in four centers of nerve clusters located at the back and front of the individual near the chest and belly region; the primary means of contact with the world is through the parents. Although physical, this contact is in no way sexual for Lawrence.

Moreover, the child needs a physical connection not just with the mother but the father as well. "But if the child thus seeks the mother, does it then know the mother alone? To an infant the mother is the whole universe. Yet the child needs more than the mother. It needs as well the presence of men, the vibration from the present body of the man. There may not be any actual, palpable connection. But from the great voluntary centre in the man pass unknowable communications and untellable nourishment of the stream of manly blood, rays which we cannot see, and which so far we have refused to know, but none the less essential, quickening dark rays which pass from the great dark abdominal life-centre in the father to the corresponding centre in the child."[7] With the coming of adolescence new centers of consciousness develop, the sexual centers. The individual breaks with the parents, and the interaction with the outside world becomes concentrated in the girlfriend and eventually a male friend as well.

All sorts of things can go wrong with the process of psychic development. Primarily, Lawrence finds in the twentieth century the mother's idealization of the child as the greatest threat to a boy's growth and conception of himself. Since the woman has lost all hope of satisfaction in the man, she tries to find fulfillment in her son. The father loses all vital contact with his son, and the mother protects and dotes on the boy. This results in the premature development of the sex-centers in the child and the incestuous desire for the mother. A vicious circle ensues. The boy desires sexual satisfaction with his mother. Yet this incestuous desire is also "mentally" repulsive to him, so that he represses his desire and eventually becomes a sexual and psychological cripple. When he grows up, his wife then turns to her son for fulfillment and the process starts all over again. Obviously, Lawrence has

*Sons and Lovers* very much in the back of his mind as he works out his theories. Importantly, Lawrence's conception of sex is not narrowly defined by the act of intercourse but extends to all man's instinctual or biological needs. Man's instincts, his "unconscious," must be the source for all living relationships, and his physical health will be the measure of his psychic "health."

For D. H. Lawrence, art records the vital, "instinctual" life of a people. We may remember the ship of death and the murals he praised so highly in his trip to the Etruscan tombs. A better medium, however, is the novel itself. The novel (which, for Lawrence, is simply any work of literature that communicates man's "whole self" and is not restricted to academic definitions of genre) is not only the supremely artistic creation but a Bible for living. As Lawrence says in his essay "Why the Novel Matters":

> To be alive, to be man alive, to be whole man alive: that is the point. And at its best, the novel, and the novel supremely, can help you. It can help you not to be dead man in life. So much of a man walks about dead and a carcass in the street and house, today: so much of women is merely dead. Like a pianoforte with half the notes mute.[8]

Although Lawrence may find his greatest expression in the short story, the expansiveness and comprehensiveness of the novel are necessary for his larger ends. Through his novels, Lawrence believes he can set man on the track to building a better society.

Durrell's conception of the "healthy" society proceeds along a similar line. Although not as fully developed as Lawrence's, Durrell's various comments about culture and civilization give enough of a clue for us to understand his vision. Like Lawrence, Durrell bases any theory of society, any theory on the individual's relationship or understanding of the world, on man's physical life. In a passage from "My Conversations with Brother Ass," Pursewarden most fully develops Durrell's theory of a "healthy" culture when he suggests that all aspects of man's thought must ultimately derive from his sexual life. "Yes, to extend the range of physical sensuality to embrace mathematics and theology: to nourish not to stunt the intuitions. For culture means sex, the root-knowledge, and where the faculty is derailed or crippled, its derivatives like religion come up dwarfed or contorted— instead of the emblematic mystic rose you get Judaic cauliflowers like Mormons or Vegetarians, instead of artists you get cry-babies, instead of philosophy semantics."[9]

Like Lawrence, Durrell has a broader meaning for sex than copulation (even the act of breathing is sexual in nature), though in the act of sexual intercourse man's instinctual needs find their greatest, most perfect expression. And all aspects of man's life, his entire understanding of the world, must be based on his bodily functions. Unlike Lawrence, however, Durrell sees man's physical life as only a beginning (though a necessary beginning) to a higher spiritual existence. Physical happiness engenders spiritual happiness; out of sexual togetherness comes the "marriage of true minds" that is love. In an interview with Kenneth Young, Durrell stresses his major difference with Lawrence: "Underneath it [Lawrence's 'blood knowledge'] I discern another attempt to foist on us Rousseau's 'Noble Savage.' My notion of the affective flow is upwards, a notion I have borrowed from the Hindus. Lawrence cuts the tree down, and emphasises only the dark roots; I would like the tree to blossom the other way round."[10] The proper expression of man's instincts is the first step toward spiritual happiness and is the solidest foundation upon which civilization can be built.

Durrell's conception of art and especially the novel is similar to Lawrence's: art is the product of culture, the record of his "whole self." As hinted in the passage from "Conversations," Durrell conceives of all citizens in a community as essentially artists, all objects made by man for that community as art, and all theories that dominate a discipline or field—whether it be science, economics, or theology—as aesthetic theories. An "unhealthy" culture produces bad art and bad theories; a "healthy" culture produces good art and good theories. Durrell, like Lawrence, believes art has a purpose other than the rendering of created form and rejects the theories of Wilde and the decadents of the nineteenth century. Art, for Durrell, serves some immediate practical function: it is a guide for "moral" behavior, presenting values by which man can live.[11]

To understand the practical value of art for man, it might be best to consider not literature, but architecture. Both Lawrence and Durrell speak admiringly of architecture and architects, and characters in their novels often see the building of monuments, houses, or dwellings as the quintessentially creative act.[12] Immediately we think of Anna and Will Brangwen's discourse on Lincoln Cathedral in *The Rainbow*. Yet Lawrence's characters never quite give as extensive a discourse on the significance of architecture as Caradoc, in *Tunc*, does in his drunken speech on the steps of the Parthenon.

Here Caradoc, the preeminent architect of the day, proposes that architecture had its beginning in man's universal desire for immortality.[13] Ancient man's conception of the afterlife, however, was based upon his life on earth. So, recognizing the body as a temple of the "living" soul, he built tombs to house the souls of the dead. "The first house, the tomb became the outer casing for the dead soul, just as the first house proper (its windows breathing like lungs) was a case for man—as indeed his mother's body had been a case to house the water-rocked embryo."[14] The "new temples" of the Greeks retained this original idea, for symbolically, the exterior of Greek temples represents the physical structure of the human body, as seen in the Parthenon and the temple of Diana.

The workmen on such temples, Caradoc suggests, had no way to remember the dimensions of the buildings they wished to imitate but knew a man's height was six times the length of his foot and a woman's height was eight times the length of her foot. They therefore built the columns of the Parthenon (male) and the temple of Diana (female) six and eight times as high as their base diameters, respectively.[15] Furthermore, on the capitals of the female columns they "introduced snails which hung down to right and left like artificially curled locks; on the forehead they graved rolls and bunches of fruit for hair, and then down the shaft they made slim grooves to resemble the folds in female attire" (*Tunc*, 86). Surrounded by such monuments of art, then, man is kept in touch with his physical self and learns how to live.

For both Lawrence and Durrell, man has become too cerebral: civilization has been organized on cultural premises that disregard man's "biological" needs. For Lawrence, western civilization has been erected on theories that spring from and promote the mind rather than the body. Durrell accepts this, but in *Tunc-Nunquam*, he narrows the focus of his attack: capitalism is the prevalent theory of modern civilization. Man, in such a civilization, conceives of himself primarily as a commodity. Therefore, human relationships are based solely on profit and gain and utilitarian self-interest. The difference between what modern civilization offers and what Durrell envisions for man can be most dramatically seen by contrasting Julian's discussion of the Firm—taken from his talk with Felix cited earlier—and Durrell's discussion of civilization in his Postface to the same novel.

Julian says to Felix in *Nunquam* that civilization is like a chain in which the weakest link is the legal and economic relationship between human beings, "'the fragile link of association of one with another, articles of faith, contracts, marriages, vows and so on'" (98). When this relationship is broken, "the primordial darkness leaks in": civilization disintegrates into chaos. For Durrell, however, civilization is not so much a chain, but a building, (again the architectural metaphor) of which the "basic brick," the very material out of which it is constructed, is "the human couple": the sexual relationship between man and woman. Once this becomes weakened or perverted the civilization topples in on itself. Durrell agrees completely with Lawrence in his conception, as seen in the depiction of Clifford Chatterley in *Lady Chatterley's Lover,* or Gerald Crich in *Women in Love,* that capitalism is the preoccupation of those modern men who have lost contact with their instinctual life.

For our purposes here, Lawrence's and Durrell's thinking should be distinguished in two other ways. First, though both fight science and technology as expressed in a Newtonian construct of the universe, Durrell is quite open to modern scientific theories, especially Einstein's theories, where the scientist proceeds from images rather than mental calculations. The epigram for *Tunc,* appropriately, is *"Deux fois deux quatre, c'est un mur."* Felix Charlock himself, the hero of *Tunc-Nunquam,* is a scientist whose inventions can be quite beneficial to man. Unfortunately, scientists and their inventions are easily manipulated by the capitalists: Felix, for instance, is bought by Julian and the Firm. Because of this, the inventions scientists create are used for the wrong purposes: technology is used to make money or to control, rather than to free, people. Lawrence sees science as much more a threat to man's living instinctually, rejecting all science's conclusions about the nature of the universe outright in the face of his own hylozoism (the sun is not a ball of gas but a soul).

Second, though both authors depict an extremely violent world, Durrell finds that man can only be at peace with himself when he acts with charity, sympathy, and goodwill toward his fellow man. These qualities, for Durrell, are inherent in man's biological makeup. Tenderness, genuine human consideration, is a vital part of man's sexual life. When Felix comes to Julian to tell him that he is going to give one of his inventions away, he bases his charity on a biological need: "'I have simply come to a point where I must make a gesture, even the feeblest of gestures, to continue breathing'" (*Tunc,* 323). Julian utterly dismisses Felix's proposal as against all the Firm stands for. Indeed, Julian's pronouncement ultimately condemns him and the civlization he represents, for it denies man's basic needs.

Lawrence, fighting the moral codes of Victorian England, often overstates his case and sees good only in the violent expression of love or hate. Although Lawrence intended that *Lady's Chatterley's Lover* be titled *Tenderness,* he felt that sympathy, love, and charity were the debilitating values of a dead age and religion: the products of the mind, not the "unconscious." When Lawrence looked within, he saw only a seething energy. In *Fantasia,* Lawrence writes, "No, there is substitute for everything—life substitute—just as we have butter-substitute, and meat-substitute, and sugar-substitute, and leather-substitute, so we have life-substitute. We have beastly benevolence, and foul good will, and stinking charity, and poisonous ideals."[16] We could not conceive of Durrell making any such statement.

## 2

In "The Man Who Died" Lawrence offers his most concise view for the future of western civilization by reinterpreting the death and resurrection of Christ. Jesus, representing modern man and the western tradition, is the intellectual, spiritual male who has forgotten about his instinctual life. When the story begins, it is Easter morning, and Christ awakens in the sepulchre after his crucifixion by the Romans. In the story Christ realizes that he was taken down from the cross too soon and has a quite natural resurrection. He also recognizes that something has been missing from his earlier preaching: namely, a life rooted in the physical world. Christ says to himself as he wanders through the countryside: "And perhaps one evening, I shall meet a woman who can lure my risen body, yet leave me my aloneness. For the body of my desire has died, and I am not in touch anywhere."[17] Finally, Jesus comes to Egypt where he meets the priestess of Isis in Search, who realizes Jesus is the Osiris she has sought, and eventually the priestess becomes pregnant. Jesus, however, fearing that the slaves of the priestess's mother will betray him to the Romans, escapes one evening by rowboat. The story ends optimistically, though, for as Jesus rows away he sees hope for a new civilization in the mystical union with the woman. "So let the boat carry me. Tomorrow is another day."[18] It is a paradigm of the Lawrencian short story.

Durrell takes the main characters of "The Man Who Died" and transforms them in *Tunc* to critique Lawrence's solution to the cultural crisis. Now Felix is "the man who died" and is, like Lawrence's Christ, the "intellectual," spiritual male—"the thinking weed" as he himself states—who requires sexual fulfillment to attain happiness. Yet Durrell's novel constantly attempts to point out the simplicity and superficiality of Lawrence's plot resolutions. Where Christ could simply escape from the Romans to some remote part of the world and find sexual fulfillment in the priestess who will have his child (symbolizing the birth of a "healthy" civilization after the inevitable destruction of the old Europe), Durrell offers Felix no such easy solution. In fact, the unified personality of the priestess has split into two distinct women, Iolanthe and Benedicta. Where the priestess had "dun blond" hair, Iolanthe has dark hair and Benedicta has blond. Benedicta, who is the daughter of Merlin (the founder of the Firm) and the sister of Jocas and Julian, is associated with modern civilization. The sexuality associated with Benedicta and the Firm is perverse, incestuous, manipulative. Julian himself has been castrated, and Benedicta tells Felix later in *Nunquam* that her father, Merlin, had her "sexually broken" by his slaves. In fact, she only marries Felix because the marriage contract ties him to the Firm as well. Iolanthe, on the other hand, with her deeply rooted sensuality, kindness, and genuine concern for Felix, is associated with a "healthy" culture. Yet both women have their attractions for Felix: Benedicta can provide him with position, money, and a family; Iolanthe can provide a satisfying "sex" life and a caring companion. Felix's choice is much more difficult than Jesus' because in either case he loses something.

The influence of Lawrence's short story on Durrell's novel goes much deeper than simply the borrowing and transformation of characters, however. The two works have parallel endings (unusual enough in themselves so that the source is unmistakable) that link them both structurally and thematically. Just as Christ escapes by rowing out into the Mediterranean at the end of "The Man Who Died," Felix escapes the Firm by rowing out into the Mediterranean at the end of *Tunc*. Julian's name and the worldwide dominance of the Firm are naturally associated with Julius Caesar and the Roman Empire. But civilization is a much more dominant force in Durrell's work simply because it has the ability through modern technology to find and destroy those who question or refuse to conform to its own standards. Iolathe, herself the symbol of a healthy sexuality and culture, dies in *Tunc* from the liquid paraffin she has injected in her breasts. Yet these injections are the only way she can maintain her "freedom" and status as a movie star as well as control of her own film company. She tries to maintain a "healthy" cultural life in modern civilization and necessarily dies for it. The futility of rebellion is further underscored when Mark, the son of Felix and Benedicta, fianlly decides not to cooperate with Julian: his only choice is to commit suicide, discharging the shotgun built into the computer Abel upon himself. Open defiance is not a viable solution for the emergence of a new culture and brings only death to those who attempt it.

The outcome of Felix's escape, then, has been adumbrated before the opening of *Nunquam*. Indeed, at the end of *Tunc*, Julian talks to Nash about Felix's disappearance and betrays some suspicions of Felix's death. It serves, too, as Durrell's commentary on Lawrence's conclusion to "The Man Who Died":

"Presumption of death isn't quite the same thing. Without a body to show for it. You need as much body to die as to live. In the case of Charlock—we will have to wait upon the evidence. At any rate the Mediterranean always gives up its bodies. I think we'll find him, if he is to be found. It's only a matter of waiting awhile." (*Tunc*, 354)

What Durrell is suggesting here is that Lawrence's diagnosis for what was wrong with civilization was right, but his plan for the rebirth of a "healthy" culture and civilization was naïve. Felix could have rowed away or had a short, romantic affair with Iolanthe, but neither of these could be permanent solutions to the rebirth of a "healthy" culture. (Benedicta tells him of the plot against his life when he is recovering in the Paulhaus.) Jesus found out that simply running away was impossible: he would either die or be found again by the Romans. In the interval between *Tunc* and *Nunquam*, Felix has been captured and placed in the hospital or Paulhaus and surgically operated on, so that he becomes a passive, almost docile, member of the Firm.

*Nunquam* is the story of what has happened to Christ, the "free man," after 1925. The intellectual, or "spiritual" male rejoined civilization—even if involuntarily—and became an active participant in its daily life. This is not to say that Europe and the West since Lawrence have given up the possibility for a "healthy" culture and civilization. Indeed modern civilization has constantly tried to associate itself with the "products" of a healthy culture. This is most obviously seen when the Firm tries to hold an impressionist exhibit at the London airport, where on one side of the concourse the paintings are displayed, while on the opposite wall are the "specimens of Merlin's choicest products."

In fact, modern civilization is in love with a "healthy" culture, as symbolized in Julian's love for Iolanthe. As has been suggested, however, a "healthy" culture cannot survive long in an "unhealthy" environment. When Julian has Felix rebuild Iolanthe, she turns against Julian and in the magnificent scene at the end of *Nunquam* commits suicide, jumping off the balustrade in St. Paul's cathedral, taking Julian with her: "They fell together into the echoing nave; in a wild and shattering moment of vision I saw them flatten out like arrows as they fell" (315–16). In a sense, then, given its opportunity a "healthy" culture would destroy modern civilization, but it is simply not a strong enough force. Julian's death has been only a minor setback to the continuation of the Firm. Where Lawrence felt that modern civilization was about to destroy itself, Durrell, from his mid-century perspective, realizes that modern civilization, left to its own devices, will endure.[19]

In order to change the civilization, in order to create great and enduring art once again, all men in the society, from those at the top of
the social scale to those at the bottom, must change how they conceive
of themselves. "It's always now or never," says Durrell, "since we are
human and enjoy the fatality of choice."

After the death of Julian, however, a unique situation arises in the
history of modern civilization, which contains hope for the rebirth
of a "healthy" culture in the West. The man in charge of the society
is the very person who has questioned and challenged the beliefs of
the Firm.[20] Christ is now in a position of power as the leader of the
society he rejected and hoped would be destroyed. Felix has become
the Firm's corporate head:

> You will see now why I had to bring all this up-to-date, in order straighten
> the record—for now the whole responsibility of the firm has fallen on my
> shoulders. These last weeks have been full of boardroom conferences,
> votes of confidence, resolutions, and so on. I have not hesitated to shoul-
> der the burden for the vanished Julian and Jocas. Outwardly, nothing
> much has changed—or else I went through everything in a sort of dream.
> (*Nunquam*, 317)

Durrell again sees it as a time for the "intellectual" male to make
a choice. Indeed, Felix at the end of *Nunquam* is about to burn the
microfilm archives that house all the contracts of the Firm. Felix hopes
that the conflagration will effectively destroy the Firm from within
and bring about the reemergence of a new society where human relationships are based on biology rather than contracts. Appropriately,
this will be done on Christmas Eve. "And we will keep on this way,
dancing and dancing," states Felix, "even though Rome burn" (*Nunquam*, 318). This is a much more feasible solution, because it does
not rely on the theoretical and natural evolution of civilization but
rather on the active participation of the men of culture.

Yet the results of the fire remain teasingly ambiguous. Durrell does
not want to give any pat answers to man's cultural crisis, nor does
he want to give any certain predictions for the future. Durrell, unlike
Lawrence in his philosophic romance, does not see himself as a
prophet for a new age but as an artist presenting the pain and human
sacrifice inherent in any struggle for a "healthy," satisfying life. There
is the suggestion, in fact, that, out of the rubble, Rome will be built
up in its old form once again. Baum, speaking for the author, states
his reservations about a new culture taking hold of the society. "'People will be afraid to take advantage of the fact that they have no contractual written obligations. They may stay put from funk or . . .'"

(*Nunquam*, 318).[21] For Durrell, we are at the very point of being able to begin anew, to destroy the old worn civilization and build on new cultural grounds. But whether we will do it and whether we have the spiritual strength to live communally after the old bonds have been broken is finally left, as it should be left, for the reader to decide.

## NOTES

1. G. S. Fraser, *Lawrence Durrell: A Study,* rev. ed. with a bibliography by Alan G. Thomas (London: Faber and Faber, 1973), 151.
2. Ibid., 151.
3. Ibid., 167.
4. Lawrence Durrell, *Clea* (New York: E. P. Dutton, 1962), 141.
5. E. D. Hirsch, *Validity in Interpretation* (New Haven: Yale University Press, 1967), 168.
6. Lawrence Durrell, *Nunquam* (New York: Penguin Books, 1979), 93–94. All subsequent references to this work will be cited by page numbers in parentheses after the passage.
7. D. H. Lawrence, *Fantasia of the Unconscious* and *Psychoanalysis and the Unconscious,* (New York: Penguin Books, 1977), 32–33.
8. D. H. Lawrence, "Why the Novel Matters," in *Phoenix,* ed. Edward D. McDonald (New York: Penguin Books, 1980), 537–38.
9. Durrell, *Clea,* 140–41.
10. Kenneth Young, "Dialogue with Durrell," *Encounter* 13, no. 6 (December 1959): 62.
11. In an interview with Joan Goulianos, "A Conversation with Lawrence Durrell about Art, Analysis, and Politics," *Modern Fiction Studies* 17, no. 2, Durrell underscores this point:

*You make a distinction between the role of the artist and the role of the citizen?*

Not really. The position is that good politics should come out of values, and the artist is busy with values not with politics. In an ideal arrangement, the artist could get on with forging the values, out of which good policy would flow. But it's fatal for him to lose himself on day to day stuff. It's simply distraction from his real job. (161)

12. In the Goulianos interview, just after the passage cited above, Durrell points out that a "healthy" culture is most easily discerned by its architecture, "because architecture takes time, and unless one has the comfortable feeling of inheritance and succession, the feeling that one has years ahead of one to build a church or a tomb or a mausoleum, one doesn't embark on it. So the best building usually represents the most harmonious and developed cultures" (Ibid., 170).
13. For a somewhat different approach to the architectural theories of *Tunc-Nunquam,* see Gregory Dickson's "Spengler's Theory of Architecture in Durrell's *Tunc* and *Nunquam,*" in Special Issue No. 1, *Deus Loci: The Lawrence Durrell Newsletter* 5 (Fall 1981): 272–84.
14. Lawrence Durrell, *Tunc* (New York: Penguin Books, 1979), 85. All subsequent references to this book will be cited by page numbers in parentheses after the passage.

15. The ideas and many of the words for Caradoc's speech are taken from Vitruvius's book on the civil architecture of the ancients, section 2, "Of the Three Orders of Columns, Their Origin, and the Proportion of the Corinthian Capitol." In *The Greek Islands* (New York: Viking Press, 1978), Durrell presents this same theory almost word for word in two quotations from Vitruvius. After the quotations, Durrell writes: "If some scholars doubt the authenticity of all this, it is at least highly suggestive, and useful to bear in mind when looking at Greek work" (225).

16. Lawrence, *Fantasia*, 143.

17. D. H. Lawrence, *St. Mawr and The Man Who Died* (1928; reprint, New York: Vintage Books, n.d.), 182.

18. Ibid., 211.

19. Lawrence W. Markert, in "'The Pure and Sacred Readjustment of Death': Connections between Lawrence Durrell's *Avignon Quintet* and the Writings of D. H. Lawrence," Lawrence Durrell Issue, pt. 2, *Twentieth Century Literature* 33, no. 4 (Winter 1987): 550–64, traces the theme of the "death drift" in modern civilization in Lawrence and Durrell. Both authors, Markert suggests, accept the inevitable destruction of civilization, but view it as a time for rebirth. But Durrell, in *Nunquam*, questions the inevitable destruction of our materialistic society and proposes instead that civilization's demise is a matter of individual choice rather than inevitability: we will go on the old way unless we, as citizens, decide not to.

20. Durrell, like Lawrence, sees the future of society determined solely by men. Men can and should incorporate the female virtues of feeling and intuition into their own being, but women do not seem capable, in either author, of taking charge of social, political, or cultural institutions.

21. J. R. Morrison, in "Memory and Light in Lawrence Durrell's *The Revolt of Aphrodite*," *Labyrs* 4 (1979): 141–53, and Tone Rugset, in *"Tunc-Nunquam:* The Quest for Wholeness," *Labyrs* 5 (1979): 155–62, see the ending of *Tunc-Nunquam* as affirmative and optimistic in tone. Both critics cite the burning of the archives as the great sign of hope, but neither considers Baum's reservations on the viability of a "new" culture.

# Part 3
# Myth, Mystery, and Dirty Tricks

# The Mystery of the Templars in
## *The Avignon Quintet*

### Michael H. Begnal

On that unlucky day, Friday the thirteenth of October in 1307, the Christian world was shocked by the arrests of all the Knights Templar in France. By order of Phillippe le Bel, king of France,[1] warrants for the arrest of probably the mightiest group then extant in all Christendom were delivered by the king's deputy Guillaume de Nogaret, and thus begins one of the strangest and most mysterious series of events in medieval history. Arguments continue to rage to this day over the guilt or innocence of the Templars,[2] and just what these knights were, or what they hoped to be, provides a central thematic consideration of Lawrence Durrell's *The Avignon Quintet*. Durrell obviously has his own view of the exact nature of the Templar heresy, or the lack of it, and it is my contention that the Order is to be resurrected in the pages of his quincunx novels. But, before looking to Durrell, it is important to understand what exactly were the charges brought against the knights.

It has never been quite clear why the Templars, a fighting force to be reckoned with, surrendered so easily, without a murmur, but the crimes attributed to them, and to which many of them confessed, sound like a scenario concocted by the Marquis de Sade. It was said that during their induction into the order they denied Christ three times, and then spat or urinated upon the crucifix. As part of the ceremony, they were to kiss their inductor upon the lips, navel, penis, and anus, and thereafter they were to engage freely in sodomy with their brother knights. During the Mass, they left out the words of consecration, and they could be absolved of any sin by their confessors. Even more bizarrely, they supposedly worshiped an idol, a head they called Baphomet, which was occasionally anointed with the fat left over from their roasting of their own illegitimate babies. Where they found the time for female concubines is not known. Whether this head was a replica of Mahomet (one theory being that the Templars were corrupted by Islam in their wars to free the Holy Land), or something connected with the secret rites of the gnostic ophites, or even a female head involved with some sort of lascivious revel, we cannot say, but heads of many sorts circulate freely through the *Quintet*.

Many of the knights confessed to some or to all of these crimes, later retracted their admissions, and again later confessed once more. Torture was used unremittingly on virtually all of the captives, and the king was intent upon their conviction. Curiously, though Phillippe and de Nogaret searched ardently through each of the chapter's temples, nothing remotely resembling a head or an idol was to be found. Just the same, it seems that the speculation will never cease, and a recent commentator, Stephen Howarth, before turning to yet another solution to the problem of the head, notes some of the more fantastic general conjectures. The Templars brought both chess and Gothic architecture to Europe—Christopher Columbus was a Templar—and the original band of Templars discovered, and may have hidden, the Ark of the Covenant. Dismissing these ideas as poppycock, he asserts that: "the Templars did possess a picture of a head, a picture which they believed had magical powers, and which they guarded with the utmost secrecy and security."[3] This picture, he intones solemnly, finally letting us in on his discovery, exists today as the Shroud of Turin.

On something of a more mundane level, it has been proposed that the sin of the Templars, the greatest banking institution of the time, was that of usury. It was said that they lined their pockets with the interest gained from lending out portions of their huge fortune, so that Phillippe le Bel, whether in righteous indignation or outright greed, was ultimately justified in bringing the order to its knees. A final, even more fascinating thesis is that the Templars were attacked because they had become adherents of gnosticism.[4]

This possibility is the bedrock upon which Toby's scholarly study rests in *Monsieur:* "there was in fact a Templar heresy, contracted perhaps in the Orient, which, on religious grounds, and from the narrowest Christian viewpoint, justified their total destruction. While they were *outremer* in the service of the Cross they became contaminated with the secret gnostic beliefs which coloured their notions of good and evil and which qualified their allegiance to the pope and Christendom."[5] In Akkad's view, there could be no possibility that the church would not react: "'Their adherents could not bring themselves to face the bitter central truth of the gnostics: the horrifying realisation that the world of the Good God was a dead one, and that He had been replaced by a usurper—a God of Evil" (*M*, 139).

Earlier, in *Tunc* and *Nunquam,* or *The Revolt of Aphrodite,* Durrell had come face to face with a world that celebrated film stars over the

Parthenon, that saw beauty in a mechanical dummy rather than in living flesh. In regard to culture, with a God of materialism firmly ensconced upon the throne, perhaps it might be best to cut one's losses and to salvage whatever that is left that is still valuable. Durrell is pragmatic rather than pessimistic here, and the problem becomes one of preserving individual insight in the midst of public indifference. In the *Quintet*, the Templar controversy and its ramifications serve as a metaphor with which Durrell attempts to structure the chaos of the past and present, and to point a way into the future. Lawrence Durrell is an artist, not a historian, and he is concerned with what will happen next much more than with what exactly happened then.

Durrell springs many of these themes upon an unsuspecting reader in the first section of *Monsieur,* suggestively titled "Outremer." Here Bruce Drexel is one of the last Templars, an exile returning home from the hinterlands to attend the funeral of his friend Piers de Nogaret, the final male descendant of the same de Nogaret who betrayed the order in the fourteenth century. Piers, whether or not he was decapitated in a ritualistic, gnostic suicide, "was a worshipper of the Templar God. He believed in the usurper of the throne, the Prince of Darkness" (*M*, 25). The following section, "Macabru," is a flashback that describes Piers's conversion to gnosticism under Akkad's tutelage, culminating in the appearance of Ophis the cobra. Toby the historian will later say of the heads or idols that the Templars supposedly revered that "their origin was probably ophite" (*M*, 253), the worship of the snake. Durrell is describing a contemporary order of gnostic Templars and a new Baphomet, but not all of the characters are taken in.

Bruce remains unconvinced, and Toby recoils in horror. Says Akkad sympathetically, " 'You saw something that looked like a brass rubbing from an English cathedral—the tomb of the Black Prince in somewhere like Canterbury. The vizor of the helmet was up, and you got scared when you stared into the black hole of the armoured head because you thought you saw the glitter of snake-eyes where the face should have been' " (*M*, 130). The problem for these modern-day seekers or pilgrims is to avoid or transcend the malevolent gaze of a twentieth-century world that will culminate in the horror of the Second World War. On one level, what Toby has seen is the face of outright evil, and Akkad will underline the connection between Satan and the horrific head: " 'You will say that we only imagine this depressing locum tenens: that he is a sort of carnival head, a totem head like the ones the Templars are supposed to have set up to replace the cross' " (*M*, 224). But Akkad knows better, and suddenly the fourteenth and the twentieth centuries have become one.

What lies at the center of *The Avignon Quintet,* rising anew out of the ruin of the Templars, are two separate and mutually exclusive quests: the material search for what might remain of the undiscovered Templar treasure, and the spiritual seeking for meaning in a world that seems to have gone mad. It is this first obsession that impells Lord Galen, the Prince, and Smirgel the Nazi to scour the countryside around Avignon for the monetary burial ground, intent upon continuing the insane, pecuniary whirl of gain that is immolating the very roots of civilized culture.

The cult of the worship of the head of Baphomet has been resurrected in all its ghoulish grotesquerie by these knights of the Treasury, and in *Constance* the Prince has a surprise for Aubrey Blanford: "He produced a large scarlet velvet-covered hatbox, the kind a conjuror might carry about, or an actor. It was a sort of oriental wig-box, in fact, but inside it there was a shrunken human head, a male head, coated heavily in resin but with the eyes open. . . . the Prince chuckled appreciatively at his reaction. 'It's the head of a Templar; it comes from the commanderie in Cyprus'" (*C,* 14). It is not long before Hitler himself is involved in the game, but, as Smirgel confides to Constance, the German leader is desirous of something else. "'It was not money or specie he thought himself hunting. . . . This is what interests our Fuhrer, a lost tradition of chivalry which he wishes to reendow and make a base for a new European model of knighthood. But of a black order, not white'" (*C,* 235).

In a more humorous vein, the debasement of both sexuality and Christianity in the modern world is demonstrated by the appearance of yet another disembodied head in Lord Galen's debauch at the whorehouse of the aptly named Mrs. Gilchrist. It seems that Galen has an inclination to be sexually crucified, and the resident young women comply with this travesty by stripping him naked and lashing his limbs to the bedposts. Stripped of his garments, except for the old Etonian tie attached to his penis to which a passing prostitute might "give a tug, crying out 'Ding-Ding!' in the accents of a passing tram" (*S,* 139), Galen's body is covered from head to toe with pictures and graffiti written in lipstick. At the height of the revels, the bed collapses, and Galen is taken down from his cross in state by the prostitutes. "Now they carried the crucified and exterminated one to a nearby sofa and laid him out in vaguely ceremonial fashion, piling cushion upon cushion on him, and leaving only his grotesquely decorated head to stick out—it was like burying a Red Indian totem pole" (*S,* 140). Religion and love have been reduced to this bizarre head, which natters on about the filth of American novels and the Catholic and Communist Indexes. As Sutcliffe wryly comments: "'And so

Galen's search for culture ended. . . . I fear . . . that this is the end of Galen the polymath and cultural dictator'" (*S*, 142). After such an abortive quest, the future of culture is not at the moment very bright.

There are quite a few of these severed heads circulating mysteriously throughout *The Avignon Quintet*. Early on, the mad Sylvie says that the nursery rhyme "Oranges and lemons, say the bells of Saint Clement's" is the song that the Templars sang: "Here comes a candle to light you to bed, here comes a chopper to chop off your head, chop, chop, chop, chop" (*M*, 88).[6] In *Livia*, when Blanford returns home exhausted from nocturnal rambling, Durrell slyly notes that Aubrey "sank to the pillow as if beheaded" (*L*, 245). After the apparent suicide of Piers de Nogaret, the above-noted descendant of the central inquisitor of the Templars, his head disappears and the body is buried without it. As we learn in *Quinx*, his alter ego Hilary was also beheaded, guillotined by the Nazis while Livia looked on.

As a double agent, working for the Egyptians as well as for the Germans, Smirgel has often been in danger of joining the rolls of the headless, were it not for Sebastian's intervention. "'We have had a long history together. I must tell you how we've saved his head more than once from Hitler's impatience and Ribbentrop's. Head for a head, so to speak'" (*C*, 271). The head that Prince Hassad has been carrying about has finally come to rest in Berlin, thanks to Smirgel. "'It is supposed to be the prophesying head of Pompey which the Crusaders believed was imprisoned in the cannon ball which tops Pompey's Pillar in Alexandria. Once in a while the thing is alleged to utter a prophecy, but in one's sleep; one has to have it beside the bed. Do you know where it is now? Beside Hitler's bed'" (*C*, 272).

Apparently, this idol of the Dark Order never spoke of anything important that Hitler could use, and his inverted dream of a Black Templar Knighthood was destroyed by suicide in an underground bunker. At the end of the war, all that is left of the new order is the band of criminals and lunatics freed from the asylum in Avignon. They are the "Crusaders of the new reality!" (*C*, 374), whom Durrell has dubbed with the names of some of the original Templars—Baudoin de St.-Just, Tortville, Jean Taillefer, Raynier de Larchant, Pairaud, and de Molay. As well, they are the new popes of the present, on their way to Rome to put an end to the Babylonian Captivity, and to raise their own Pandemonium. "'To Rome!' they shouted, growled and piped. 'Onwards to Rome!'" (*C*, 377). In their insanity, in their obsession, they may be explained by the comment Durrell makes about Mnemidis, the deranged murderer of Sebastian: "The mad must be people without selves: their whole investment is in the other, the object. They are ruled by the forces of total uncertainty" (*S*, 160). The darker quest has proven to be just as fruitless as will the search of the caves beneath Avignon.

Yet we still must look to the other quest, the quest for the light that involves Constance and Sebastian, Rob Sutcliffe and Aubrey Blanford. Commenting on the evolution of *The Alexandria Quartet,* Lawrence Durrell says: "I wanted to set my novel in a purely historical plane, using Alexandria as a foundation, one of the real nerve-centres of our civilization. And as I went along, through all this ordure, through this orgy, I stumbled on what is perhaps the most interesting part: the pure and dedicated quest for a new asceticism."[7] Avignon provides the nerve center for the search in these quincunx novels. For Durrell, the Templar is a Gnostic is an Artist.[8] Early in *Monsieur,* Akkad pointed the reader in the right direction: "'The poets have shown us the way. For those, in every age, who feel the deeply humiliating condition of man and nourish any hope, I won't say of ever changing it, but even ameliorating it. . . . they sense the great refusal as necessary'" (*M,* 140). Quatrefages the clerk is on to something: "'I think there is no treasure; I think Phillippe le Bel got it all. . . . but our search for the quincunx of trees concerns another sort of treasure'" (*L,* 163).

The Templars lost, but the artist may not. Sebastian Affad is a gnostic; when he goes before a council of his peers, the place is called "The Crusaders' Chapel" (*S,* 36). He explains the string he wears around his neck to Constance in this way: "'The little thread is flax, grown on the Nile. . . . It's the sign of the yogi, of his frugality and mental chastity. The Templars wore it as a belt—and those idiot Inquisitors took it for some secret sexual symbol arguing a homosexual affiliation. Idiots! The double sex was quite another thing, a syzygy of the male and female affect'" (*C,* 298). Much later, Blanford will come to virtually the same conclusion in almost the same words: "'They had become infected first by the old Gnosticism so rampant in the Middle Orient *(outremer);* and then secondly and definitively by the practices of yoga—as the thread woven from millet round their waists so clearly showed'" (*Q,* 54).

Though certainly Blanford is not an outright practitioner of yoga or gnosticism, the novel he is working on is rooted in the Templar controversy and the need for a new vision. Blanford re-creates himself in *Livia* as an alter-ego of the historian Toby: "I pictured myself doing a definitive book on some aspect of medieval history" (*L,* 30). He describes his novel's genesis in words that consciously or unconsciously recall Sebastian's gnostic thread: "'I was led to it by a lot of sporadic and scattered reading first of all: by the mystery of the Templar's abject surrender and their obvious guilt. It was Affad who told me they were simply gnostics dedicated to cross swords with Monsieur instead of putting up with his rule. Then I took up the threads [!] right there in Alexandria. They are not joking you know! The cult of the human head is with us even today'" (*C*, 345). The struggle against the omni-present Prince of Darkness is now to be waged by the artist in a battle for the preservation of culture. As Akkad asserted earlier: "He [Satan] is only troubled when a poet gives him the lie. Then for a moment he feels himself shrivelling in the flames" (*M*, 143).

Blanford is writing a different kind of novel: "'a book full of spare parts of other books, of characters left over from other lives, all circu-lating in each other's bloodstreams—yet all fresh, nothing second-hand, twice chewed, twice breathed. Such a book might ask you if life is worth breathing, if death is worth looming'" (*C*, 122). As Blanford realizes, opposed to the gnostic thread in his novel is the rope of the wasteland's hangman. "'Reality is a running noose, one is brought up short with a jerk by death. It would be wiser to cooper-ate with the inevitable and learn to profit by this unhappy state of things—by realizing and accommodating death! But we don't, we allow the ego to foul its own nest. Therefore we have insecurity, stress, the midnight-fruit of insomnia, with a whole culture crying itself to sleep. How to repair this state of affairs except through art, through gifts which render us language manumitted by emotion, poetry twisted into the service of direct insight?'" (*C*, 343).

Durrell's manipulation of the pieces and the resonances of the Templar-gnostic puzzle is reflected in the mirror of Blanford's double Rob Sutcliffe, who is linked directly to the Templars. Beginning as a figment of Aubrey's imagination, Rob soon assumes the status of a character in his own right. The Knights were supposed to have ad-hered to a set of blasphemous commandments called the "Secret Rule of the Brothers-Elect," though most scholars now agree that the list is a much later forgery, as bogus as the "Protocols of Zion" that Dur-rell alludes to in *Constance*. In *Livia*, Rob Sutcliffe, the artist with the sense of humor Blanford lacks, declares that "'nobody could contra-vert my twelve commandments—the indispensible prerequisites for those who wish to make works of art'" (*L*, 18).

Thus Sutcliffe, in a mock-heroic way, aligns himself with the contemporary band of emerging artist-Templars. Sutcliffe's set of precepts, in slangy French, is included in an appendix,[9] but he has sub-stituted for commands to kiss the various parts of the initiator's anat-omy with such whimsical rules as number one: "One must pump the mummy allegorically"; number five: "One must anoint the Grand Master's gorgonzola"; and number nine: "One must caress ineluctably the Great Eggplant of our day." Number eleven, "One must stare at reality by dint of supposing or presuming," sounds suspiciously like an allusion to Durrell's own *On Seeming to Presume*. This new set of rules, funny though they may be, demonstrates an awareness on Sutcliffe's part that art and the Templars' quest are intertwined.

As was mentioned above, Blanford seriously notes the omnipresence of the human head, and it surfaces again in a hilarious and astounding way with Sutcliffe. Rob too possesses a magical red box, which parallels the Prince's with its mummified head, but the artist's contains something totally different. "With him he carried the battered scarlet minute-box with the monogram of the Royal Arms on the lid; it contained his novel—the 'other' one" (*C*, 351). Rob is a secret messenger, on his Durrell's service. If Hitler will listen in vain for words of wisdom from his idol in Berlin, it becomes clear that art, the novel, can provide the insight that the legion of light is seeking. Here the yogic Templar thread will serve a new and different function. "The commonplace book began to fill up once more with what Sutcliffe called 'thimbles' or stray thoughts, and Blanford 'threads.' He wrote: 'Pearls can exist without a thread but the novel is an artefact and needs a thread upon which to thread not so much the pearls as the reader!'" (*Q*, 50).

The writing of the work, and the reading of it as well, become almost a sacred duty. All along, Constance has insisted: "'No, the book will not lose its place or its preciousness for it is a privileged communication between two spirits and the link it forges is vital to the culture of the heart and mind, and hence to man'" (*M*, 300). Durrell has woven the strands of the Templars and the gnostics tightly into the fabric of *The Avignon Quintet*. The transition from gnosticism to yoga to artistry is embodied in the prototypical novel upon which Blanford and Sutcliffe are collaborating in *Quinx*.

It should be noted as well that the oneness implicit in the work of art is complemented in Durrell's view by the physical and spiritual coming together of the male and female. It is the lovemaking of Constance and Sebastian, and later that of Constance and Aubrey, that triumphs over the Nazi destruction, or at least provides a ray of hope. The knowledge dawns upon Constance, complete with a Molly Bloom–like affirmation: "Yes, with all this she had suddenly, dramatically assumed herself, her full femininity—something which had remained always a sort of figment, a symbol which gave off no current. . . . To achieve some understanding of the role of the female— why, it chimed with her art, it was implicit in the craft of her job. The female was the principle of renewal and repair in the cosmic sense, it was she who made things happen, made things happen, made things grow" (*C*, 273). The emphasis on "made things happen" underlines the active sense of her role.

Though Constance is not an artist of the written word, she is in many ways a practitioner of just what art is supposed to do, in Durrell's scheme of things. Just as Aubrey's work evolves, in one way out of Einstein, Constance has taken her cue from Freud. In her involvement as a Freudian therapist, she will set Sebastian's son Affad upon the road to recovery from his autism. Her accidental wearing of his mother's perfume causes the first breakthrough: "Then one day the magical weeping started, the fruitful tears began to flow. . . . it was as if the whole of reality rushed in like a Niagra of feeling—suddenly the weeping started, weeping of such violence and abandon that it was as if his little psyche had exploded like a bomb" (*S*, 71). Assuming the mantle of a mother, Constance is able to put the boy back in touch with his own emotions, and, at Sebastian's funeral, both son and surrogate mother make the giant leap of being able to face the reality of death together, joining hands as they view the imposing coffin.

For Durrell, art cannot exist in a vacuum—it must be put into practice in the real world. Constance had snapped, "'they spoke about art as if it were some sort of vitamin. . . . It's when the mind strays out of touch with its own caresses—its own catlicks upon the body-image of itself—then it loses the power to cherish and restore itself through self-esteem'" (*C*, 344). The art object cannot be accomplished until the psyche is at one with itself. Just as Blanford will slowly recover physically from the injuries he suffered when mistakenly shelled by British mortars on the ill-fated picnic in the Egyptian desert, so too will his emerging love for Constance bring him back to spiritual health. As he says, "'I had to have my spine shot into holes before I realized that the only way to deal with the Socratic voice is to concretise it, let it live, manifest itself. Then it becomes a harmless ghost, it passes off in a fever, it writes the classic phrase for you. It can do everything but love. That you must do for yourself'" (*S*, 5). In such a fusion, in such a resolution of opposites, is the cultural quest of the *Quintet* to be finalized.

There may be an echo of Constance Chatterley in Durrell's woman,[10] and it is just possible as well that her name recalls ironically the Council of Constance, held in 1417, which unified the papacy and returned it to Rome. Whatever meaning in existence that may be left is to be found in the lovers Constance and Aubrey, who ultimately make the reversed journey back to Avignon, an overt parallel to Bruce's trip in *Monsieur*. In *Quinx*, Blanford seems to have solved the mystery of the Templars, at least to his own satisfaction, when he decides that "'The real secret treasure was the Grail, the lotus of insight'" (*Q*, 54). He describes the style of his novel as akin to the technique of jumpcutting in film, and he sees as its essential end the fusion of opposites. "'The old stable outlines of the dear old linear novel have been sidestepped in favour of soft focus palimpsest which enables the actors to turn into each other, to melt into each other's inner lifespace if they wish. Everything and everyone comes closer together, moving towards the one'" (*Q*, 99).

The completeness of the man and the woman is to be balanced by the completeness of the work of art: "'a narrative apparently dislocated and disjointed yet informed by mutually contradictory insights—love at first insight, so to speak, between Constance and myself'" (*Q*, 166). One result of the novel to be written will be the dethroning of the satanic head of Ophis, and its replacement with something different. The novel's purpose will be "To celebrate the mystical marriage of four dimensions with five skandas so to speak. To exemplify in the flesh the royal cobra couple, the king and queen of the affect, of the spiritual world. 'My spinal I with her final she'" (*Q*, 198). One Templar treasure may have been lost, but an infinitely greater and more important one has been found in *The Avignon Quintet*. It seems that the Sacred Order, transformed, is still alive and well.

## NOTES

1. For a basic account of the story, see G. Mollat, *The Popes at Avignon, 1305–1378* (London: Thomas Nelson and Sons, 1949), and Edward J. Martin, *The Trial of the Templars* (London: George Allen & Unwin, 1928).

2. Two sides of the controversy are offered by G. Legman and Henry Charles Lea in *The Guilt of the Templars* (New York: Basic Books, 1966).

3. Stephen Howarth, *The Knights Templar* (New York: Atheneum, 1982), 310.

4. Two articles by James P. Carley provide background, "Lawrence Durrell and the Gnostics," *Deus Loci* 2 (September 1978): 3–10, and "An Interview with Lawrence Durrell on the Background to *Monsieur* and Its Sequels," *Malahat Review* 51 (1979): 42–46.

5. Lawrence Durrell, *Monsieur* (New York: Viking Press, 1974), 248. Further citations will be drawn from this and the following editions and included, abbreviated, in the text: *Livia* (New York: Viking Press, 1979); *Constance* (New York: Viking Press, 1982); *Sebastian* (New York: Viking Press, 1984); *Quinx* (New York: Viking Press, 1985).

6. It is interesting, in the way that Durrell's characters become avatars of one another, that Justine recalls the same nursery rhyme for Darley at their final meeting. "She turned, and standing in front of me with a serious face, as if playing a game with a child, she softly patted her palms together, intoning the names, 'Pursewarden and Liza, Darley and Melissa, Mountolive and Leila, Nessim and Justine, Narouz and Clea. . . . Here comes a candle to light them to bed, and here comes a chopper to

chop off their heads.'" Soon she asks: "'The sort of pattern we make should be of interest to someone; or is it just a meaningless display of coloured fireworks, the actions of *human* beings or of a set of dusty puppets which could be hung up in the corner of a writer's mind?'" (Lawrence Durrell, *Clea* [New York: E. P. Dutton, 1960], 60).

7. Marc Alyn, ed., *The Big Supposer* (New York: Grove Press, 1974), 17.

8. As Reed Way Dasenbrock observes: "Artists and gnostics alike are heretics whose heresy is the acceptance of death, though neither commits suicide: they kill their friends instead, though the artist murders only vicariously through the agency of his art" ("The Counterlife of Heresy," in *Critical Essays on Lawrence Durrell*, ed. Alan W. Friedman [Boston: G. K. Hall, 1987], 226). For an interesting view of the *Quintet*, see William L. Godshalk, "*Sebastian: or Ruling Passions*: Searches and Failures," *Twentieth Century Literature* 33 (Winter 1987): 536–49.

9. I am indebted for the translations here to my colleague Michel Pharand.

10. After this was written, Lawrence W. Markert has also noticed the similarities between the two Constances in "The Pure and Sacred Readjustment of Death: Connections between Lawrence Durrell's *Avignon Quintet* and the Writings of D. H. Lawrence," *Twentieth Century Literature* 33 (Winter 1987): 550–64.

# Writer as Painter in Lawrence Durrell's *Avignon Quintet*

## Susan Vander Closter

Lawrence Durrell's experiments with narrative structure are executed on a grand scale. Not content with manipulating time and space in a single volume, Durrell has achieved a simultaneity of varied perspectives by creating several novels that interact with each other, as in *The Alexandria Quartet* (1957–60) and *The Avignon Quintet* (1974-85). In the *Quartet,* Durrell first used multiple volumes to disturb the convention of a linear narrative whose truth is privileged and unquestioned. *Balthazar*'s response to *Justine* demonstrates that there is more than one side to a story, that an image's meaning fluctuates as a result of the viewer's relationship to it. Interart analogies are common in Durrell scholarship because this use of multiple surfaces and angles of perception finds its equivalent in the visual arts, and, as a painter, Durrell makes frequent allusions—both verbal and visual—to the painted image. The multivolume novel form as conceived by Durrell demands that the reader eventually see its parts simultaneously as if the volumes were panels set in three-dimensional rather than linear arrangement, a structure that is dramatically plastic and related to the perceptual tricks of the modernists in cubism or, in another medium, like jazz, with its reliance on variations and the fluidity of thematic expression.[1] In its conception and execution, the Avignon series is without question the most ambitious of Durrell's fiction.

Durrell's use of the painted image as a structural model increases the complexity of his experimentation. In a sense, he is revising the novel's traditional means of representation by rendering pieces of the narrative in pictorial ways that force them into relief, instead of allowing them to blend and therefore to become the invisible means of developing the plot. At times, these pieces are figural or purely descriptive images that interrupt abstract or somber discourse and offer a temporary escape, reinforcing Durrell's recurring perception of art as a consolation. In general, however, the verbal picture is discursive and must be the visual means toward idea. This pictographic power places Durrell in the tradition of Poussin, who hoped, as Norman Bryson explains, that French painting "would not be physical at all, but the communication of ideas from one consciousness to another across an image that is altogether transparent."[2] Like Poussin, Durrell seems to be taking us into the realm of the senses so that sight may lead to insight.

The discursive images of the *Quintet,* archetypal in their depiction of peace and war, are stylistically varied. The past is romantically portrayed and exaggerated as an Eden where childhood innocence is experienced in a fertile, prewar Provencal landscape. With war, this same landscape is sterile and scarred. In German-occupied France, Constance and Nancy Quiminal will see "civilians hanging on the branches of a plane tree opposite the Papal city. Or in another part of the town a dog and a youth hanging from a first floor balcony."[3] These images, reminiscent of Goya's *Disasters of War,* work as powerful complements to the idyllic portraits of peace and untroubled youth and exemplify what Mary Ann Caws defines as "superpositioning." Related to Durrell's use of layering or the verbal palimpsest, this technique assumes that two or more scenes separated by space in the text are "meant to be reconsidered together, with evident reference points: instead of being read in an ordinary linear movement, the episodees are seen to work in cumulative and progressively more significant superpositioning, one scene easily pictured as placed directly above the preceding one, to which it looks back in retrospective reframing."[4] Combined in this way, childhood purity and potential that are reflected in the landscape are seen to be overwhelmed by the violent and deformed impulses of adults who have fallen from innocence. In *Sebastian* and *Quinx,* Durrell's prose takes the metaphysical turn of Chirico toward a concealed but accessible other reality where individuals can heal themselves and can achieve sexual, psychic, and therefore artistic well-being.[5] These bordered segments of the text can be approached in two ways, much as Durrell's writer Sutcliffe and Blanford approach painting, Sutcliffe "to bathe his wits in colour" so that he can silence the ideas rattling "around in his noodle like nutmegs in a tin," and Blanford to convince "by thrilling the mind and the optic nerve simultaneously."[6]

The most striking example of the *Quintet*'s pictorial structure is the dream sequence in *Constance.* Its two major images are compared within the dream itself to Chirico's *The Parting* and to the "masterpiece of Clement," a work frequently mentioned in the quincunx. The reader is asked to study the iconography of these paintings so that the acts of pictorial and dream interpretation become one and the same process. Constance's references to painting suggest that, for her, "paintings are to bring calm," to bring chaos to order as dreams order experience (281). Before Constance has her painterly dream, she has struggled through a painful return to the past and has been forced to confront Sam's death, the reality of the German occupation, and her sister Livia's suicide. During her visit to Tu Duc, Constance has a "sombre vision" that "stands forever as a marker" illustrating the nature of Nazi brutality (221–22). At dusk Constance and Nancy Quiminal see a halted train whose doors are open and frame "pale exhausted faces in abstract expressions of estragement or grief" (222). When they attempt to feed the children loaves of bread, the two are beaten and chased away. Soon after this experience and immediately before fleeing Provence, Constance finds her sister hanging in what was once her bedroom in Tu Duc. In Geneva, Constance finds hope and a release from those dark experiences through her lovemaking with Affad. On the stark white surface of the masseur's settee and later in the bath, she begins to move away from death and to discover "an attachment where the physical and the mental made common cause" (269). Having discovered herself and the female as "the principle of renewal and repair," Constance finds her parting from Affad agonizing. She falls asleep at her office desk, feeling "deeply shaken," and dreams "archaic dreams of haunting incoherence" (280).

The first frame finds Constance in the healing context of a hospital bed surrounded by white screens. On this surface, Chirico's *The Parting* is projected, "with its clinical rigour, its glacial detachment which freezes the optic nerve like anaesthetic" (281). Chirico's palette and tone, she reflects, befit "partings where grief bit too deep for expression." Superimposed on this image of clarity is a "mental foliage of rusty wire ... from which one flies into comfortless futures of thought." Constance recalls her deep union with Affad— the text punctuated by what Affad had earlier referred to as the "primal vision of man and woman, the primal fig leaf, the primal asterisk" (268). Apparently, Constance's tension and pain are caused by the possibility of this union's being interrupted, by "comfortless futures of thought ... the lovers' goodbye, the turning away, the imprint of the primal crime, the original fall." While dreaming, Constance addresses her fears, concluding that "the meaning of lovecraft only grew out of parting." Before the image dissolves, the lovers are harmonious and inseparable. It is clear that in dream Constance is expressing her apprehension that the healing, primal union with Affad that she has experienced will be destroyed as a result of interference or separation, hence the archetypal references to mankind's expulsion from the garden and the soothing evocation of Chirico's *Parting*. As a Freudian, Constance realizes the work that can be accomplished during the dream. Sitting on Freud's "old analytic sofa" while revisiting Avignon, she quotes to herself, "In dreams begin responsibilities" (208).

The second framed dream image is many layered and extremely complex. The interpretive difficulties this image poses seem to stem from the image's being more significant and emblematic to Durrell and the *Quintet* as a whole than to the dreamer. After the first painting fades, we are told that "in its place there shone out from the heart of Avignon, lambent like the Grail, the old smoky masterpiece of Clement" (283). Constance remembers *Cockayne* as the painting Smirgel cleaned, and she sees it as a "weird mixture of elements—a sort of *Paradise Regained* painted upon a gossamer veil." Durrell is known for creating layered surfaces or palimpsests, and here the text asks us to visualize the typical composition of a *Last Supper* but to place above it a revision that in many respects is an inversion of the original.[7] *Cockayne* is presented with great clarity and detail despite its being part of a dream:

> The sleepers were asleep in their chairs, the candles had melted and run all over the place. Strangely enough it was outside in a grassy meadow, sheltered by a coloured marquee. There were gold coins lying about in the grass, handkerchieves, articles of wear. Parts took place in the seventeenth century, Christ had the head of Spinoza. Judas looked with a conger's gaze. The wine had been doped, perhaps? Had they all fallen asleep at the table? Maybe the gypsies had sneaked up and cut their throats while they slept? (282)

The apparent shift from ritual to disorder constitutes the inversion. The movement of the figures outdoors recalls Christ's agony in the garden before his arrest, since often the disciples are asleep, having left Christ to face Judas alone. Here, Judas's "conger's gaze" identifies him with the evil serpent, and the scattered coins remind us that he was paid in coin for his betrayal. Speaking of the intent of this fictional painting, Durrell remembers using an old edition of an encyclopedia to study the development of the *Last Supper* from a sacred to a secular and even orgiastic rendering of the human experience.[8] His main objective, it would seem, is to express culture's entropic nature, but his image of betrayal in the garden is contradicted by its titles, including *Paradise Regained* and *The Land of Plenty* (*Constance*, 282, 331).

This contradiction persists if we locate the sources of the images in the dreamer's experience in Avignon. There are reasons to link the Judas figure with Smirgel and Livia because both, in Constance's mind, are associated with Nazi Germany, and, like Judas, Constance's sister will hang herself as a result of her disillusionment. When Constance first sees Smirgel, she is peering through her kitchen window and sees a sleeping German officer whose eyes are "doubly hooded" by "heavy vulture's eyelids" and eyeglasses (232). Her perception of the painting as a radiant Grail probably stems from Smirgel's description of Quatrefages's interest in the Templar treasure. He explains to Constance that Quatrefages "felt himself to be on the track of the Grail, the Arthurian Grail. . . . it could have been the cup out of which Jesus drank at the Last Supper," and Smirgel also mentions Hitler's desire to establish a black chivalric order (235–36). Others, however, are like Judas in their lack of interest in the symbolic treasure and in their pursuit of the buried Templar fortune. Constance's dream image reads as if she were contemplating an Eden invaded by the powers of darkness: are these figures, she wonders, asleep, doped, or have they had their throats cut? (232) Because Constance later defines herself as an expression of the seventeenth century (290), the painting must be important to her as a reflection of the present. One may speculate that, although the images are generated by her journey to Avignon and may be an echo of the first painting's expression of threatened pleasure, she is associating the Last Supper with the self-sacrifice and betrayal that precede the regaining of paradise.

To complicate matters, Durrell reminds the reader of Clement's masterpiece as if it were emblematic of the *Quintet*'s stylistic and thematic concerns. Later in *Constance,* Pia and Trash will be working on a tapestry whose subject is "Clement's celebrated painting from Avignon, The Land of Plenty: Cockayne, which had been commercialized by Gobelin" (331). The painting also possesses meaning for Quatrefages, the historian who sees the past and present as variations on the theme of persecution. In "The City's Fall," Quatrefages' angle of vision is brought into sharp focus. Human behavior repeats itself, and "History triumphantly describes the victory of divine entropy over the aspirations of the majority" (363).

The new inquisition has its precedents. Like Constance, Quatrefages is bombarded by images from the past that appear on his wall like a slide show, "projections of troubled memory, once full of armoured knights . . . now the same space peopled with dark-robed exemplars of the new Inquisition" (365). This double layering or revised configuration resembles the technique employed by Clement, and Quatrefages too notes the importance of this work:

> He laughed aloud, for with all the cars and tanks passing the wall went on and off in cinematic fashion, and each time it was a new picture. A feeling of continuity resided only in the fact that the one that repeated was the old Crucifixion of Clement—the land of Cockayne. . . . it was

quite a celebrated work of art; so much so that Smirgel had managed to get a half-size colour print of it which he pinned to the wall of the nearby cell in the Danger Ward where he composed his despatches. (365)

After the bombing, Quatrefages compares history's tendency to repeat itself—with variations—to "a negative of which one was the print, the positive." "'Variations on themes,' he repeated aloud, 'Just as a diamond is a variation on carbon, or a caterpillar on a butterfly'" (378). Durrell's invented work by Clement expresses this idea of the historical palimpsest as does the *Quintet* as a whole with its juxtaposition of the thirteenth- and twentieth-century inquisitions. Seen in this way, the painting not only shines like the Grail in Constance's dream, but it can be located as the centerpiece of the quincunx, a reminder that it is art that creates order and insight.[9]

Like Clement's painting, the *Quintet*'s landscapes are also carefully designed and set in relief to reinforce Durrell's thematic concerns. The seemingly figural paintings of prewar and postwar Tu Duc in summer and winter, reminiscent of the "massive water paintings of the Italian school" that depict "imaginary landscapes during the four seasons of the year," become discursive when set in juxtaposition to each other (*Livia*, 108). At *Livia*'s beginning, Blanford, distraught by Constance's death, travels back to the Avignon of the past "to sum it all up—from the point of view of death," and he is encouraged by Sutcliffe to remember that "it is the small things which build the picture" (12, 30). The small things that Blanford crowds onto his canvas are colorful and enviable. The Rhone journey by barge—with bronzed and blond Constance signifying summer—is an apt preface to the Avignon vacation. Blanford recalls the slow spinning of the sun, silhouetted against "the arc of a sky of utter blue" and the water's turn toward "a dark shade of amethyst verging on ultramarine" (33, 36). The mulberries of Lyon become "olives, shivering and turning in the mistral" as Constance, Aubrey, Sam, and Hilary move past picturesque, turreted, "rosy baked little towns" toward "the coves and *calenques* of Cassis" (44). In late evening, they see Avignon at its most magical, "magnetically lit by moonlight pouring over it from the direction of the Alpilles" (47). Like the city, Tu Duc, dilapidated but charming, is picture-book perfect: there are moonlit swims in the lily pond, milky *pastis,* and, during the day, the scents of sand, sea, or rosemary and thyme.

From the sunny balcony where breakfast waited they could see the swifts stooping and darting, how beautifully the birds combined with gravity to give life to this wilderness of garden which Constance had sworn never to have tidied and formalized. It was full of treasures like old fruit trees still bearing, strawberry patches, and a bare dry section of holm-oak—a stand of elderly trees—which had a truffle bed beneath. (*Livia,* 112)

This fecundity, described in the chapter "Summer Sunlight," reflects the poetic richness of their experience. Sam and Constance are falling in love, and a gypsylike Livia initiates Aubrey and teaches the insomniac Felix to appreciate Avignon. These, as all of the imagery suggests, are halcyon days.

The fall of this Eden is charted in *Constance* where the point of view shifts from Blanford's nostalgic recollections to an omniscient eye's relentless documentation of a landscape ravaged by war. The color scheme or palette changes dramatically as if the only appropriate shade is gray, Blanford's "omega grey . . . the almost black of death" (*Livia,* 196). War and winter seem to arrive together with the cold mistral and the rehearsing aid-raid sirens. In "Tu Duc Revisited," Constance returns to Provence, now a wintry countryside "ominous and beleaguered." The manor, like occupied France, seems abused and mournful, its exterior "damp-stained and unpainted" (*Constance,* 205). "Everywhere gutters oozed and dribbled"; the garden is in "ruinous isolation" (206).

With Sam's death unresolved, Constance finds herself painfully alone, and Avignon is "no longer the sun-golden, leisurely town she had known. The winter wind, the whirling leaves, the seething river . . . all went to make up a revised image against which she now had only the fact of her loneliness to place" (211). Durrell continues to set this visit in contrast to the first sunlit summer. Instead of light and growth, there is twilight, rations, curfews, fear, and executions "in this rather barren, backward land of austere towns and empty heaths" (244). Outside the gray church of Montfavet, Constance will meet Livia, "a figure in a field-grey uniform" who had lost an eye and who will return "like a hunted animal" to the Tu Duc "burrow which had once been hers . . . in that forgotten summer" (240, 249). The image of Livia bathing at dawn in the lily pond, her head like a statue, is replaced by her pale figure hanging from a rope. The trains, once filled with black bulls on their way to Nimes, now carry cold, starving prisoners, young children who cry for food as if they were seagulls (222). Throughout, the text evokes that twilight grayness which is the prelude to blackness, "a winter twilight populated by Germans" (211).

Given this thematic manipulation and literary use of landscape, Durrell's tribute to Turner is appropriate.[10] In *Livia,* we have already witnessed the remembered love scene between Blanford and Livia in Avignon's little museum when we read of Prince Hassad's similar celebration of love and beauty at the Tate. Fawzia's appreciation for

Turner excites the prince, who proposes to her while she sits in the painter's chair and gazes "past the balconies of The Swan to where, on a level horizon and fretted by forest, an unframed Turner sunset burned itself slowly, ruinously away into a fulginous dusk, touched here and there with life as if from a breath passing over a bed of embers" (*Livia*, 220). For the prince, art, represented by Turner's paintings, is an aid to perception, for he seems to come to nature by means of painting. Both this natural beauty and Turner's work provide refuges from the tensions of war as well as from his fear of impotence and consequent marital unease. Returning from Germany, he heads for St. Mary's, where the rain gives way to an enflamed sky. Such beauty, like art, defiles time. "It was as if Turner himself had come back to welcome him, to give him a last sunset before the end. . . . It was like watching a stained-glass window being slowly shattered" (229). Beauty, he discovers, is a great consolation, inspiring him to trust that, while power is ephemeral, "the real Empire was in the primacy of the imagination" (229).

Durrell exploits not only the metaphoric power of the landscape but also the visual power of the portrait. The reader must collect and superimpose or make a collage of the scattered two-dimensional and fragmented images to compose these portraits, because descriptive pieces are separated in the text and also exist on various levels of reality within the fiction. In *Constance*'s brief Author's Note, Durrell claims to have painted World War II with "impressionistic accuracy," and certainly his portrait of Von Esslin, the Nazi, is a critical segment of this larger impressionistic picture and an important discursive tool. The Nazi's image alone represents the psychic and sexual disturbances that typify the archetypal man of war. Several sections of *Constance* are devoted to him in an attempt to comprehend "this calamitous historic process," what Constance sees as the mystery of worldwide self-destructiveness. When she and the prince arrive in Avignon, Constance examines the red death-sentence posters "upon which the crooked cross had been overstamped" and wonders "how human beings with so short a span of life at their disposal should seek in this way to qualify and abbreviate it with their neurotic antics" (185).

Representing the puppet generals under the Fuhrer's command, the neurotic Von Esslin is set in contrast to Fischer, the "blond Mephisto" (111). While Fischer is as cold and insensible as an empty-eyed Roman statue or neon sign, Von Esslin must create an exterior that belies his sentimentality and his insecurity. In addition to his short Hitlerian mustache, he begins to wear his gold-rimmed monocle to appear "aristocratic and forbidding" and to hide the seething mass of contradictions within (172). His paternal inheritance is militaristic and romantic. His father, also a general, died of a broken heart after his daughter, and, most significant, Von Esslin's twin died from multiple sclerosis. Describing the German's family as "of the Junker breed," Durrell notes that this obduracy is mixed with piousness and a "special weakness" for music (29). Von Esslin retains a strong attachment to his Katzer-Mutter, whom he sentimentalizes from a distance, and fantasizes about Germany's victory over Poland when he is taken into his Polish maid's bed.

There, he dreams "of his big, playful tanks nosing about like sheepdogs in the dust and clutter of the farms they had knocked down" (38). Childish and confused, he zealously adopts and rereads Goebbels's recommended texts—the Protocols of Zion and Will of Peter the Great—in the hopes that drowning himself in the large gray mass of nazism will quell his apprehension. "It was best to think nothing, to say nothing—to throw oneself into the marvellous liberation of blind action; to become part of this vast steel juggernaut aimed at Poland, and leave the thinking to others who knew more than he did" (43). Von Esslin finds that hearing news of the Polish maid's suicide and watching executions threaten his blind commitment: he suffers from constipation and colitis. He longs to confess even though SS officers torment him with hints "that one could not compromise between God and Hitler" (212). He is completely isolated when Krov, a Polish slave-prisoner, shows him the kindness of a son before betraying him. In a classic Oedipal power play, Krov tries to kill Von Esslin. An icon of nazism, he is left blind, despondent, and helpless. In *Quinx*, we will see a reflection of Egon Von Esslin in the crippled Egon Von Lupian, the Austrian who hunts gypsies and prefers as his victim a woman with a child at her breast (79–82).

Sylvie's portrait is less conventional and more striking as a technical achievement. Her image in *Monsieur*, the fiction within the fiction, is a composite of others in *Livia, Constance, Sebastian*, and *Quinx*. In *Livia*, Sylvie's portrait is one of the "three smoky heads" remaining in Tu Duc's gallery: "one could make out the word Piers on the portrait of the pale young man . . . and the word Sylvie below that of the dark intense girl, who might have been his sister" (64). The blond blue-eyed third figure, like the "chateau de Bravedent" scrawled on the back of one of the portraits, invites Blanford to invent and to "incorporate their story in a book which had nothing to do with real life" (65). In *Constance*, Blanford meets Sylvaine Le Nogre, whose name and participation in a love triangle including her brother Bruno and Dr. Drexel, all of whom plan to retire to their chateau in Villefoin after the war, will inspire *Monsieur*'s Piers and Sylvie de Nogaret and their lover Bruce Drexel, M.D. Sylvaine reminds Blanford of "a dark girl" he remembers seeing in the rose garden of Montfavet (*Constance*, 185).

In *Sebastian,* Constance allows Sylvie, her patient, to love her. Sylvie's Genevan pavilion is tucked in the midst of a pine forest and is decorated "with brilliant hangings and old-fashioned carved furniture of heavy Second Empire beauty." The room's focal piece is a medieval tapestry whose hunt-of-the-hart motif has a female twist: the female stag has been raped and left "panting and bleeding in tears like a woman," and Sylvie, we are told, "was not unlike the animal" (194). The story of the two blond lovers, Constance and Sylvie, is continued in *Quinx.* Sabine's tale of the gypsy woman hunted like a stag, an event that horrifies young Von Lupian and forces him to commission many oils titled *Gipsy Pursued by Hounds,* reinforces the theme of male and female conflict, the image of the male pleasure to be found in the destruction of the female. When Constance leaves Sylvie, Blanford's rival takes refuge in Montfavet, where we find her in *Monsieur.*

The portrait in *Monsieur* is in several respects a palimpsest. In retrospect, the reader sees Sylvie as a collection of the aforementioned images, and Durrell uses the painting within a painting, a familiar iconographic device, to enrich the thematic power of the image. Bruce Drexel, the lonely narrator of "Outremer," travels to *Montfavet-les-Roses* to visit Sylvie, who has retreated from the world after her beloved brother's suicide.

> The authorities had allowed her to move in her own graceful furniture from the chateau, carpets and paintings, and even a large tapestry rescued from the old ballroom. . . . She worked under the great tapestry with its glowing but subdued tones—huntsmen with lofted horns had been running down a female stag. After the rape, leaving the grooms to bring the trophy home, they galloped away into the soft brumous Italian skyline; a network of misty lakes and romantic islets receding into the distance along the diagonal; fathered by Poussin or Claude. The stag lay there, panting and bleeding and in tears (211).

As it does in *Sebastian,* this tapestry draws attention to Sylvie's violation, to the gnostic sacrifice of her brother, the destruction of the Verfeuille dream, and the indifference of the world responsible for these losses. Throughout the *Quintet,* nature is violated. In the tapestry, the abandoned stag is left in the foreground while the hunters victoriously ride toward "misty lakes and romantic islets." The text's portrait of Sylvie is a reflection of this dynamic: we imagine her within her refuge or romantic prison with, in the background, high French windows revealing the garden in the distance. In front of this landscape and enclosed, Sylvie appears to be safe, but she is unable to venture out of this haven lest she be made vulnerable once again to the violence of the outside world. Within, she has collected beautiful objects, an "old Portuguese writing desk with its ivory-handled drawers, the rare bust of Gongora, the autograph of Gide enlarged and framed above the piano. . . . a bundle of manuscripts, and a tangle of notebooks lying about in a muddle on the carpet" (21). Collectively, the detail encourages us to see an artist exiled in "a private country" (129) or introversion as an escape from "a world in which we are each other's food, each other's prey," a world ruled by the Prince of Darkness (138).

Like the landscapes and portraits, Durrell's descriptions of events are elaborately detailed and framed. These segments of the narrative, frequently referred to by Durrell scholars as set-pieces, are analogous to genre paintings. Several scenes visually stand out from the text—The Spree (*Livia*, 250), The Confession (*Quinx*, 76), and the Mini-Satyrikon (*Quinx*, 181)—but two companion pieces from *Monsieur* clearly illustrate the painterly quality of Durrell's construction. The two events, Christmas Dinner and the Funeral, are representations of Provencal rituals that are rendered in the same style and point of view. In mood, of course, the two are quite different, the well-being and companionship of the Christmas gathering being contradicted by the somber journey to the family burial ground.

Saving his memories from the ravages of time, Drexel dreams and writes about his Christmas holiday at Verfeuille. "It was not," he recalls, "a place or time easy to forget. . . . I must have unconsciously memorized it in great detail without being fully aware of the fact at the time. I knew of no other place on earth that I can call up so clearly and accurately by simply closing my eyes" (56). In great detail, he paints the chateau's central hall with its stone floor strewn with herbs, its ten-foot-wide fireplace topped by "tall bottles of luminous olive oil" and "burnished copper vessels," its rush-bottomed and wicker chairs, and its long table. Our senses are seduced by the fragrance of the fish ragout and by the "longbrown loaves," which "cracked and crackled under the fingers of the feasters like the olive branches in the fireplace" (58). The room is warmed by fire, wine, brandy, and coffee, and, as a whole, the entire Christmas scene is traditional, including the peasant dress, old Jan's serene prayer, and the elaborate creation of the creche. The painting provides a feeling of light, warmth, and safe enclosure.

Working in the manner of the Old Masters, Durrell takes us out into a chiaroscuro and snowy night for the funeral. As Drexel notes, "the colourful strangeness" (66). The pyre in front of the chateau does not shelter the mourners from the dampness and cold but illuminates the scene, throwing light on peasants awkwardly dressed in Sunday clothes, on the harnessing of farm horses, and on the "homemade

hearse," a cart with "a picture of angels ascending into a blue empy-
rean." The horse sports "a glossy black plume" (67)a. The quiet pro-
cession, many mourners frustrated by Piers's gnostic renunciation of
Christianity, descends toward the cypress-surrounded vault by lantern
light, "a long glowworm of light" gradually forming behind the cart
(69). The burial spot is depressingly detailed, from the dark enclosed
canopy created by overgrown shrubs to the "dilapidated urns," the
"cowwebbed side-chapels" of the family tomb, the grim, silenced
Abbe, and the whimpering wind and screeching coffin screws (71).
In comparison to the warmth of the Christmas piece, its atmosphere
is appropriately cold and dark. War destroys both of these moments,
turned into spectacle by Drexel's memory, and no one has the luxury
of observing a holiday or of marking a death. Like the underlying
image of *Cockayne,* these companion pieces, when placed in relationship to the *Quintet*'s images of war, suggest the world's frightening
entropic movement toward absurdity and chaos.

These framed pieces—the dreamed masterpiece of Clement, the
landscapes, portraits, and genre paintings—are beautifully conceived
and demonstrate Durrell's skill in translating the techniques of one
one medium into another. Controlled and atmospheric, the images
consistently reinforce the *Quintet*'s thematic patterns and serve an important discursive function. It is tempting to connect André Gide's
observations about Nicolas Poussin to the quincunx, for he celebrates
the French painter's integration of the sensual and the cerebral, claim-
ing that Poussin was *"avant tout compositeur."* Working in and actually
redefining the form of the multivolume novel, Durrell too deserves
recognition as a *"compositeur."* Gide's comment on the integration of
idea and design applies: of Poussin, he remarks that he *"etait et reste
le plus conscient des peintres, et c' est aussi par la qu'il se montre le plus
francais. . . . La pensee preside a la naissance de chacun de ses tableaux."*[11]
In the *Avignon Quintet,* we see a Poussin-like stretch of pictorial language that is a highly sensual means for expressing ideas. Durrell depicts the loving and the cruel and the light and the dark nature of
human experience. In this realm of the senses, we, like Blanford, come
to realize the quintessential and to comprehend the meaning of art
inspired by "the old force-field quinx" (*Quinx,* 15).

## NOTES

1. Michael H. Begnal's "The Narrational Complexities of the *Avignon Quintet*"
examines the quincunx's multiple levels of reality and argues that "ultimately the
*Quintet* will have to be treated as a five-dimensional novel" and approached like a
multilevel chessboard (unpublished paper, Third International Lawrence Durrell

Conference, 13–14 April 1984). In "The Quincunx Quiddified: Structure in Lawrence Durrell," Ian S. MacNiven sees *Monsieur*—the novel that "spans everything"—as the centerpiece of the "quincuncial pattern" (*The Modernists: Studies in a Literary Phenomenon,* ed. Lawrence B. Gamache and Ian S. MacNiven [Rutherford, N.J.: Fairleigh Dickinson University Press, 1987]).

2. Norman Bryson, *Word and Image: French Painting of the Ancien Regime* (New York: Cambridge University Press, 1981), 61.

3. Lawrence Durrell, *Constance* (New York: Viking, 1982), 215. Further citations from this edition will be included in the text.

4. Mary Ann Caws, *Reading Frames in Modern Fiction* (Princeton: Princeton University Press, 1985), 28. Caws's descriptions of framing techniques and superpositioning have helped me articulate the perceptions I have had of Durrell's pictorial prose structure. Durrell's palimpsests in *The Alexandria Quartet* have been analyzed by Carol Peirce in "'Wrinkled Deep in Time': *The Alexandria Quartet* as Many-layered Palimpsest," *Twentieth Century Literature* 33 (Winter 1987): 485–98. Peirce isolates the layers of history, myth, and literary allusion and draws our attention to Durrell's comments about this technique in Marc Alyn, ed., *The Big Supposer* (New York: Grove, 1974).

5. Lawrence Durrell, *Sebastian* (New York: Viking, 1984) and *Quinx* (New York: Viking, 1985). Further references will be included in the text.

6. Lawrence Durrell, *Monsieur* (New York: Viking, 1974), 197, and *Livia* (New York: Viking, 1979), 245. Further references will be included in the text.

7. Ian S. MacNiven discusses thematic inversion in the *Quintet* in "The Quincunx Quiddified." At this point, it is also important to note the various titles of Clement's work that result from subjective recollection and to recall other revisions of traditional representations. The most dramatic attempt to translate a religious painting into contemporary terms must be Sutcliffe's idea for "a film about the filming of the Crucifixion" (*Monsieur,* 280–81). Point of view determines imagery and style in the *Quintet,* and while Blanford discusses his ideas for redesigning the novel, Sutcliffe makes the most references to painters (see "The Venetian Documents" in *Monsieur*).

8. Lawrence Durrell, Fourth International Lawrence Durrell Conference, April 1986.

9. Michael H. Begnal establishes the connection between the Templar treasure and art in the preceding essay, "The Mystery of the Templars in *The Avignon Quintet.*" Begnal defers to Blanford's solution of the mystery: "'The real secret treasure was the Grail, the lotus of insight'" (*Quinx,* 54).

10. The novel's tribute to J. M. W. Turner seems inevitable given the analogies between his intentions and Durrell's thematic and structural goals in the *Quintet.* In the "Introduction to the First Edition" of *The Paintings of J. M. W. Turner* (New Haven: Yale University Press, 1984), Evelyn Joll remarks on Turner's "sustained attempt . . . to raise the role of landscape . . . to a level of importance which placed it beside paintings of historical, allegorical, mythological and religious subjects—and of portraits" (xv). Turner learned from, but experimented with, the work of the old masters, and, as an architectural draughtsman, he brought an "underlying sense of structure" to his painting. Often labeled the first impressionist, Turner did not paint out of doors but painted landscapes that are "a synthesis of recollection" (xvii).

11. André Gide, *Poussin* (Paris: Au Divan, 1945), 5.

# The Risen Angels in Durrell's Fallen Women: The Fortunate Fall and Calvinism in Lawrence Durrell's *Quincunx* and *The Alexandria Quartet*

JAMES R. NICHOLS

In his study of Lawrence Durrell's oeuvre through *The Alexandria Quartet,* John Weigel notes quite correctly that there can be "no one single truth in a space-time novel." Weigel goes on to quote from *Balthazar:* "Everything is true of everybody."[1] Because it is so clearly tautological, Durrell's statement at first might seem innocuous, a grand gesture, a momentary bit of sprezzatura by a young writer feeling his oats. Yet, the comment is not only central to Durrell's understanding of the artist and his art, as Weigel and so many others have suggested, it is also for Durrell a complex and intense admission of the constant changes and paradoxes that define human experience. Indeed, G. S. Fraser has given silent assent to such an analysis by asserting that "*The Alexandria Quartet* is a cosmic myth set within the framework of the psychological novel. . . . The epistemology of which insists that there is neither absolute error nor absolute truth."[2]

For Durrell, all human experience is vital, not static, and thus Fraser's point is even more intriguing than it is descriptive. If Fraser is correct, then Durrell evidently understands the substance of human experience to be psychological, and its meaning to be mythic. Such a reading explains why Durrell, aggressive Lawrencian sensualist that he is so often labeled, has evidenced such a lifelong intellectual and artistic interest in religion: in hermaneutics, gnosticism, Copts, Buddhism, and so on.

Surprisingly enough, Durrell is a very religious writer, even if, as Reed Way Dasenbrock has noted, his religion is the redeeming value of heresy.[3] For Durrell, religion is an explanation in vital form of human desire, fear, joy, and tragedy. It is not religious dogma that is vital, however, but religious myth—the stories, not the laws. This has been especially true for Durrell's women, who again and again defy convention and social conformity in an effort not only to realize themselves, but also to assert their compassion. Durrell's women submit to no dogma except living itself, and they assert life by accepting death. They discover strength through submission. Most important, they attain virtue in a realization of sin. Like Milton's Eve in *Paradise Lost,* Durrell's women, primarily in the *Quartet* and the *Quintet,* are the means by which man both falls from grace and is simultaneously assured of Paradise. Throughout the *Quintet,* the paradox of the Fortunate Fall has become more and more central to both the structure and the substance of Durrell's fiction.

The Christian concept of the Fortunate Fall has been around for a long time, but for technical reasons let me outline once more its major features. Man in Eden is originally good, but without knowledge. Without knowledge he is without free choice, and, therefore, his goodness is of no moral consequence. Thus, both Heaven and Hell are denied him, as is the divinity of his own humanness. The fall into sin is, importantly enough, the happy, happy sin of both the medieval church and of the gnostics (but for different reasons, as I will point out). It, the sin of Adam visited upon him by Eve, is morally ambiguous. Adam and Even gain knowledge, disobey God to do so, fall under the power of Satan, discover themselves as separate individuals separated from God's will, gain the power of free choice, and are punished and cast out of the Garden, only to have ensured by their sin (and God's limitless mercy) Mary, the Virgin Birth, Christ on the Cross, Salvation, and the certainty of Heaven for their progeny.

The long list of Western authors who have approached and investigated the paradox runs from a 17th-century, Calvinistic Milton, for whom man's "freedom" is the inestimable luxury of doing God's will, to a 20th-century Joyce Cary, whose philosopher/artist, anti-hero Gulley Jimson sees the "Fall into Freedom" not as the first act of redemption, but the final act of creation. As opposed to such complex intellectuals as Darley and Aubrey Blanford, Gulley has learned almost perfectly how to avoid useless thought and unproductive spirituality.

In all its transformations, however, woman plays the central role in the Fall. She is both evil and good, gnostically both virgin and viper, the cause of damnation and the instrument of redemption.[4] She is both perfect bliss, "with thee conversing I forget all time," and world destroyer. For Durrell, as for Lawrence, she is the giver of both life and death.

In the *Quintet,* the great paradox of the Fortunate Fall is not that the sin of Adam, visited upon him by Eve, leads to good, the eventual restoration of man to God through Christ's sacrifice, but that Eve's sinful betrayal of Adam to her own body is good itself, a reflection, in clear gnostic terms, of a false God and his equally false laws of the dead spirit. The Fall is clearly a fall into freedom of the more fecund, productive, and life-giving laws of the flesh. It is a theme nascent in much of Durrell's earlier work, such as *The Black Book* and *The Alexandria Quartet*.

Freedom is Durrell's key concept, and more specifically a "free" woman his central vision. Rob Sutcliffe notes this in *Monsieur* when he says of Piers, Bruce, and Sylvie:

> In this context my trio of lovers must present the prototype of a new biological relationship, foreshadowing a different sort of society based upon a free woman. (199)

We cannot wait for lightning to strike. Durrell parodies the Trinity by replacing God the Father with God the Mother and Lover. Two pages later Durrell makes sure that we understand exactly what his "Freedom" is when Akkad writes:

> And freedom, which is simply the power of spending—its prototype the orgasm—was shackled in the mind and later the body. (201)

"The power of spending." No lady of the night could want more justification. In Durrell's world, it is Eve who saves and Mary who inverts. Melissa in the *Quartet* is the first clear example of Durrell's argument. She saves Darley by the force of her "charity."[5] Her rescue of Darley from his debt to Capodistria is an early proof of the war that Akkad insists is central to the twentieth century, "sperm against specie" (*Monsieur,* 223). And Melissa knows this when she tells Darley:

> Justine would have paid your debt from her immense fortune. I did not want to see her increase her hold over you. Besides . . . this was the least of sacrifices. (*Justine,* 35)

For all her weaknesses and problems, Melissa is the central woman of the *Quartet,* more so than Justine or Clea. She freely spends not only for Darley, but for Nessim, for Cohen, and later (in actual time but not fictional time) for Sebastian, the banker from whom she refuses to accept money after their lovemaking.[6] Melancholic and alone, she spends of herself freely for all the men in her life. She leaves Sebastian with his Juliet cigar-wrapper marriage-ring and her own contraceptive pessary sponge. And while it would be foolish for anyone to insist that Melissa is the totally "free" woman, it is her freedom and human compassion that make the inversion of redemption not only unnecessary but undesirable.

Earlier in *Monsieur*, Akkad says of his gnosticism:

> We have let sperm stand in place of excrement, for our world is a world not of repression and original sin but of creation and relaxation, of love and not doubt.

> Self-realization is an imperative.

> that self-perpetuating cycle of joy which was the bliss of yesterday. (130)

Durrell's fallen women are not prostitutes working for money, but increasingly free women opposing the twentieth century's materialistic prostitution of both spirit and flesh. Finally, Justine cannot be counted among them, for she is never able to live freely, without man, as Constance insists *she* can after Sebastian.[7]

As James B. Carley notes, Durrell uses "gnostic philosophy as a means of exploring his own disillusionment with Christianity."[8] It is gnosticism, this "disease" of Christianity, that Durrell's women address. Durrell does not defend the cynicism and reality of evil as exposed in a gnostic doctrine that Durrell's women rise above. Instead, they insist upon self-discovery and reject the simplistic duality of both Christianity and gnosticism.

Clea, the final woman of the *Quartet*, is substantially free. She insists upon her fall when she begs Pursewarden, another artist, "to *depuceler* me, please, because I can't get any further with my work unless you do."[9] In spite of Pursewarden's laughter and wounded vanity (*he* needs to be wanted), Clea has correctly divined her own problem. Virginity is a ghastly Christian inversion, essentially sexless, joyless, and totally uncreative; a kind of living death for the artist. Clea cannot abide such stagnation, such a hoarding of sperm and egg, a denial of her own womanhood and, therefore, humanhood. One does not hoard, one invests, as she and Darley are to do for one another later in the novel, and as Sebastian and Constance (and later Constance and Aubrey) accomplish in the last two books of the *Quintet*.

Not only does Darley save Clea from drowning and then give her life and a new hand (supplied by Amaril) with which to paint, but, as importantly, Clea, through the free spending of herself, leads Darley toward his own self-realization. While drifting into sleep, Darley hears the voice of a distant muezzein praising God and thinks, "the buoyancy of a new freedom possessed me. . . . I knew that Clea would share everything with me, withholding nothing" (*Clea*, 90).

Quite correctly, Jennifer Linton Fruin has pointed out that Clea is the "realized love of the hermetic paradigm. She exists on the fourth and amatory level in which all experience is understood as divine and good."[10] In the *Quartet,* it is the virtuous woman who has nothing to give her lover, neither life nor knowledge. Melissa, the prostitute, is the archetypal fecund woman, both giving to and knowing of Darley as a man. She educates, provides and sacrifices for, the nascent artist. Bereft of Calvinistic virtue, she is all virtuous. She spends and does not hoard. Clea culminates the sequence, needing to be ravished before she can create and become an artist herself (loss of hand as well as hymen).

The *Quintet,* centrally in the figure of Constance, completes Durrell's anti-Christian, gnostic argument. If it is knowledge that reveals to man his own humanness and ultimately his Godliness, then experience and sin *are* man's salvation, not just a means to it. Eve seduces Adam, and so man triumphs over sin, just as Constance seduces Sebastian from his gnostic views in book 4. And, equally, Sebastian's death at the hands of Mnemidis, who uses the same knives that the nuns use to slice bread (the symbolic referent of which is the body of Christ, more sardonically God himself, in edible slices), is a moral victory committed by a madman. Mnemidis takes on the disguise of a nun in his escape from the hospital, and seduces a truckdriver while wearing the habit. The lesson is clear. Virginal purity is a hideous inversion of man and woman, a rejection of humanity's fellow sympathy and love, and a denial of the creative and lifegiving Godhood of man.

This is why the Renaissance sonneteers, especially Dante and Petrach, become such an important image pattern in the *Quintet.* The sonneteers praised adulterous love and the paradox of human exaltation and ascension up the Platonic ladder to perfect knowledge of perfect Godhood. Durrell ends the journey abruptly with human love itself. Petrach's sojourn in Avignon ends when he discovers the perfection of man's physical beauty at church in the person of the green-robed Laura, green for the endless cycle of birth and death to which Laura's physical life is tied (*Monsieur,* 213).

Even poor Sutcliffe, who suffers so at the hands of Pia (as Aubrey does before Livia), has his unlucky chance encounter with Sister Rosa, the nun.[11] Sutcliffe asks, "How? When? Where?" on the endpapers of his hymnal (hymenal?—the pun is too attractive). He does not ask "How much?" because "after all she was a bloody nun." But, as always with poor invented Sutcliffe, this is a false start. Sister Rosa began the affair because she was justifiably bored, and Sutcliffe messes it up in vaudevillian style by stealing into the Mother Superior's cell instead of Rosa's. The chaste, virtuous Mary becomes a false redeeming fig-

ure, having lost all the qualities that mark her as a woman, and so she
is incapable of either giving to or saving her man. She hoards virtue,
spends no human love, and thus becomes the symbol of perverted
greed, and the horrible inversion of self-love.

Constance, of all the women in the *Quintet,* moves toward completion, fulfillment, and self-knowledge. In doing so, she avoids the extremes to which many of Durrell's women go in denying man in order
to achieve selfhood. Unlike the comic prostitute Iolanthe in *Tunc* and
*Nunquam,* who is at first a woman used as a mechanism, then a female
mechanism created by man for man, and finally a fully free woman
because her mechanisms have worked so well, Constance develops
along more complex and clearly human lines. She has three major
lovers—Sam, Affad (Sebastian), and Aubrey Blanford. From the novel's beginning, Durrell insists that she is an emancipated scientist, a
psychologist whose initial sexual shyness is due to an inherent sensitivity of spirit as well as an understandable lack of experience.

She ministers to the men in her life, however, by bringing sin (sex
and human experience) to them. Unlike her quixotic sister Livia, Constance is not driven to isolated self-discovery and social rebellion. She
moves predictably and surely (for the reader if not for herself),
through stages of self-discovery and fulfillment that deny greed
and self-centered virtue, and build toward womanly self-confidence,
human discovery, and the paradox of complete freedom through sexual sharing. Constance attains the final "dual control" of the sex act
itself, when in *Quinx* she gives of herself so completely as to accept
the male role and psychologically castrate Blanford in order eventually
to allow him to respond fully to her.[12] It is a "dual control" for which
Aubrey knows he must thank the dead Affad and Sabine.

Durrell, who insists upon the phrase, outlines the culmination of
sexual love in the twentieth century as the progressive "conquering"
of "the loving amnesia of the orgasm and expanding its area of consciousness." If we make the relatively easy assumption that "consciousness" need not mean intellectual awareness, then Durrell's "dual
control" is nothing more nor less than what Constance Chatterley experiences "beyond shame" during that wonderful night with Mellors
that has so fascinated modern readers for so long.

If woman is to be fully woman, she must throw off the debilitating
concept of Christian virtue. "The aching root," says Durrell, "is guilt
over uncommitted sins" (*Quinx,* 180). Again, here is the paradox. To
be fully human, we must sin, "oh, happy, happy sin." "Civilization
[Christian] is a placebo with side-effects," we are told. Constance, a
woman who began her sexual journey with the goodhearted but sim-
pleminded Sam, and after his death became swept into the incredibly

complex inversions of Affad's gnosticism, finally makes love with Aubrey Blanford, "secure in this despairing knowledge."

The free woman has conquered all, or at least most all. Constance has won through a war that took Sam from her. And we must remember that Sam admits to Aubrey that nothing can compete with war, not even lovemaking that seems merely a charming adventure (*Constance*, 72–73). Constance, as well, has seen the humane and free Nancy Quiminal murdered by the very people that woman has helped save. She has overcome the inversions of Affad's gnosticism and brought him to a commitment to life before he was murdered. Finally, she and Aubrey, with a shiver, ready themselves to enter the first Templar cave at *Quinx*'s end. Her "loving triumph" over Blanford in Quinx is that of a teacher over a student, who only waits for the student to equal and surpass her (14–15), in insight but never in dogma.

In "Provence Anew," the first chapter of *Quinx*, Constance insists very early upon the thematic center of the book, and by extension the entire *Quintet*, when she says:

> And birth is no trauma but an apotheosis: here I part company with my Viennese colleagues for they were born into sin. But in reality one is born with bliss—it is we who cause the trauma with those mad doctrines based on guilt and fear. Pathology begins at home. Instinct has its own logic which we must obey.

She then tells the story of Julio, the legless man with the great member, and concludes, "sex is not dying, it is coming of age with the freedom of the woman" (17–19). It is no accident that Julio is savaged by a bull, the quintessential image of his traditional manhood, and only becomes truly male when he must be taken by his partners—when he presents no threat to them other than that which they willingly accept.

In truth, Durrell's fallen woman is a reflection of the excessive Puritan mentality of Protestant Christianity more than of a Mediterranean cultural ambiance (which he has always loved). In *Quinx*, Aubrey specifically wants his great work to avoid "excessive puritan morality" (13). Durrell implicitly denies a Calvinistic world much more than he does a more broadly Christian one. It is Calvinism, with its insistence upon double predestination and the consequent loss of personal freedom, creation, and the imagination, that is most repugnant in the *Quintet*.

Implicitly, Durrell sees Protestant Calvinism as a dogma that wholly denies the reality of this physical life—of the "bliss" of the body and birth. For Durrell, Calvinism is, finally, a religion without human compassion in that it insists upon judgment over mercy, faith and ignorance over understanding and knowledge, stasis over change, and virtue over love. In Durrell's terms, Calvinism hoards specie and refuses to give sperm. It is *merde,* offal, a denial of human freedom and joy.

In a clear reversal, Durrell's fallen woman refuses to accept dead dogma. Instead she becomes risen angel (responsible for man's erections, as he for her lactation), and she gives her lover that sin which fulfills man as God unto himself. She is the spirit alive and only alive in the flesh—the original sin of that fallen angel Lucifer, who would have no God above him. Having avoided self-centered and personal virtue, she has asserted her common, loving humanity.

Lovers, mothers, sisters, goddesses, and witches, Durrell's women—Justine, Melissa, Clea, Iolanthe, Livia, Constance, and Sappho—like Pater's Mona Lisa, subsume time and judgment. They are older than the rocks upon which they sit, the embodiment of man's experience and the symbol of his possibility.

## NOTES

1. Lawrence Durrell, *Balthazar* (New York: Dutton, 1966), 108.

2. G. S. Fraser, *Lawrence Durrell: A Critical Study* (New York: Dutton, 1968), 135.

3. Reed Way Dasenbrock, "Death and the Counterlife of Heresy in Wyndham Lewis and Lawrence Durrell," *Deus Loci* 4, no. 1 (September 1980): 16.

4. Lawrence Durrell, *Monsieur* (New York: Viking Press, 1974), p. 127. Further references will be included in the text.

5. Lawrence Durrell, *Justine* (New York: Dutton, 1966), p. 18.

6. Lawrence Durrell, *Sebastian* (New York: Viking Press, 1984), p. 46.

7. Lawrence Durrell, *Constance* (New York: Viking Press, 1982), p. 347.

8. James B. Carley, "Lawrence Durrell and the Gnostics," *Deus Loci* 2, no. 1 (September 1978): 9.

9. Lawrence Durrell, *Clea* (New York: Dutton, 1966), p. 99. Further references will be included in the text.

10. Jennifer Linton Fruin, "The Importance of Narouz in Durrell's Hermetic Paradigm," *Deus Loci* 2, no. 6 (June 1979): 5.

11. Lawrence Durrell, *Livia* (New York: Viking Press, 1979), p. 60.

12. Lawrence Durrell, *Quinx* (New York: Viking Press, 1985), pp. 169–170. Further references will be included in the text.

# Lawrence Durrell's Game in
## *The Avignon Quintet*
### William L. Godshalk

Lawrence Durrell strikes me as one of our most playful novelists. Along with—say—James Joyce, John Fowles, John Barth, and Thomas Pynchon, Durrell is at play in a field of words, ideas, and forms, and, as with the works of these novelists, part of the fun is Durrell's violation of the basic rules of the verbal game he is playing. The realist critic may object that he's cheating, but Durrell might very well reply that he is conforming to a universal law, since in *Quinx*, the narrative voice claims, in italics: *"The universe is playing, the universe is only improvising!"*[1] The universe itself is not bound by strict laws, but is ruled by the art of the improviser. Throughout his career Durrell has extolled artistic playfulness, and I feel that the qualities of play and game are especially evident in *The Avignon Quintet*.

Huizinga in his classic study of "play" comments that "the *fun* of playing . . . resists all analysis, all logical interpretation,"[2] but that the basic qualities of play can be isolated and discussed. First, "play is a voluntary activity" characterized by its freedom, and this freedom separates play "from the course of the natural process" (7). Second, "play is not 'ordinary' or 'real' life. It is rather a stepping out of [the] 'real' . . . into a temporary sphere of activity with a disposition all of its own"; it is "an *interlude* in our daily lives." At the same time, this pretend quality of play "does not by any means prevent it from proceeding with the utmost seriousness" (8–9). As paradoxical as it may seem, play is a serious procedure. Third, play is limited by certain confines of time and space. "It contains its own course and meaning. . . . It is transmitted, it becomes tradition. . . . In this faculty of repetition lies one of the most essential qualities of play" (9–10). Huizinga's "playground" is more extensive than a field upon which children play; it takes on cultural overtones, and he suggests that arenas, card tables, stages, and screens are fields of play—and he might well have added the novel to his list.

Huizinga's fourth characteristic of play is that "it creates order."

"Inside the play-ground an absolute and peculiar order reigns." We sense a "rhythm and harmony." But, concurrently, there is an element of "uncertainty," and this uncertainty yields a feeling of "tension" (10). We do not know how the game will end. Finally, "all play has rules" that govern the temporary world circumscribed by play. "The rules of a game are absolutely binding and allow no doubt" (11). Huizinga's characteristics presuppose a spectator sport, where one segment of society plays, while another enjoys watching; but both segments in their separate ways participate in the game.

What I find interesting about Huizinga's definition of play is that it may be applied to the art of the novel. The novelist is a "player," the novel a "game," and the reader a "spectator." The novel takes the reader/spectator outside his daily life. The novel—like any playfield—is limited in space, and—like any game—limited in time. The novel is orderly, rhythmic, harmonious, and yet it maintains a sense of tension in that the reader/spectator is generally kept in suspense (if not surprised) by the outcome. And, as the narratologists have taught us, novels—as narratives— do have definite rules.[3]

But Huizinga's argument goes beyond the production of art. "A certain play-factor," he contends, is "active all through the cultural process and . . . it produces many of the fundamental forms of social life" (173). Thus, my contention that Durrell is a playful novelist is—if we accept Huizinga's arguments—not very meaningful. Durrell is not simply one of a select group of novelists that I consider "playful," but shares his creative playfulness with all of us who are engaged in the cultural project—including priests, soldiers, and lawyers. From Huizinga's perspective, all novelists are game players, and so what makes Durrell's playing significant is not *that* he does it, but *how* he does it. I hope to define the style of his game, to discover just what sort of player he is, and to describe and explain this novelist *ludens*.

Part of Durrell's game is—as I see it—the conscious and effective violation of ordinary rules. In a narrative fiction, we expect a primary reality. The characters and situations, the time and space, of this primary reality we accept as *real;* in the world of the fiction, what happens to the characters *really* happens; we tend to get caught up in their stories and in the *donnés* of their worlds. In science fiction, for example, we accept "hyper-space" as a fact. And within this primary reality, we have learned, as readers, to accept the possibility of a secondary reality such as in Shakespeare's *Taming of the Shrew,* a play that begins in the "real" English world of Christopher Sly and then modulates into the "fictional" Italian world of Kate and Petruchio. As readers and spectators, we accept the idea that "real" characters in the primary fictional reality can become engaged—in much the same fashion as we have become engaged—by "fictions" from a secondary reality. And artists as diverse as Shakespeare and Borges have been tempted to play with this regression into fictions within fictions, creating Chinese boxes of art.[4]

But what Durrell does in *Monsieur* is to work backward, to begin in the secondary reality of Bruce Drexel and then in the final section of the novel to move to what the reader assumes to be the primary reality of Aubrey Blanford, the creator of the secondary reality. As a reader geared to conventional expectations, I was confused and upset by the realization that the narrative of Bruce, Piers, and Sylvie is a secondary fiction, not the primary reality of the novel. I had become engaged by and with these characters, and my realization of their secondary status forced me to make a radical readjustment of my feelings about them. I was annoyed by Durrell's game, thrown off balance, perhaps a little angry. I was alienated, for Durrell initially urges upon me the reality of Bruce's world, and then, without notice, urges me to accept Bruce's world as a fiction. My contrary urge was to have Bruce *real*—as far as reality is possible in a fictional world. My next reaction was more considered: I expected that the *Quintet* was going to be about the writing of *Monsieur*, that the following novels were going to show me the *reality* out of which Blanford—the real novelist—had created the fictional world of *Monsieur*. I expected the conventional juxtaposition of primary and secondary realities where fiction is duly separated from fact. What I got was—for me—the disturbing interpenetration of primary and secondary realities— "encysted in each other."[5] While reading the first pages of *Livia*, I thought that Blanford's talking to the "fictional" Sutcliffe indicated Blanford's mental instability; *he* was confusing fiction and imagination with reality, much as he does at the end of *Monsieur* when he dines with the missing duchess of Tu. But as the series progressed, I realized that other characters—Constance and Affad, for example— could also see and talk with both Sutcliffe and Toby. As reader, I could accept Blanford's madness much more easily than I could accept the idea that characters from the secondary reality of *The Prince of Darkness* (Sutcliffe's version of *Monsieur*) had stepped into the primary reality of the *Quintet*.[6] Durrell questions and challenges our assumptions about fictive reality and our demand as readers to know what is "real" and what is "fiction." Durrell makes difficult—or impossible—our conventional readerly habit of identification with the protagonist of the primary reality when he makes it perfectly evident to his reader that both "fiction" and "reality" are merely part of an elaborate narrative game, a game controlled by the novelist.

Perhaps the reason I am most disturbed as a reader by this secondary invasion is that Durrell's primary world seems to be mimetic rather than fantastic. The world of the *Quintet* appears to be set firmly in the Midi, in Egypt, in Switzerland; it is a world of history as we know it—the rise of Hitler, the fall of France, and the collapse of Nazi Germany. These are places we can find on the map, events we can locate in history books. In a created world that seems to reflect our world so precisely, we expect things to happen as they ought to happen—no ghosts, no extraterrestrial beings, and certainly no characters stepping out of novels. We expect a reflection of the mundane reality with which we are familiar; but this is *not* what Durrell consistently gives us.

Along with the ever-present possibility of art transmigrating into reality, Durrell also suggests the infinite regression into art: reality in the Quincunx novels is always susceptible of being transformed into art—the Chinese-box effect that I mentioned above. Durrell writes about Blanford who writes about Sutcliffe who writes about Drexel who, in turn, writes about Sutcliffe, who writes about Sylvia, who writes. . . .[7] What we get is a two-way street where art can become reality and reality can be transformed by the artist into art. The Quincunx world is completely unstable in its identification of "reality," and any distinction it may make between the imaginary and the real is unclear and disquieting.

I sense that Durrell is playing with my readerly expectations and challenging the ordinary conventions of formal narrative. The end of *Quinx* is a perfect example of my expectations being rather playfully denied. I expected—perhaps naïvely, but certainly guided by the usual conventions of narrative—to find some kind of conclusion, some kind of closure; what I get is prophecy and probability: as Sabine tells Felix Chatto, "statistically it falls out as I see it [i.e., as Gypsy fortune teller] about seven times out of ten" (*Quinx*, 187). At the end of the *Quintet*, the reader is left with the same sense of indeterminacy—and a series of unanswered questions. The Templar treasure, for example, has been a leading motif throughout the five novels, and the existence of that treasure has been tied to the image of the quincunx. Recurrently the reader is led to the mysteries surrounding the Templars and their supposed treasure, and the reader is also led to believe that Durrell will provide an answer—if only a fictional one. The reader is deceived, and the mystery remains a mystery.

Durrell's game is extremely reader oriented. Blanford notes in his commonplace book: "the novel is an artefact and needs a thread upon which to thread . . . the reader!" (*Quinx*, 50). Earlier Blanford had discussed the growth of meaning: "Happily meaning has a tendency to accrete in time around an enigma. I don't know why. As if nature could not rest without offering a gloss. In poetry the obscure becomes slowly invested with meaning as if by natural law. The big enigmas of art, simply by dint of continuing to exist, finally accumulate their own explanations by force of critical projection" (*Quinx,* 24). The concept underlying Blanford's thought is that the reader—the audience—invests art with meaning, and thus the reader is invited to play her—or, in my case, his—active part in the verbal game.

Let me consider for a moment my metaphor of playing a game, which, as you see, is consciously chosen and mirrors my thoughts about Durrell's fiction. The text is both the playing field (for the writer) and the game (for the reader). Durrell is the player whose purpose is to perform for the reader/spectator. But as Blanford's comment indicates, the reader is not to be passive; he or she is actively to engage in interpreting, commenting upon, and judging the player's game. The game—like a videotape—can be played again and again, and each time the spectator can see and appreciate new facets of the player's skill and style. My metaphor, of course, may break down here and there, but it does give me a way of placing the novelist, the text, and the reader in a cultural context that suggests something about Durrell's art—his style of playing the narrative game.

If a major part of that style is geared toward keeping the reader off balance, and keeping the tension high, another part is geared toward teasing the reader's memory—*again* demanding the active participation of the reader in the narrative game. A constant experience I have while reading Durrell's narratives is *déjà vu;* I vaguely remember a reference, a sentence, an idea. Sometimes Durrell is alluding playfully to another author. (See, e.g., *Quinx,* 29 and 33, for allusions to John Donne.) But more often he is alluding to himself, creating his own verbal context, and challenging his reader to recall or to find the earlier passage. In *Quinx,* for example, Constance finds herself "at last in the side chapel under the oil-painted witnesses, so gauche and awkward. On the wall at her back was a plaque with an inscription commemorating the death of some now forgotten priest" (114). In this case it basically repeats the passage in *Quinx*—and to the wary suggests a connection between the "real" Constance and the "fictional" Sylvie.

In other places, the allusion is vaguer—and more teasing—and a whole lot harder for the reader to locate. At the end of *Livia,* for example, the male guests at the prince's party "were all dressed in dark suits which were uncomfortably warm for the time of the year" (256). When I first read this passage, I found the idea familiar, and searching back through *Monsieur,* I found that Jourdain sports "dark suits even in summer, when they must have been stifling to wear" (24). The

allusion—after all the trouble to find it—does not seem terribly en-
lightening. (Another teasing reference is to the one-eyed person: *Monsieur,* 93; *Livia,* 100; *Quinx,* 114.) In contrast, *Livia* (5) has a passage
that purports to be quoted from one of the earlier novels—but, as
far as I can find, is not. The reader with a good memory is recurrently
forced to consider whether or where, or both, in Durrell's narrative
or elsewhere he's read these words, encountered this idea or that
image.

I do not wish to suggest that all Durrell's repetitions (or pseudo-
repetitions) are aimed simply at teasing the reader's memory, to provide a meaningless echolalia.[8] The echo-chamber effect more often
reinforces central concepts in the narrative. For example, there is
the recurrent configuration of the three lovers beginning with Piers,
Sylvie, and Bruce, and Toby, Sutcliffe, and Sabine, and that includes
Constance, Affad, and Blanford, then modulates into Constance,
Sylvie, and Blanford. Blanford and Sutcliffe both have lesbian wives—
Livia and Pia—who have female lovers, Trash and Thrush—thus creating two more love triangles. Livia's lover Smirgel finds that Livia
really loves her brother Hilary. These three-way lovers are often incestuous, adulterous, or homosexual. And the reader keeps finding
them: the Quincunx world is filled with tripartite love affairs. This
repetition emphasizes the significance of the amorphous sexuality
to be found on Durrell's playground. (For Sutcliffe's analysis, see
*Monsieur,* 220–21.)

What these repetitions tell me about Durrell's style of play is that
it is very self-reflexive. He is consciously and constantly underlining
the fact that his narrative is a playful construct, and he emphasizes
that he is playing, seriously playing. I seem to get this message: the
playful artistic performance is not to be confused with the real thing.

Regarding the real thing—as we have seen—Durrell keeps reminding his reader of the historical past: the Templars, the Babylonian
Captivity, the Second World War reminded us that Durrell's fictional
present is firmly grounded in an historical past—a real past that becomes fictionalized as part of the Quincunx. The architecture of the
past is recurrently noticed, described, and forms a dense historical matrix in which Durrell places his fiction. One thinks of the intricate
description of Angkor Wat (*Monsieur,* 265). If Durrell has art interpenetrating reality, he also has history interpenetrating fiction. It is,
of course, impossible for the general reader—I include myself—to be
able always to tell where one ends and the other begins, and Durrell
himself underscores the mysteries of historicity. Defending his uses
of history in fiction, Blanford writes: "The distortions and evocations
are thrown in to ask a few basic questions like—how real is reality,

and if so why so?" (*Quinx*, 100). Perhaps Blanford may speak for Durrell as well. In any case, the playing with history and fiction is certainly part of Durrell's style.

Durrell's emphasis on the historical matrix of his fiction suggests another facet of his narrative style: his insistence on temporality.[9] The water seller in Macabru holds a mirror "to our faces to remind us that we were mortal and must die" (*Monsieur*, 107). But what interests me most is the temporal distortions and improbabilities of the Quincunx world. In *Quinx*, directly after World War II, while France is just beginning to recover and return to normality, Felix Chatto returns from China, a China that already has a "Marxist Ministry of Finance" and "an American adviser called O'Schwartz" (59). Now we know that historically China did not fall to the Communists until 1949, and that the United States did not normalize relations with China until the administration of Richard Nixon. So O'Schwartz's promise that "all America" will "rush to visit China" under the proper conditions is very improbable in the context of the late 1940s. In fact, Chatto's story—recounted by Sutcliffe—seems thirty years out of place, and thus one of Blanford's "distortions."

Blanford's back—or rather the history of his recovery from the possibly symbolic wound—also poses a temporal problem for me. In *Monsieur*, Blanford thinks of himself as a "lovely big dollie, with a D.S.O. and Bar, and a spine full of shrapnel fragments, and a male nurse for a mama" (296). You will recall that the narrative voice tells us that this thought occurs *after* Constance (here called the duchess of Tu) has died. In *Livia*, the narrrative voice tells us of "the new orthopaedic waistcoat-brace" that "might allow Blanford one day to throw away his crutches" (4), and by the time we get to *Quinx* (147, 152), Blanford is walking on his own—and swimming and making love. Constance tells him: "I know now that the wound is healed and while there are some muscular movements that you can't make there is no more pain or stress. You can go the whole hog and act without thinking or hesitating" (170). All indications are that Blanford is getting better and better as the narrative progresses, *but*, in terms of the abstract "story" (rather than the "plot" or "discurse"),[10] the events recorded in *Quinx* happen *before* those recorded in the opening pages of *Livia*, and all of *Livia* temporally precedes *Monsieur*. We apparently have an inverted time scheme, an idea also suggested when, in *Quinx*, the narrator tells us that Piers and Sylvie are "of the past" (192). And there are other hints in *Quinx*, as well as in *Livia* (3, 8), that *Monsieur* (or *The Prince of Darkness*) has already been written. But this is improbable when we learn in the first novel that *Monsieur or The Prince of Darkness* is completed only *after* the death of Constance. In *Quinx*,

Constance is still young and very much alive. Durrell is obviously playing with our usual sense of temporal flow, and he is setting "story-line" against "plot-time."

The ages of the central characters are also problematic—and Durrell seems to be playing with long and short time, much as Shakespeare does in *Othello*.[11] Blanford recalls, "Their [Hilary's, Sam's, and his own] youth enabled them to escape the trenches [of World War One] —in 1918 they were still just under military age, though Sam nearly managed to join up by a subterfuge; but he was found out and sent back to school; whence, to Oxford where the three, though so different, became inseparable" (*Livia*, 28). It seems that the three were born about the beginning of the century *if* they were up to Oxford in or around 1918; and if Sam almost got into the army in that year. And yet later in *Livia* we are told by the narrator that "Sam had only a few days' leave before returning to Oxford and the war" (169)—but the war here is the Second World War, and thus Sam and his friends have been students at Oxford for at least twenty years! And, of course, the young men and women who came to vacation in France in the '20s (or perhaps the '30s—see *Livia*, 123) are now almost forty years old. And yet they are presented as fair young folk with all of life before them. Here temporal distortion points toward temporal improbability.

In *Quinx*, the new Prefect of Police notices that "some" of the guests at the final gathering come "from other time-fields or other contingent realities" (192). Taking this hint, I speculate that Durrell's narrative sequences are to be read as temporally distinct, that they are to be seen as "contingent realities," each with its own "time-field." Bruce Drexel argues for temporal relativity: "From that point forward day merged with day and night with night to such an extent that time became fluid, distances illusory; we are moving from one dream to another, merging from one truth into another in a way that gave the lie to the banal chronology of Piers' diary, which tried to segment our lives in so untruthful a fashion" (*Monsieur*, 154–55). And the possibilities within the temporal field are numerous: "We each have as many destinies stacked up inside us as a melon has seeds," Sabine explains. "They live on *in potentia* so to speak" (*Quinx*, 169). The various narratives embody these potentials. They do not form a temporal sequence as we ordinarily think of temporal sequence. Blanford perhaps suggests this when he describes his concept of a quincunx of novels: "Though only dependent on one another as echoes might be, they would not be laid end to end in serial order . . . but simply belong to the same blood group" (*Livia*, 11). In any case, I suggest that this unique use of temporality is a conscious part of Durrell's game plan.

But if Durrell plays with temporality in the Quincunx novels, he also plays with space. "Literature," Gabriel Zoran claims in a difficult but extraordinarily suggestive article on narrative space, "is basically an art of time. Although no one today would state this as badly as Lessing . . . did, the dominance of the time factor in the structuring of the narrative text remains an indisputable fact."[12] Zoran, of course, is wrong in thinking that the primacy of time has not been disputed, since Durrell's narrative structures are aimed at making space as important as time in the narrative act. The Quincunx novels are related spatially rather than temporally. Although each reader will explain this spatial relationship in a different way, I see the novels set out so that they approximate the form of the quincunx.[13] *Constance* is the center. The first novel—*Monsieur*—and the fourth novel—*Sebastian*—are related by subject: Egyptian gnosticism, the suicide pact, and the deaths of Piers and Affad. These two novels form one arm of the quincunx. The second novel—*Livia*—and the fifth novel—*Quinx*—again are related by subject: Blanford's love affairs with the two sisters, the dark Livia and the blond Constance, and both novels end significantly with a festival at the old Roman aqueduct. These novels form the second arm of the quincunx. And the two arms intersect to form the Greek letter chi: the chiasma, the cross. (I learn this fact from Frank Huntley who explicates Sir Thomas Browne who in turn is explicating Plato.)[14] For the mystagogue, this quincunxial chi symbolizes spiritual life, and for the Christian, specifically Christ. But we are here looking at the quincunx in terms of plane geometry. In terms of solid geometry, we can see the quincunx as two intersecting circles. Huntley tells us how to construct one: "make two strips of paper into two circles, then place one circle within the other so that each bisects the other as the equator bisects the meridian at zero and 180."[15] Looked at from above, the two circles still form a chi, but, looked at from the side, they form a theta, which suggests, for the mystical interpreter, *thanatos,* or death. The circle of the theta is symbolic of perfection, immortality, God, while the straight line intersecting this circle symbolizes linear time, the body, divisibility, and death.

Durrell is here building for his narrative a new kind of playground, a new space, a new area in which to conduct the narrative game. Here the serial novel approximates geometrical forms, forms that have thematic meanings that in turn reflect and refract the thematic concerns of the text. Form and meaning are thematically linked. The duality inherent in the form (chi/theta) is also a major part of the verbal structure as Durrell dialectically opposes art against reality, spirit against flesh, life against death, certainty against doubt, and so on, without—at any time—resolving these oppositions, but making their tension an inherent part of his text, just as they are inherent in the quincunxial form itself. This special use of symbolic space helps us further to define Durrell's narrative game.

If Durrell plays with time and space, he also plays with ideologies, presenting elaborate intellectual and religious systems only to question and challenge them—playfully. Affad firmly espouses the gnostic suicide cult, but he is ironically murdered by a psychotic who takes Affad for Constance. Blanford and Constance glorify the cult of sexual orgasm, and Constance convinced Blanford "of the existence of lovers as philosophers, and of the need for a joint approach to time through the atom of their love" (*Quinx,* 176). The narrator wryly notes that "this sometimes made them both a bit of a bore" (176). Psychoanalysis fares little better. Schwartz, the great analyst, commits suicide; Constance violates medical ethics by falling into lesbian love with a patient; and Dr. Joy (Freud) and his Sofa are a constant object of jest. At first yoga is present positively, and then undercut by the satirical Sutcliffe. The narrator agrees that "Sutcliffe was right to reproach [Blanford] with all the brain-wearying lumber he had taken aboard— all this soul-porridge, all this brain-mash of Hindu soul-fuck" (*Quinx,* 83). Indeed, the novels are "informed by mutually contradictory insights" (*Quinx,* 166), and, perhaps echoing Bakhtin, Blanford comments, "men and women are polyphonic beings" (*Livia,* 41).[16] Diversity, dialogue, and dialectic seem to be at the core of Durrell's play.

The two novelists Blanford and Sutcliffe seem to embody the conflict between the romantic and the classic, between the enthusiast and the cynic. Blanford's romanticism is set against Sutcliffe's penetrating skepticism. But even Sut runs afoul of the human need for some kind of positive value, and he appears to find that value in love—his love for Pia, and finally in his abiding love for Sabine, a love consummated once again in *Quinx.* The point for me is that no character can maintain a complete distance from all belief, that these characters ultimately need something in which they can have at least a modicum of faith. Although dialectical play may be fine for the narrator, although he may be able to maintain his playfully ironic distance, his characters require a firmer grounding.

But that playful, playing narrative voice demands our closer attention. Some years ago, Wayne Booth indicated that in *Mountolive* Durrell uses the unreliable third-person narrator—a narrator who only *apparently* directs the reader to the truth of the matter.[17] I suggest that the narrator of the *Quintet* is similarly unreliable. "Good writing should pullulate with ambiguities," we find in the polyphonic pastiche that begins chapter 5 of *Quinx* (133), and the narrator orchestrates this pullulation. For example, he tells us that it is the tribal mother, the *puri dai,* who tells the fortunes of Galen, the prince, and Sylvie (74, 86–88), and yet, in the final chapter, Galen and the prince make it clear that Sabine herself has been the fortune-teller. Galen says: "I'm on the look-out for that Sabine lady . . . to try to get a really detailed and authoritative reading of her. She was rather unsatisfactory last time when we went to the Saintes Maries; and yet there was sufficient truth in what she said to be very striking" (*Quinx,* 185). Moreover, the narrator tells us that the prince "as a good Egyptian . . . believed in the other world of alchemy and divination" (*Quinx,* 95), but, earlier, the narrator assures us that the prince "was less prone to believe in soothsayers" than Galen (88). Even earlier we find that the prince has consulted a "soothsayer" (66), but he assents to Galen's comment that fortune-telling is "not very *sound*" (65). Later, however, the narrator informs us that the prince's "fortunetellers had predicted the death of the Princess, and he had begun to dream of the funeral cortege" (*Quinx,* 173). Obviously the narrator has not made up his mind about certain facts in the story nor about certain attitudes of the characters. The narrator (apparently) tells us, "Listen, nothing that SUT has to say about BLAN should be taken seriously" (*Quinx,* 27–28). The same might be said *more generally* about the narrator.

At another place in *Quinx,* a voice tells us—I assume that it is the narrative voice—"I have made a discovery but I can't tell you what it is because the language in which to express it has not been invented. I know a place but there is no road to it—you must swim or fly—thus the mage Faustus. What's to be done? Why, we must push on with reality, living in the margins of hope" (178). The voice then goes on with a poem that ends, "tickle my arse and call me Chomsky!" (178). The reference to modern linguists is apparent, but this is not the narrative voice that the reader has come to expect in what Sutcliffe calls "the average novel" (*Quinx,* 23). The narrator here is gnomic and playful, and hardly inspires the confidence of the reader.

Also, unlike the narrative voice of most novels, Durrell's voice can at times be overheard by the characters. (This fits in with Durrell's playful use of the ordinary conventions of fictive reality.) Commenting on Blanford's new novel, the narrator says, "it was a hopeless task, for what is to be done with characters who are all the time trying to exchange selves, turn into each other? And then, ascribing a meaning to point-events? There is no meaning and we falsify the truth about reality in adding one" (*Quinx,* 167). At this point, Sutcliffe, the skeptic, stops the voice: "Who knows all this? You should say, in the interest of clarity." The voice responds: "I leave you to guess," and Sutcliffe guesses, "Sabine?" And the voice of Sabine continues with a long paragraph on the "game of destiny" (*Quinx,* 168).

I find this exchange interesting because of the unanswerable questions that it forces me to ask. I wonder whether the narrator speaks with the voice of Sabine, or whether he merely expresses her ideas. In the text, the narrator's comments are not in quotation marks; Sutcliffe's and Sabine's responses are. It is unclear where Sabine comes from. So far, Blanford and Sutcliffe have been talking—apparently alone. It seems to me that here the narrator does not at all help the reader reconstruct the immediate scene. Far from it. The narrator himself becomes part of the phantasmagorical quality that recurrently surfaces in the *Quintet*—and especially in *Quinx*.

Throughout the *Quintet*, the narrator is problematic. Unreliable, limited, shifty, and shifting, the narrator seems to change from novel to novel. In *Monsieur* he appears only in the last twenty pages, while in *Constance* his voice and eyes hold the narrative together. My major point here is that Durrell's use of the narrative voice—like his use of other narrative conventions—is unpredictable, and thus keeps the reader constantly active in the narrative game. The narrator does not give the reader a vision of *the truth,* but merely one idiosyncratic version of what is going on in the "story."

Durrell presents us with a pluralistic, polyphonic world where truth is contingent, multiple, and relative, and Durrell's game plan tends toward the fragmentary and the contradictory, toward the tangential and the inconclusive. "And pray, why not an aberrant prose style to echo the discordance at the heart of all nature?" (*Quinx*, 22). *Obiter dicta* are apparently thrown without reason on to the page. In parentheses the reader is told: "If the communication between the sexes falters the whole universe, which is imaginary, is put to risk!" (*Quinx*, 92). On first reading, I paused to assess the truth of the aphorism, only to find it denied in the next sentence: "Of course it is pure impudence to think like this" (*Quinx*, 92). I find this two-sentence assertion and denial a general paradigm for Durrell's style of play. Durrell seems to be speaking for himself when he has Blanford say, "I was hoping . . . to free the novel a bit from the shackles of causality with a narrative apparently dislocated and disjointed yet informed by mutually contradictory insights" (*Quinx*, 165–66). And Blanford treats the concept of the unified ego with the same disdain as he treats the unified plot: "in the course of the few years . . . every cell in the body of this 'I,' this individual, has been modified and even replaced. His thoughts, judgements, emotions, desires have all undergone a similar metamorphosis! What then is the permanence which you designate as an 'I'?" (*Quinx*, 176).

Durrell's game plan does not give a clear and intelligible vision of story and character, but questions and challenges whether such a clear and intelligible vision is possible. On Durrell's multiformed play-ground, the relationship of "story" to "plot," of "narrator" to "charac-ter," is extremely problematic, and the reader becomes a spectator of a narrative game that he or she must constantly reassess, as he or she must constantly reassess his or her own relationship to the game he or she is watching. What we have in the *Quintet* is a narrative of striking originality presented by a player with dazzling style, on a playground of his own creation, with a game plan that demands the intelligent and active participation of the spectator.

## NOTES

1. Lawrence Durrell, *Quinx or The Ripper's Tale* (London: Faber, 1985), 67. Fur-ther references will be included in the text. The American edition (New York: Viking, 1985) has the same pagination.

2. Johan Huizinga, *Homo Ludens: A Study of the Play-Element in Culture* (Boston: Beacon, 1955), 3. Further references to this study will be included in the text. Huizinga completed this study in 1938. Some of my points are anticipated by Keith Brown's brief, perceptive review of *Quinx*, "Up to the Pisgah-sign," *TLS*, 31 May 1985, 597.

3. E.g., Gerard Genette, *Narrative Discourse: An Essay in Method*, trans. Jane E. Lewin (Ithaca: Cornell University Press, 1980), and Seymour Chatman, *Story and Discourse: Narrative Structure in Fiction and Film* (Ithaca: Cornell University Press, 1980).

4. See Jorge Luis Borges, *Labyrinths*, ed. Donald A. Yates and James E. Irby (New York: New Directions, 1964), and Tony Tanner's comments in *City of Words* (New York: Harper & Row, 1971), 42.

5. Lawrence Durrell, *Livia or Buried Alive* (New York: Viking, 1979), 17. Fur-ther references will be included in the text. The American edition is a page-by-page reprint of the British (London: Faber, 1978). The Penguin edition (1984) follows suit.

6. Fictional characters entering a real world is perhaps more acceptable in drama. Cf. Pirandello's *Six Characters in Search of an Author* and Woody Allen's *The Purple Rose of Cairo*. A real character entering a fictional world may be traced back to Odysseus's fantastic adventure story and includes Alice's adventures in Wonderland.

7. Lawrence Durrell, *Monsieur* (New York: Viking, 1974), 309. Further refer-ences will be included in the text. The Penguin edition (1984) follows the American edition's pagination. The British edition, *Monsieur or The Prince of Darkness* (London: Faber, 1974), has this material on p. 296.

8. Cf. Susan Suleiman's "Introduction: Varieties of Audience-Oriented Criti-cism," in *The Reader in the Text* (Princeton: Princeton University Press, 1980), 43. She is quoting M. H. Abrams.

9. The classical study of temporality in the novel is A. A. Mendilow's *Time and the Novel* (1952; reprint, New York: Humanities Press, 1972), a study that does not mention Durrell.

10. Chatman makes this distinction clearly, in the above noted *Story and Discourse*, 19–22.

11. See, e.g., M. R. Ridley's "The 'Double Time Scheme,'" in his edition of *Othello* (London: Methuen, 1958). He feels that Shakespeare "knew to a fraction of an inch how far he could go in playing a trick on his audience" (lxx).

12. Gabriel Zoran, "Towards a Theory of Space in Narrative," *Poetics Today* 5 (1984): 310.

13. The relationships among the five novels is far more complex than I indicate here. I simplify in order to suggest one possible arrangement.

14. Frank Livingstone Huntley, *Sir Thomas Brown* (Ann Arbor: University of Michigan Press, 1962), 207.

15. Ibid., 207–8.

16. For an exposition of Bakhtin's concept of "polyphony," see Katherina Clark and Michael Holquist, *Mikhail Bakhtin* (Cambridge: Harvard University Press, 1984), 240–42, *et passim*.

17. Wayne Booth, *The Rhetoric of Fiction*, 2d ed. (Chicago: University of Chicago Press, 1983), 493.

# Bibliography

## THE FICTION OF LAWRENCE DURRELL

*Pied Piper of Lovers*. London: Cassell, 1935.
*Panic Spring*. London: Faber & Faber, 1937.
*The Black Book*. Paris: Obelisk, 1938.
*White Eagles Over Serbia*. London: Faber & Faber, 1957.
*Justine*. London: Faber & Faber, 1957.
*Balthazar*. London: Faber & Faber, 1958.
*Mountolive*. London: Faber & Faber, 1958.
*Clea*. London: Faber & Faber, 1960.
*Tunc*. London: Faber & Faber, 1968.
*Nunquam*. London: Faber & Faber, 1970.
*Monsieur, or The Prince of Darkness*. London: Faber & Faber, 1974.
*Livia, or Buried Alive*. London: Faber & Faber, 1978.
*Constance, or Solitary Practices*. Faber & Faber, 1982.
*Sebastian, or Ruling Passions*. London: Faber & Faber, 1983.
*Quinx, or The Ripper's Tale*. London: Faber & Faber, 1985.

## SECONDARY SOURCES

Alyn, Marc, ed. *The Big Supposer*. New York: Grove Press, 1974.

Andrewski, Gene, and Julian Mitchell. "Lawrence Durrell: The Art of Fiction XXIII: An Interview with Lawrence Durrell," *Paris Review* 22 (Autumn–Winter 1959–60): 32–61.

Antrim, Harry T., and Eugene Lyons. "An Interview with Lawrence Durrell," *Shenandoah* 2 (Winter 1971): 42–58.

Attridge, Derek, and Daniel Ferrer, eds. *Post-structuralist Joyce: Essays from the French*. Cambridge: Cambridge University Press, 1984.

Barthes, Roland. *Image/Music/Text*. Translated by Stephen Heath. New York: Hill and Wang, 1977.

Begnal, Michael H. "Lawrence Durrell." In *Dictionary of Literary Biography* 15, 87–97. Detroit: Bruccoli, Clark, 1983.

Berger, John. *The Success and Failure of Picasso*. New York: Pantheon Books, 1980.

Boothe, Wayne. *The Rhetoric of Fiction*. 2d ed. Chicago: University of Chicago Press, 1983.

Brewer, Jennifer L. "Character and Psychological Place: The Justine/Sofia Relation," *Deus Loci* 5 (Fall 1981): 234–41.

Brigham, James A. "An Unacknowledged Trilogy," *Deus Loci* (1979): 3–12.

Brown, Keith. "Up to the Pisgah-sign," *TLS*, 31 May 1985, 597.

Brown, Sharon Lee. "*The Black Book:* A Search for Method," *Modern Fiction Studies* 13 (Autumn 1967): 319–28.

Bryson, Norman. *Word and Image: French Painting of the Ancien Regime*. New York: Cambridge University Press, 1981.

Budge, E. A. Wallis, ed. *The Book of the Dead: The Papyrus of Ani*. New York: Dover Books, 1967.

Burns, J. Christopher. "Durrell's Heraldic Universe," *Modern Fiction Studies* 13 (Autumn 1969): 375–88.

Card, James Van Dyck. "'Tell Me, Tell Me': The Writer as Spellbinder in Lawrence Durrell's *Alexandria Quartet*," *Modern British Literature* 1 (1976): 74–83.

Carley, James P. "An Interview with Lawrence Durrell on the Background to *Monsieur* and Its Sequels," *Malahat Review* 51 (1979): 42–46.

———. "Lawrence Durrell and the Gnostics," *Deus Loci* 2 (September 1978): 3–10.

———. "Lawrence Durrell's Avignon Quincunx and Gnostic Heresy," *Deus Loci* 5 (Fall 1981): 284–304.

Cavendish, Richard. *The Tarot*. New York: Harper and Row, 1975.

Caws, Mary Ann. *Reading Frames in Modern Fiction*. Princeton: Princeton University Press, 1985.

Chapman, R. T. "'Dead or Just Pretending?': Reality in *The Alexandria Quartet*," *Centennial Review* 4 (Fall 1972): 408–18.

Chatman, Seymour. *Story and Discourse: Narrative Structure in Fiction and Film*. Ithaca: Cornell University Press, 1980.

Clark, Katherina, and Michael Holquist. *Mikhail Bakhtin*. Cambridge: Harvard University Press, 1984.

Clark, R. T. Rundle. *Myth and Symbol in Ancient Egypt*. London: Thames and Hudson, 1978.

Coleman, John. "Mr. Durrell's Dimensions," *Spectator*, 19 February 1960, 256–57.

Creed, Walter G. "'The Whole Pointless Joke?': Darley's Search for Truth in *The Alexandria Quartet*," *Etudes-Anglaises* 27 (April–June 1975): 165–73.

Dare, H. "The Quest for Durrell's Scobie," *Modern Fiction Studies* 10 (Winter 1964–65): 379–83.

Dasenbrock, Reed W. "Death and the Counterlife of Heresy in Wyndham Lewis and Lawrence Durrell," *Deus Loci* 4 (Sepember 1980): 3–18.

DeBary, William, T. *The Buddhist in India, China, and Japan*. New YorK: Random House, 1969.

Dewey, John. *Art as Experience*. New York: Minton, Balch and Co., 1934.

Dickson, Gregory. "Spengler's Theory of Architecture in Durrell's *Tunc* and *Nunquam*," *Deus Loci* 5 (Fall 1981): 272–84.

Eastman, Richard M. *A Guide to the Novel*. San Francisco: Chandler, 1965.

Eco, Umberto. *Opera aperta*. Milan: Bompiani, 1962.

Eskin, Stanley G. "Durrell's Themes in *The Alexandria Quartet*," *Texas Quarterly* 5 (Winter 1962): 43–60.

Evans-Wentz, W. Y., ed. *The Tibetan Book of the Dead*. London: Oxford University Press, 1960.

Foucault, Michel. *The Order of Things*. New York: Random House, 1973.

———. *Raymond Roussel*. Paris: Gallimard, 1963.

Fraser, G. S. *Lawrence Durrell: A Study*. New York: Dutton, 1973.

Fraser, Sir James G. *The New Golden Bough*. Edited by T. H. Gaster. New York: S. G. Phillips, 1959.

Friedman, Alan W., ed. *Critical Essays on Lawrence Durrell*. Boston: G. K. Hall, 1987.

———. *Lawrence Durrell and The Alexandria Quartet: Art for Love's Sake*. Norman: University of Oklahoma Press, 1970.

Fruin, Jennifer L. "The Importance of Narouz in Durrell's Hermetic Paradigm," *Deus Loci* 2 (June 1979): 3–10.

Fry, Edward F. *Cubism*. London: Thames and Hudson, 1966.

Genette, Gerard. *Narrative Discourse: An Essay in Method*. Translated by Jane E. Lewis. Ithaca: Cornell University Press, 1980.

Godshalk, William L. "Some Sources of Durrell's *Alexandria Quartet*," *Modern Fiction Studies* 13 (Autumn 1967): 316–74.

———. "*Sebastian: or Ruling Passions*: Searches and Failures," *Twentieth Century Literature* 33 (Winter 1987): 536–49.

Gossman, Ann. "Love's Alchemy in *The Alexandria Quartet*," *Critique* 13 (1971–72): 83–96.

Goulianos, Joan. "A Conversation with Lawrence Durrell about Art, Analysis, and Politics," *Modern Fiction Studies* 17 (Autumn 1971): 159–66.

Graves, Robert. *The White Goddess*. New York: Vintage, 1960.

Grebstein, Sheldon N., ed. *Perspectives in Contemporary Criticism*. New York: Harper and Row, 1968.

Guenther, Herbert V., and Chogyam Trungpa. *The Dawn of the Tantra*. Berkeley and London: Shambhala, 1975.

Harari, Josue V., ed. *Textual Strategies*. Ithaca: Cornell University Press, 1979.

Hirsch, E. D. *Validity in Interpretation*. New Haven: Yale University Press, 1967.

Hollahan, Eugene. "Nemerov's Definition and Proust's Example: A Model for the Short Novel," *Studies in the Novel* 11 (Summer 1979): 41–67.

Howarth, Stephen. *The Knights Templar*. New York: Atheneum, 1982.

Huizinga, Johan. *Homo Ludens: A Study of the Play-Element in Culture*. Boston: Beacon, 1955.

Kellman, Steve. *The Self-Begetting Novel*. New York: Columbia University Press, 1980.

Kershaw, Alister, and Frederic-Jacques Temple, eds. *Richard Aldington: An Intimate Portrait*. Carbondale: Southern Illinois University Press, 1965.

Kersnowski, Frank. "Paradox and Resolution in Durrell's *Tunc* and *Nunquam*," *Deus Loci* 7 (September 1983): 1–13.

Kruppa, Joseph E. "Durrell's *Alexandria Quartet* and the 'Implosion' of the Modern Consciousness," *Modern Fiction Studies* 13 (Autumn 1967): 401–16.

Laporte, Paul M. "Cubism and Science," *Journal of Aesthetics and Art Criticism*, March 1949, 243–46.

———. "The Space-Time Concept in the Work of Picasso," *Magazine of Art*, January 1948, 26–32.

Lawrence, D. H. *Fantasia of the Unconscious.* New York: Penguin, 1977.

Legman, G., and Henry C. Lea. *The Guilt of the Templars.* New York: Basic Books, 1966.

Lemon, Lee. *Portraits of the Artist in Contemporary Fiction.* Lincoln: University of Nebraska Press, 1985.

Lévi-Strauss, Claude. *Les structures elementaires de la parente.* Paris/La Haye: Mouton, 1967.

Levitt, Morton P. "Art and Correspondence: Durrell, Miller, and *The Alexandria Quartet*," *Modern Fiction Studies* 13 (Autumn 1969): 299–318.

Loraux, Nicole. *"Ce que vit Tiresias."* In *L'Ecrit du Temps 2,* 104–10. Paris: Minuit, 1982.

Machery, Pierre. *A Theory of Literary Production.* Translated by Geoffrey Wall. Boston: Routledge and Kegan Paul, 1978.

MacNiven, Ian S. "The Quincunx Quiddified: Structure in Lawrence Durrell." In *The Modernists,* edited by Ian S. MacNiven and Lawrence B. Gamache, 215–38. Rutherford, N.J.: Fairleigh Dickinson University Press, 1987.

Markert, Lawrence W. "The Pure and Scared Readjustment of Death: Connections between Lawrence Durrell's *Avignon Quintet* and the Writings of D. H. Lawrence," *Twentieth Century Literature* 33 (Winter 1987): 550–64.

Martin, Edward J. *The Trial of the Templars.* London: George Allen and Unwin, 1928.

Mendilow, A. A. *Time and the Novel.* New York: Humanities Press, 1972.

Merrell, Floyd. *Pararealities: The Nature of Our Fictions and How We Know Them.* Philadelphia: John Benjamins, 1983.

Miller, J. Hillis. *Deconstruction and Criticism.* New York: Seabury Press, 1979.

Mollat, G. *The Popes at Avignon 1305–1378.* London: Thomas Nelson and Sons, 1949.

Moore, Arthur, K. *Contestable Concepts of Literary Theory.* Baton Rouge: Louisiana State University Press, 1973.

Moore, Harry T., ed. *The World of Lawrence Durrell.* New York: Dutton, 1964.

Morrison, J. R. "Memory and Light in Lawrence Durrell's *The Revolt of Aphrodite*," *Labrys* 5 (1979): 141–53.

Mortimer, John. "Comus, Durrell, Wain, and Kavan," *Encounter* 57 (1958): 80–87.

Neumann, Eric. *Art and the Creative Unconscious.* New York: Harper and Row, 1966.

Nichols, James R. "Sunshine Dialogues: Christianity and Paganism in the Works of Lawrence Durrell." In *On Miracle Ground II: Second International Lawrence Durrell Conference Proceedings,* ed. Lawrence W. Markert and Carol Peirce, 129–33. Baltimore: University of Baltimore Press, 1984.

Pandit, M. P. *Kundalini Yoga.* India: All India Press, 1970.

Peirce, Carol. "'Wrinkled Deep in Time': *The Alexandria Quartet* as Many-Layered Palimpsest," *Twentieth Century Literature* 33 (Winter 1987): 485–98.

Pinchin, Jane Lagoudis. *Alexandria Still: Forster, Durrell, and Cavafy.* Princeton: Princeton University Press, 1977.

Pritchett, V. S. "The Sun and the Sunless," *New Statesman,* 13 February 1960, 223–24.

Read, Phyllis. "The Illusion of Personality: Cyclical Time in Durrell's *Alexandria Quartet*," *Modern Fiction Studies* 13 (Autumn 1967): 389–99.

Reis, Timothy J. *The Discourse of Modernism.* Ithaca: Cornell University Press, 1982.

Rose, H. J. *Gods and Heroes of the Greeks.* New York: Meridian Books, 1958.

Rugset, Tone. "*Tunc-Nunquam:* The Quest for Wholeness," *Labrys* 5 (1979): 155–62.

Schillip, Paul A., ed. *Albert Einstein: Philosopher-Scientist.* New York: Harper, 1959.

Schwerdt, Lisa. "Coming of Age in Alexandria: The Narrator," *Deus Loci* 5 (Fall 1981): 218–30.

Suleiman, Susan. *The Reader in the Text.* Princeton: Princeton University Press, 1980.

Tanner, Tony. *City of Words.* New York: Harper and Row, 1971.

Taylor, Chet. "Dissonance and Digression: The Ill-Fitting Fusion of Philosophy and Form in Lawrence Durrell's *Alexandria Quartet*," *Modern Fiction Studies* 17 (Summer 1971): 167–79.

Thomas, Alan G. *Spirit of Place: Letters and Essays on Travel.* New York: Dutton, 1969.

Unterecker, John. *Lawrence Durrell.* New York: Columbia University Press, 1964.

Vander Closter, Susan. *Joyce Cary and Lawrence Durrell: A Reference Guide.* Boston: G. K. Hall, 1985.

Walker, Benjamin. *Gnosticism: Its history and Influence.* Wellingborough: The Aquarian Press, 1983.

Weatherhead, A. K. "Romantic Anachronism in *The Alexandria Quartet*," *Modern Fiction Studies* 11 (Summer 1964): 128–36.

Wedin, Warren. "The Artist as Narrator in *The Alexandria Quartet*," *Twentieth Century Literature* 18 (July 1972): 175–80.

Weigel, John A. *Lawrence Durrell.* New York: Twayne, 1965.

Wickes, George, ed. *Lawrence Durrell and Henry Miller: A Private Correspondence.* New York: Dutton, 1963.

Young, Kenneth. "A Dialogue with Durrell," *Encounter* 13 (December 1959): 61–68.

Zimmer, Heinrich. *Philosophies of India.* New York: Meridian Books, 1956.

Zoran, Gabriel. "Towards a Theory of Space in Narrative," *Poetics Today* 5 (1984): 298–301.

# Contributors

CORINNE ALEXANDRE-GARNER is Maitre de Conférence at the University of Paris, where she teaches English. Along with essays on literature and psychoanalysis, she has published *Le Quatuor d'Alexandrie: Fragmentation et Ecriture,* and she is currently working on a study of Durrell's fiction to be published in English.

MICHAEL H. BEGNAL is Professor of English and Comparative Literature at the Pennsylvania State University, where he is also Director of Graduate Studies. He has written widely on modern and contemporary literature, and his most recent book is *Dreamscheme: Narrative and Voice in Finnegans Wake.*

CHIARA BRIGANTI, from the University of Pisa, is the author of several articles on nineteenth- and twentieth-century British and American fiction. She is currently finishing a book on Jane Austen, Charlotte Brontë, and Charles Dickens.

CANDACE FERTILE teaches at the University of Alberta. She has done the bulk of her writing on Lawrence Durrell and Henry James.

WILLIAM L. GODSHALK's books include *Patterning in Shakespearean Drama* and *The Marlovian World Picture.* A Professor of English at the University of Cincinnati, he is editor of the Garland Shakespeare Bibliographies and has recently completed a detective novel, *In Quest of Malloy.*

EUGENE HOLLAHAN is Director of Lower Division Studies in the Department of English at Georgia State University (Atlanta). His recent books are *Philosophical Dimensions of Saul Bellow's Fiction* and *Centenary Revaluation of Gerard Manley Hopkins.*

DONALD P. KACZVINSKY earned his master's degree at the University of Virginia, and he is completing his dissertation on Lawrence Durrell's novels at The Pennsylvania State University.

206

FRANK KERSNOWSKI, president of the Lawrence Durrell Society, is Professor of English at Trinity University. He has published on a variety of British, Irish, and American writers, including Durrell, Graves, Yeats, Joyce, and Hemingway.

IAN S. MACNIVEN, who teaches at SUNY Maritime College, is the editor of *The Durrell-Miller Letters* and the coeditor of *Literary Lifelines: The Richard Aldington–Lawrence Durrell Correspondence* and *The Modernists: Studies in a Literary Phenomenon.* He is currently writing an authorized biography of Durrell.

JAMES R. NICHOLS is head of the English and Philosophy Department at Georgia Southern College. Along with studies of the British novel, his books include a novel and a selection of poems. He has begun a full-length study of paganism in Lawrence Durrell's work.

CAROL PEIRCE is a Professor of Renaissance and Modern Literature at the University of Baltimore. She has written several articles on Durrell, coordinated the first international conference on Durrell in 1980, and was the first President of the Lawrence Durrell Society.

SUSAN VANDER CLOSTER is an Associate Professor of English at the Rhode Island School of Design. She is the author of *Joyce Cary and Lawrence Durrell: A Reference Guide,* and she pursues literary interests in contemporary literature, art, and film.

DAVID M. WOODS lives in Athens, Georgia.

# Index